Discourse Analysis
and
Pragmatics
Issues in Theory and Practice

Discourse Analysis and Pragmatics
Issues in Theory and Practice

Edited by

Gbenga Ibileye

Malthouse Press Limited
Lagos, Benin, Ibadan, Jos, Port-Harcourt, Zaria

© Gbenga Ibileye 2017
First Published 2017
ISBN 978-978-959-723-9

Published and manufactured in Nigeria by:

Malthouse Press Limited
43 Onitana Street, Off Stadium Hotel Road,
Off Western Avenue, Lagos Mainland
Website: www. malthouselagos.com
malthouselagos@gmail.com
Tel: +234 (01) 0802 600 3203

All rights reserved. No part of this publication may be reproduced, transmitted, transcribed, stored in a retrieval system or translated into any language or computer language, in any form or by any means, electronic, mechanical, magnetic, chemical, thermal, manual or otherwise, without the prior consent in writing of the publishers

This book is sold subject to the condition that it shall not by way of trade, or otherwise, be lent, re-sold, hired out, or otherwise circulated without the publisher's prior consent in writing, in any form of binding or cover other than in which it is published and without a similar condition, including this condition, being imposed on the subsequent purchaser.

Dedication

This book is dedicated to the loving memory of my dad, Pa. Emmanuel Ibileye, who believed so much in and nudged me on passionately

Acknowledgements

I am greatly indebted to an innumerable number of persons, from whose virtues, I have drawn inspiration and strength in the course of my development as a scholar. Top in the scale of such individuals is Prof. Adebayo Joshua of the Department of English and Literary Studies, Ahmadu Bello University, Zaria, at whose feet I cut my academic teeth and under whose tutelage I grew into maturity. I am also indebted to Prof. Taiwo Gani-Ikilama of the same Department for her support and words of inspiration that always spur me into action and productivity. Prof. T.Y. Surakat, Prof. G.Y. Sadiq, Prof. Dili Ofuokwu, Dr. Folasade Frank-Akale, Dr. Samson Abaya, Mr. Ode Ekpeme, Dr Jonah Amodu, Dr. Saminu Isyaku and all my former colleagues in the Department of English and Literary Studies, Ahmadu Bello University, Zaria deserve special mention for the quality of intellectual discourse both at Departmental seminars and in the course of our professional interactions which spanned close to three decades. It was in the richness of those academic interactions and intercourse that the conception of this endeavour was birthed. I am indeed indebted to you.

I thank all the contributors to this volume especially Prof. Ayotunde Ayodabo, Dr. Solomon Oreoluwa, Dr. Nahum Butari, Dr Adewole Alagbe and Dr. John Acheoah all deserve special mention. I also wish to acknowledge Prof. Akin Odebunmi of the University of Ibadan for providing me with a lot of intellectual inspiration and support. Thank you

I owe the late Prof. Joseph Sunday Aliyu. the pioneer Head of the Department of English and Literary Studies, Federal University Lokoja for being such an inspiration and intellectual pillar. Similarly, I acknowledge Prof. Hassan Rafindadi, the pioneer Vice Chancellor of the University for providing me with the enabling environment to thrive and flourish. I also owe Prof. Angela Freeman Miri, the current Vice Chancellor for her support and encouragement.

Prof. David Irefin, Dean, Faculty of Arts and Social Sciences, Federal University Lokoja deserves a world of gratitude for his supportive disposition and encouragement. Also deserving of appreciation are Prof. Muhammed Sulaiman Audu, Dr. Remi Akujobi, Dr. Abel Joseph, Dr Ayodele Bamidele, Dr. Adesina Lawal, Dr, Peter Okpeh, Dr. Sunny Okpeadua, Dr Philip Olaniyi, Mr Olaoluwa Duro Bello, Mrs Josephine Ohieme, Ms Bunmi Balogun and Mrs Winnie Olaniru all of the Department of English and Literary Studies, Federal University Lokoja for the richness of our relationship which provided the fertility for my ideas. My friend and brother, Mr Emmanuel Ikpelemoh deserves special mention for being supportive and inspiring. I similarly acknowledge Ms Dora Mbu, Ms Ify Okolo, Mr Abdullazeez Jatto, Mr Theodore Shey, Mrs Kemi Dada. I also owe Mrs Alero Richard-Ominyi for always being dependable and helpful. She it was who processed many of the manuscripts of the papers submitted for this book.

Over the years, I have taught and interacted with generations of students at the different levels of my involvements at the Ahmadu Bello University, Zaria, Universite Gaston Berger, St Luis, Senegal, Kaduna State University, Usmanu Danfodiyo University, Sokoto, Kogi State University, Anyigba and Nasarawa State University, Keffi. My many intellectual activities as External Examiner to various universities such as University of Ilorin, Bayero University, Benue State University, Modibbo Adama University of Technology, University of Nigeria, Nsukka, University of Jos, and Ibrahim Badamasi Babangida University where I had the privilege to share multiple perspectives on the subject matter of this book, left imprints on my mind for which I am grateful. I am also greatly indebted to my students at Federal University Lokoja for providing me with the learning platform and the urge to always strive for greater heights.

I am specially indebted to my wife and soul mate for enduring the many days of sharing her affection with my computer and for carrying on with tasks which naturally are in my place to discharge. I also thank King, Okiki and Dara, my lovely children for being so wonderful and for providing me with the sweet family platform supportive of my intellectual endeavour. My siblings, Mrs Oshe, Funmilayo Kayode, Foluke Owolabi and Toyosi Ibileye have been supportive all through. Thank you. I also appreciate Prof. Dafe Otobo for lending me his shoulder to lean on and Malthouse publishers for producing this work satisfactorily.

Finally, I return all praise to the Almighty and all-knowing God for the divine enablement and grace to undertake this task.

Preface

Previous works on Discourse Analysis and Pragmatics have either been dominantly focused on theory or on practice without much balance and attention to both theory and analysis. The present volume seeks to strike a balance between the two closely related disciplines on the one hand, and between the study of theory in the two disciplines and on issues of methodology and application in specific areas of enquiry on the other.

The book seeks to provide a cross-sectional view of scholarship in these areas, specifically from the perspective of how the intersection of theory and practice enables Nigerian scholars of Discourse Analysis and Pragmatics to understand and analyse texts that have pan-Nigerian peculiarities.

The scope and outlook of the book are therefore guided by this general devotion of the themes discussed. Broadly speaking, the book is divided into two parts, Discourse Analysis and Pragmatics. Each broad area is further arranged with sensitivity to the two general issues of theory and practice, such that theoretical chapters in Discourse Analysis as Gbenga Ibileye's chapter on discourse, Upah Butari's on context, Solomon Oreoluwa's on conversational analysis, and Christiana Rakiya Ogidi-Andrew's chapter on Deixis are featured before the more practical/analysis-based chapters, like Ayotunde Ayodabo's chapter on President Goodluck Jonathan's telephone conversation conceding to General Muhammadu Buhari, presidential candidate of the All Progressives Congress in the 2015 General Election in Nigeria. A similarity exists between Ayodabo's chapter and John Emike Acheoah's and it is the focus on a speech act analysis of a mobile-phone call. Specifically on the subject matter of pragmatics, two chapters, Rita Bossan's history and scope of pragmatics and Jonah Amodu's concept of presupposition, explore theoretical issues in pragmatics and provide some basis for the chapters concerned with analysis both in discourse analysis and pragmatics.

Some recent developments in discourse analysis and pragmatics were given adequate focus. Peter Okpeh's chapter on critical discourse analysis (CDA) is one of such chapters. The chapter explores the scope and subject matter of CDA. The second chapter in this category is Olaoluwa Duro-Bello's on Forensic Linguistics. Olaniyi Oladimeji and Abiodun Jombadi's joint-chapter on the application of CDA to the analysis of Boko Haram text provides the bridge between theory and practice in this regard.

There are fringe issues explored too. Adewole Alagbe's and Joy Aworo-Okoh's chapters provide some insight into the diversity and depth of issues to which discourse analysis and pragmatics could be applied.

Editor

Ibileye, Gbenga - Professor Ibileye lectures in the Department of English and Literary Studies, Federal University Lokoja. His close to three decades of scholarship, spanning many institutions in Nigeria and Senegal, has been focused on research in (Critical) Discourse Analysis, especially, legal and constitutional documents; Pragmatics, Applied Linguistics and Forensic Linguistics.

Contributors

Acheoah, Dr John Emike - Dr Acheoah lectures in the Department of English, Federal University, Birnin Kebbi. He has published extensively in the general area of pragmatics and discourse analysis.

Alagbe, Dr. Adewole - Dr Alagbe is the Dean, Faculty of Arts, Nasarawa State University, Keffi. He specialises in the syntactic and pragmatic description of legal and quasi-legal documents. He has four books on the general theory and analysis of language.

Amodu, Dr. Jonah - Dr Amodu lectures in the Department of English and Literary Studies, Ahmadu Bello University, Zaria. His major area of research is the pragmatics of advertisement. He has published extensively in this area.

Aworo-Okoh, Dr. Joy - Dr. Joy Aworo-Okoh lectures in the Department of English, Nasarawa State University, Keffi. Her research interest cuts across the broad spectrum of Linguistics, but specifically, Discourse Analysis of the language of sports. She has published a number of books on Discourse Analysis, Pragmatics and Stylistics.

Ayodabo, Professor Ayotunde - Professor Ayodabo is an acclaimed scholar whose interests cut across the major areas of Pragmatics,

Discourse Analysis and Stylistics. He is the Editor in Chief of Issues in Language and Linguistics: Perspectives from Nigeria which has published three volumes. He lectures at the Crowther University, Oyo, Nigeria.

Bosan, Dr. Rita - Dr. Bosan specialises in new media discourse. She has written extensively on the structure of internet and social media language. She is a senior lecturer in the Department of English and Drama, Kaduna State University.

Butari, Dr Upah Nahum - Dr Butari is a senior lecturer in the Department of English and Drama, Kaduna State University with interest in Pragmatics, Semantics, Discourse Analysis and Stylistics. He has conducted extensive research into the linguistics of some indigenous languages in northeast Nigeria, especially Jukun, the semantic fields of which he has compared with those of English.

Duro-Bello, Olaoluwa - Olaoluwa Duro-Bello is a PhD candidate in English at the University of Nottingham Malaysia Campus. In the last five years he has taught linguistics to undergraduate students at Federal University Lokoja, Nigeria. His research interests span forensic linguistics, discourse analysis and language use in social contexts of politics, conflict and insurgency. His current research investigates the representation of Boko Haram in the speeches of Nigerian presidents.

Jombadi, Abiodun - Abiodun Jombadi is a doctoral student of Discourse Studies and a lecturer of Language courses at the English Unit in the Department of Linguistics, African & European Languages of the Kwara State University, Malete. He has written and published articles in Discourse Analysis.

Lawal, Dr O. A. - Dr Lawal is a lecturer in the Department of English and Literary Studies, Federal University Lokoja. His major area of scholarship is Pragmatics with specific interest in media discourse.

Ogidi-Andrew, Dr. Christiana Rakiya - Dr. Andrew-Ogidi has about eighteen years of lecturing experience starting from the Nigerian Airforce School of Air Intelligence Makurdi , 1999 to 2002, Ground Training Centre, Nigerian Airforce Base Kaduna from 2002 to 2008, Nigerian Airforce Institute of Technology Kaduna 2008 to 2015 and

Nigeria Defence Academy till date. Her major areas of scholarly interests are Mophology, Semantics and Pragmatics.

Okpeh, Dr Peter Ochefu -Dr Okpeh lectures in the Department of English and Literary Studies, Federal University Lokoja. His research interest is in Pentecostal discourse and the linguistic description of metaphor. He has devoted a lot of scholarly attention to the ideological orientation of metaphor in Christian discourse and specifically, in the sermons of major Christian speakers in Nigeria.

Oladimeji, Dr Olaniyi - Dr. Olaniyi Oladimeji teaches Syntax, Phonology and Applied Linguistics in the Department of English and Literary studies of the Federal University Lokoja. He has written and published articles in Pragmatics and Discourse Analysis.

Table of Contents

Dedication
Acknowledgements
Foreword
Preface

CHAPTERS

1. **Discourse** - Gbenga Ibileye - **1**

2. **Context** - Nahum Upah Butari - **15**

3. **Conversational Analysis** - Solomon Oreoluwa Abraham - **35**

4. **History and Scope of Pragmatics** - Rita Bossan - **45**

5. **Speech Acts as States-of-affairs: A Pragmatic Overview of a Mobile-Phone Message of August 31st 2012** – John Emike Acheoah - **79**

6. **Deixis** – Christiana Rakiya Ogidi-Andrew - **99**

7. **The Concept of Presupposition** - Eneojoh Jonah Amodu - **117**

8. **A Pragmatic Analysis of Truth Value in Selected Nigerian Newspapers** - Lawal Olarewaju Adesina - **133**

9. **Speech Act analysis of President Goodluck Jonathan and General Mohammed Buhari's 31st March 2015 Telephone Conversation** - Joel Olatunde Ayodabo - **155**

10. **The Discourse of Language of Public Relations (PR): A Case Study of Nasarawa State University, Keffi** - Adewole Adigun Alagbe - **183**

11. **Critical Discourse Analysis: An Overview** - Peter Okpeh - **201**

12. **Contextualizing An African Brand of Terrorism in The Eye of Critical Discourse: a Case of Nigeria's Boko Haram Islamic Sect -** Oladimeji Olaniyi - **215**

13. **Forensic Linguistics -** Olaoluwa Duro-Bello - **229**

14. **A Multimodal Discourse Analysis of Selected Campaign Posters in Abuja -** Joy Aworo-Okoroh - **239**

Index - **255**

Chapter 1

Discourse

-Gbenga Ibileye

Discourse, the theoretical basis of the emergence of the field of discourse analysis, is a pervading phenomenon, which governs human life and daily activities sometimes in an unconscious way. Discourse has been variously conceived by scholars as the authentic product of human interaction as well as being the concrete aspect of the abstractness of communication. Scholars such as Stubbs, Coulthard, and Gee submit that discourse defines the human essence as it reflects what a speaker wants, who the speaker is and what the speaker does. In other word, discourse shows us humans as using language to do things and to depict our identity in the discourse that we so produce. This is why studying discourse has a vast potential of revealing the true nature and essence of human relations.

Gee particularly sees discourse as something beyond the material to also include the structure of human communication. He segments discourse into two types. The first type sees discourse in *terms of structure*, something more or less like syntax: Discourse is the sequence of sentences. It is the ways in which sentences connect and relate to each other across time in speech or writing...Discourse concerns how various sentences flowing one after the other relate to each other to create meanings or to facilitate interpretation.(18)

The second conception of discourse is that it is *language in use*. On this second meaning of discourse, Gee submits that 'we study language not just as an abstract system ('grammar'), but in terms of actual utterances or sentences in speech or writing in specific contexts of speaking and writing or writing and reading'(19). This latter meaning of the term discourse clearly distinguishes its preoccupation from the task of structural linguists by focusing on language within its context of use. Gee further avers that discourse is an encompassing concept through which we disentangle people's identities, As he submits, 'people build identities and activities not just through language, but by using language together with other '"stuff" that isn't language.' (45)

To this extent, Gee submits that different spheres of life necessitate people speaking the 'right' language, acting and dressing in the 'right' way. People also need to engage, or at least, behave as if engaging in ways of thinking, acting, interacting, valuing, feeling and behaving that are characteristic of those spheres of life like being a corporate lawyer, marine sergeant, radical feminist, or a regular at the local bar (45). Interestingly, Gee states that one person might act in one context that shows that he/she is a lawyer, but in another context he acts in a way that shows that he is a father or a member of a religious organisation. These contexts of acting typify what is meant by discourse as each context of acting shows talk which is specific not only to the topic, but also the role specific relationship of the speaker.

Indeed, Halliday (following Firth and Malinowsky) had argued that language, being the product of human communication, should be studied in its context of situation. It is this that makes language to yield its true essence of indirectness. Three broad elements were identified in studying language in its context of situation. These three parts are: *the field* (what is being spoken about); *the tenor* (what are the relationships among or between the participants); *the mode* (what are the circumstances in which the language communication takes place) (e.g. spoken or written language) (Collerson, 1994)

Scholars with orientation towards the study of language in its context of situation, affirm that circumstances dictate the level of language used, such as: the formal, the informal, the colloquial and slang (Collerson). An example of context of situation could take place in a shop. The field could be the price of a certain item; the tenor would be a slight deference on the shop assistant part towards the customer because of a potential sale; the mode would be that of spoken inquiry: question, answer, response.

As is mentioned,[1] context of situation forms part of context of culture. By context of culture is meant the meanings and assumptions we share as a community of people. It also incorporates "the culturally evolved expectations of ways of behaving" and getting things done (Hammond et al., 1992, p.2). For example, the buying and selling of

---

[1] *https://resource.acu.edu.au/acuskills/critlit/glossary.html#contextsituation*

goods will vary from culture to culture. In some cultures bartering is always acceptable but in Australia selling goods at fixed prices is the usual expectation. We must keep in mind, however, that a society like Australia has a multi-cultural strand in which different cultural assumptions interact but that in some Australian settings, it is possible for a common set of meanings and assumptions to operate

Studying language in this way also shows that language, like Stubbs also avers, is designed for use in face to face interaction. This is mainly why, unlike structural linguists who strip language of its contextual value, preferring to idealize data based on introspection, discourse analysts rely on data produced as the authentic product of human interaction. Discourse analysts, just like Firth, Malinowsky and their succeeding generation of critical linguists, believe that if language is stripped of its context of situation, what ensues is a meaningless junk of human expression. Materials produced in this way, which facilitate interaction within different domains of human interaction, are generally covered by the term discourse.

Discourse, therefore, is central to the preoccupation of the discourse analyst, and it therefore merits a considerable amount of attention in theoretical explanation. A discourse can be conceived of as a text which forms a fairly complete unit of expression either in writing or in speech. Crystal believes a discourse to mean 'a continuous stretch of (especially spoken) language larger than a sentence, often constituting a coherent unit, such as a sermon, argument, joke or narrative'. Brown and Yule also define discourse aptly as 'language in use' (1), while Cook sees the term as referring to 'stretches of language perceived to be meaningful, unified and purposive'. The three features mentioned in Cook's classification deserve some evaluation.

For a piece of language to be described as discourse, it must be considered meaningful, first from the encoder (speaker or writer) and more importantly, by the decoder (hearer or reader). The features that make the expression meaningful are determined by the structural rules of the language. This tends to suggest that discourse analysis does not supplant existing approaches to the study of language; rather, it utilizes the insights provided by some of the approaches for its validation. In other word, syntax for instance will help to ensure that interlocutors speak the same language and imbue their expression with the conventional meaning in that language. The second criterion proposed by Cook is unity. For a piece of language to be considered as a discourse, it must be unified.

Another way to describe this is to borrow from the Halliday approach which talks about coherence and by extension, cohesion. A piece of language, no matter how short, whose components do not demonstrate harmony cannot be considered to be a discourse. In other word, whether short or long, for a piece of communication to be termed a discourse, its parts must demonstrate unity. Here unity might be structural or thematic such that the piece of language is seen as one. This is the kind of unity that allows language users to look at a book of hundreds or probably thousands of pages as constituting a discourse so long as the respective words, sentences, pages and chapters show unity.

The centrality of an understanding of the concept of discourse cannot be discountenanced as it constitutes the main thrust of the discourse analyst's interest in language. The analyst's interest in this way precludes much reliance on introspection and intuition as the major recourse for validation, much in the tradition of structuralists who believe not in the authentic language events as the raw material for linguistic enquiry.

Johnstone (44) concurs with the above position when she affirms the centrality of discourse and its preference in the analysis of language over and above the structure or form of language. While not advocating for the structure of language to be discountenanced, Johnstone affirms that true meaning resides in the study of discourse. She advocates for the study of 'actual instances of talk, signing, and writing rather than an idealized description of the knowledge that people draw on as they talk, sign, or write. In other words, instead of asking how the grammar and vocabulary of a language affect, and are affected by, the ways speakers of that language conceive of the world, we could ask about how the thing people do when they talk, sign , or write influence, and are influenced by their knowledge about language and the world as they experience it'. Johnstone's assertion underscores the situational or contextual orientation of discourse analysis as an approach to the study of language within its context of use.

Discourse analysts believe that the real value of human language is that it is used by humans in real communicative situations. It is in the contextual ideation of language in this way that the real essence of language emerges. In saying this, we are mindful of the situation of language as being created by persons, in some physical, psychological, cultural or social contexts. When language is created in this way, we talk about discourse, or its related concept of text, which is a term describing fairly similar issues but being preferred by text linguists.

In maintaining that discourse analysis has as its major preoccupation the concept of discourse is by no means asserting the monolithic nature of the concept. Indeed, discourse could be of various kinds depending on what the interest of the creators of the communication is, the subject matter and the nature of social relationship between them. We can then talk in terms of discourse genres, a term which captures the variety that exists in the raw material which humans create in the process of communication. In describing the genres of discourse, we could align with Brown and Yule's broad categorization of discourse genres into two, the transactional and interactional functions of discourse. While the transactional discourse genre mainly passes information from a speaker/writer to a hearer/reader, the interactional discourse genre is used for the maintenance or sustenance of social relationship. This categorization, although limited, does underscore the variegated nature of human communication which are conditioned by contextual and communicative need factors by language users. This again sets the discourse analyst apart from the structural linguist whose interest does not take into account contextual considerations in the generation of data for linguistic analysis.

Our discussion of discourse above should not be construed as meaning that discourse is like a portmanteau, complete in itself. Rather, we can assert that no discourse is self-contained, complete in itself and without recourse to other 'discourses'. Every discourse is a part of a universe of discourses which contribute tiny bits of completeness to the particular discourse in point. Every discourse makes reference, in some immediate or remote way to other discourses that had gone before and it is by reference to such previous discourses that the meaning of the new discourse is understood and interpreted.

This cross-reference is what Gee has captured in four ways as representing the conceptualization of discourse and which he roughly terms 'intertextuality'. According to Gee (46) 'when we speak or write, our words often allude to or relate to or even quote other 'texts' or certain types of 'texts', where by 'texts'...mean words other people have said or written'. He cites the example of *Wired* magazine as follows:

> *Wired* magazine once printed a story with the title: "The New Face of the Silicon Age: Tech jobs are fleeing to India faster than ever: You got a problem with that?" (February 2004). The sentence, "You got a problem with that?" reminds us of "tough guy" talk we have heard in many movies

or read in books. It intrigues us that such talk occurs written in a magazine devoted to technology. This sort of cross-reference to another text or type of text I refer to as "intertextuality". In instances of intertextuality, one spoken or written text alludes to quotes, or otherwise relates to another one. (46)

Similarly, Fairclough (84) conceives of intertextuality as being 'basically the property texts have of being full of snatches of other texts, which may be explicitly demarcated or merged in, and which the text may assimilate, contradict, ironically echo, and so forth.'

The point remains that, as noted by Yule, our entire life is dominated by talk. However, from the point of view of our conceptualisation of intertextuality, we tend to suggest that all the talks that we engage in are connected in some direct or loose ways and they reinforce, challenge, contradict or even refute each other. Any text or discourse that a discourse analyst seeks to understand therefore, has its life based on this intricately interwoven web of connections. Therefore, discourse analysis functions within the context of the situation of talk exchanges as members of that network of connections called intertextuality.

The assertions and arguments above about the nature and essence of discourse, and by extension, the text, are supported by Johnstone (9) who affirms the centrality of discourse as the major tool of the discourse analysts' enterprise. In doing this, Johnstone asserts that 'the basic question the discourse analyst asks is "Why is this stretch of discourse the way it is? Why is it no other way? Why these particular words in this particular order?" In other word, the task of the discourse analyst revolves around his understanding of the working of discourse.

In answering the questions above, Johnstone asserts:

We obviously need to think about what our "text" is about, since clearly what a person is talking about has a bearing on what is said and how it is said. We also need to think about who said it, or who wrote it or signed it, who is thought, in its particular socio-cultural context, to be responsible for what it says, who the intended audience was and who the actual hearers or readers were, because who the participants in a situation are and how their roles are defined clearly influences what gets said and how. We need to think about what motivated the text, about how it fits into the set of things people in its context conventionally do with discourse, and about what its medium (or media) of production has to do with what it is like. We need to think about the language it is in, what that languages encourages speakers and writers to do and what it is relatively difficult to do in that language. We need to think about the text's structure, and how it fits into larger structures of sets of texts and sets of interactions. (9)

The views of Johnstone above conflate with similar questions posed as constituting the focus of discourse analysts by Michael McCarthy, Christian Mathiessien and Diane Slade (53). In their view, because the endeavour of the discourse analyst differs somewhat markedly from that of the structural linguist or the formalist, the discourse analyst asks questions which expectedly differ from those asked by the structuralist. Therefore, the discourse analyst asks the following questions:

i. Who are the participants in the discourse, that is, the writer and reader(s), the speaker(s) and listener(s)? What is their relationship? Is it one between equals? Are there differences in power or knowledge between the participants? What are their goals? (A formal grammarian does not usually take any of these factors into account when working with out-of-context sentences).

ii. How do we know what writers and speakers mean? More specifically, discourse analysts ask 'what does this piece of language mean in this context? and 'what does the speaker/writer mean by this piece of language?' What factors enable us to interpret the text? What do we need to know about the context? What clues are there in the surrounding text which will enable us to apprehend the meaning? (In contrast, a formal grammarian can ask the question 'What does this sentence mean?', and a lexicologist can ask 'What does this word mean, independently of context?)

Johnstone further asserts that discourse is shaped by its context and that discourse shapes its context. This assertion he breaks down into six ways in which discourse and context regulate each other: (10)

1) Discourse is shaped by the world, and discourse shapes the world.
2) Discourse is shaped by language, and discourse shapes language.
3) Discourse is shaped by participants, and discourse shapes participants.
4) Discourse is shaped by prior discourse, and discourse shapes the possibilities for future discourse.
5) Discourse is shaped by its medium, and discourse shapes the possibilities of its medium.

6) Discourse is shaped by purpose, and discourse shapes possible purposes.[2]

We might also wish to distinguish between discourse and conversation. While the former has been extensively discussed in the preceding portion of this chapter, it is the latter that we need to shed further light on. We can anchor our understanding of the concept of conversation on Gee's who has viewed it from two broad perspectives. According to Gee, the first kind of conversation is that which takes place within specific context of talk, correlating roughly with our understanding of discourse, but dovetailing towards the informal non-institutional category of verbal exchanges. The other category, which I perceive to be more suited as a tool for social science research, is what Gee (72) realizes with a capital 'C'. According to Gee, when we talk about things like the general societal discussion around issues; like abortion or smoking, we are using the word 'discussion' in a partly metaphorical way, of course. We are talking about the public debates that swirl around us in the media, in our reading, and in our interactions with other people, not any one specific discussion among specific people.

On certain issues (e.g., abortion, smoking, gambling, feminism, affirmative action, etc.), Gee affirms, we know what the 'sides' are, how they are talked about, and what sort of people tend to be on specific sides. Some of these sorts of issues are known by nearly everyone in a society, others are known only by specific social groups. Gee (72) calls 'such public debates, arguments, motifs, issues, or themes "Conversations" with a capital "C', speaking metaphorically as if the various sides in debates around issues like abortion or smoking were engaged in one big grand conversation (or debate or argument, whatever we want to call it). Of course, this big Conversation is composed of myriad of interactional events taking place among specific people at specific times and places.

It is in the broadness of its reference and coverage that Conversation (which of course encompasses conversation in its isolation) finds convergence with discourse as the preoccupation of discourse analysis. Indeed, an understanding of the intersection between the two terms will yield much result as no text can be seen to be analyzable and complete in itself without cross reference to other texts that might have been created

---

[2] How discourse is shaped by its context, and how discourse shapes its context. Source: Barbara Johnstone, 2008 (10)

before it. This also yields reference to the concept of intertextuality as reference to one text shows its place in a larger maze of inter-related texts.

Discourse Analysis

Discourse Analysis broadly defined as 'the study of language viewed communicatively and/or of communication viewed linguistically' (Hugh Trappes-Lomas 134) has a very long history. Dairo and Onadeko report that the origin of Discourse Analysis is traceable to ancient Greek rhetoricians of over two millenia who construed the text as a typical representation of intension (van Dijk 1988a; 1988b; Weiss and Wodak 2003; Wodak and Meyer 2001; Fairclough 2003). Although, the ancestry of Discourse Analysis could be traced to classical rhetoricians, the first use of the term 'discourse analysis' in English dates back to the mid-twentieth century. Dairo and Onadeko further report that the origin and growth of the subject had heavy influence from disciplines in the humanities and the social sciences as well as from theorists among whom were Vladimir Prepp, Claude Levi-Strauss, Dell Hymes, John Gumperz, Ferdinand de Saussure, Antonio Gremci, Michael Foucault, Jacques Derrida, Mikhail Bakhrin as some of the major contributors. Scholars (for example, Mathias R. Mehl 143), have linked the emergence of Discourse Analysis to the Second World War when governments which were opposed to Nazi Germany made deliberate efforts to analyse the propaganda contents of Nazi messages. However, the 1960s which featured a blossoming of insights in Discourse Analysis, was a time that witnessed a reaction, in Linguistics, against structuralism which had dominated research in the discipline. The point of conflict between structuralism and discourse analysis was that while the former focused squarely on the grammatical properties of language while ignoring its social (macro) properties, that latter takes into account the social structure within which language is constructed and used. Discourse analysts believe that the context and use of language determine its structure. Linguistic scholars such as Halliday and Hasan, van Dijk who had shown interest in Discourse Analysis in its early stages focused more on the micro-analysis of linguistic features including words, sentence structure, cohesion and coherence.

Another major point of departure between structural linguistics and discourse analysis is that while the former focuses on the formal structure of language thus relying on the possibility of obtaining linguistic evidence and data through reliance on the intuitive knowledge of the native speaker, the latter offers new insights and approach to text analysis as it shows interest in real life, naturally occurring 'language in use' rather than invented or contrived samples to suit the linguist's purpose of analysis. This new orientation of Discourse Analysis, shifted attention of mainstream linguists away from language as an abstraction to language that functions within real-life context and as used by real speakers in communication. The fascination of Discourse Analysis as perhaps a concrete aspect of linguistics and the social sciences, attracted scholars into multi-disciplinary collaborations. Discourse analysis can therefore be said to be multi-disciplinary in nature with a diverse range of interests which has provided useful tools for description of the structure and function of language within text and talk. Discourse Analysis incorporates the finest aspect of structuralism and social analysis in analysing the different aspects of discourse. The above explanation tallies with Lyons' (32) view that while other forms of language study are committed to the formal properties of the language, discourse analysis is primarily concerned with the investigation of what that language is used for. Lyons. Similarly, Mey (33) sees discourse analysis as the study of an utterance, text unit or a communicative event that is generally perceived as having a varying theme, topic or setting.

Similarly, other scholars have defined and described discourse analysis from a variety of perspectives. Discourse analysis is like other allied disciplines, e.g. law, and even language, which are devoid of a specific definition. Discourse analysts have not come up with a practical and generally acceptable definition of this phenomenon. For instance, Brown and Yule (1983:1) state that

The analysis of discourse, is necessarily the analysis of language in use. As such, it cannot be restricted to the description of linguistic forms independent of the purpose, or functions which their forms are designed to serve in human affairs.

Brown and Yule claim further (1983: viii) that discourse analysis

> Has come to be used with a wide range of meanings which cover a wide range of activities. It is used to describe activities of the intersection of disciplines as diverse as socio-linguistics, psycholinguistics linguistics and computational linguistics.

As observed by Dairo and Onadeko {2008) the usefulness of this definition is limited by seeing discourse analysis as sociolinguistics itself rather than an aspect of it. They emphasize on specific perspective toward language, functional versus structural, which is tied to a focus on de

Saussure's 'parole' and 'langue'. The definition is also faulty in that it does not give allowance for differentiation between discourse analysis, on the other hand, and its other sister disciplines like pragmatics, semantics, on the other hand.

Stubbs (1983:1) observes that discourse analysis is a conglomeration of attempts to study the organization of language above larger linguistic units, such as conversational exchanges or written texts. It follows that discourse analysis is also concerned with language in use in social context and in particular with interaction or dialogue between speakers.

This observation emphasizes on particular unit of analysis (above the sentence) which leads him towards a similar pragmatic emphasis on "language in use" of Brown and Yule's definition. Despite this shortcoming, Stubbs narrows down his definition to "organization of language above the sentence or the clause and therefore to study larger linguistic units, such as conversational exchange". We concur with Dairo and Onadeko when they assert that it would have been more appropriate and more practical if Stubbs has restricted it to organization of exchanges in spontaneous conversations (face to face) or written conversation, rather than 'or written text', which is ambiguous in that one tends to interpret his 'written text' to include any written text or just a written dialogue only. To include 'written text' in general is to lump discourse analysis with Textlinguistics (as the German linguists do, see Sandulescu 1976) and pragmatics.

To accentuate the above inseparability further, Richards *et al.* (1985:83-84) observe that "sometimes the study of both written and spoken discourse is known as Discourse Analysis" However, some researchers attempt to separate written text from spoke text. They opine that the analysis of spoken discourse is sometimes called Conversational Analysis, while the analysis of written discourse is Textlinguistics. According to these authorities, discourse analysis is the study of how sentences in spoken and written language form larger meaningful units such as paragraph, conversations, interviews, etc. They assert further that the content of discourse analysis should include:

a) The relationship between utterances in a discourse as in adjacency pairs and coherence (See Schegloff, 1968)
b) The moves made by speakers to introduce a new topic, change the topic, or assert a higher role relationship to the other participants (see Barry, 1987; Onadeko, 1999)

Schiffrin (1987:1-2) claims that since Giglioli (1972), Leech (1983:10), Levinson (1983: Chapter 6), Bauman and Schetzer(1974) have interwoven discourse analysis with pragmatics and sociolinguistics, discourse analysis is too vast a discipline to be compartmentalized. She opines that:

It should not really be surprising that discourse analysis is so vast and diffused like pragmatics and sociolinguistics. It has its intellectual roots not only in linguistics, but in the social science and philosophy.

Perhaps instructive is Dairo and Onadeko's attempt to diatinguish between discourse analysis and pragmatics. They assert that although discourse analysis is related to pragmatics and sociolinguistics, it is absurd and not very correct to give both the same attributive properties.

Tannen (1984) opines that discourse analysis is not more than a deconstructive reading and interpretation of a problem or text. Tannen (1984) asserts that discourse is an attempt to study language beyond the grammar level. It studies chunks of language as they flow together in a speech event. Furthermore Thomas (1995:23) claims that discourse has much to do with language making meaning out of utterance. He states that:

> ...meaning in interaction...The different contributions of both speakers and hearer as well as that of utterance and context to the making of meaning.

What he is saying is that discourse analysis is related with meaning making in interaction in social context. However, this does not mean that discourse analysis is the same discipline as semantics or pragmatics.

We are fascinated by Dairo and Onadeko's submission about the autonomy of discourse analysis as a discipline. They argue that as fluid, dynamic and diffused a phenomenon discourse analysis seems, it is a distinct and unique discipline which cannot be subsumed under any already existing discipline. Even though, it may have some interface with disciplines like sociolinguistics, psycholinguistics, semantics and pragmatics, etc. it is a distinct field with its own specific framework. It is a discipline that will enable and consequently reveal the obscure motivation behind a naturally occurring talk or behind the choice of a particular method of research in order to favourably interpret the talk. Discourse analysis is the specific study of naturally occurring and spontaneous conversation (or what is intended to be so rendered in written mode) which exists between at least two participants in a social context. When face-to face discourse is reduced to writing, especially in a novel, it includes its narrative tags that explain who said what, his action and his preparations for the speech (Onadeko, 1994). Consequently, a novel's sentences, for instance, could be divided into narrative sentences and conversational pieces, e.g.

It was like that first night when he had met Leah.	1
They did not say much but they understood.	2
She had known he was alright just by looking at him.	3
So it is with people in the country	4
They understand and they know	5
And now it was like that again	6
"You are a good one", he said and took her arm	7

(Peter Abraham's Mine Boy, p. 85)

In the above except, Sentence 1 through 6 are narratives, while Sentence 7 is said and done by a person in the text. The first clause is uttered by a participant, the second clause is said by a reporter (obviously the novelist) and the third clause is an action performed by the character in the story, who uttered the first clause. Strictly speaking, Sentence 7 is the chief concern of a discourse analyst if we are to restrict the term discourse analysis to its rightful domain. Discourse analysis involves all verbal and nonverbal actions that take place during a speech event. It has basic properties: i) it has its own specific structure, ii) it centres on meaning making, and iii) it focuses on the accomplishment of action.

References

Austin, J.L. (1962) *How to Do Things With Words* London: Oxford University Press.

Brown, G. and G. Yule (1983) *Discourse Analysis*, Cambridge: Cambridge University Press.

Coulthard, M. (1985) *An Introduction to Discourse Analysis (new ed)* London: Longman.

Crystal, D. and D. Davey (1969) *Investigating English Style* New York: Longman

Dairo, A. L and T. Onadeko (2008) *Understanding Discourse Analysis and Pragmatics*. New York: Peace Concept.

Johnstone, B. (2008) *Discourse Analysis* Oxford: Blackwell Publishing.

Fairclough, N. (1980) *Language and Power*. Essex: Longman.

Gee, J. P. (2005) *An Introduction to Discourse Analysis Theory and Method*. London and New York: Routledge.

Halliday, M.A.K. and R. Hasan (1976) *Cohesion in English*. *London: Longman.*

Halliday, M.A.K. (1970) *A Course in Spoken English Intonation.* Oxford: Oxford University Press.

Mey, J. L. (2008) *Pragmatics: An Introduction.* USA, UK; Australia: Blackwell .

Stubbs, M. (1983) *Discourse Analysis* Oxford: Blackwell.

Chapter 2

Context

- Butari Nahum Upah

Introduction

Other than the traditional examination of just the structures of language alone, Pragmatics and Discourse Analysis focus on a more balanced way of studying language. This is done with the common belief that there is a great deal of relationship between language and the society where language use is generally influenced by the social context. Language use therefore refers to the use of linguistic codes in the context of social life. It is that realization of studying language in its social context that has attracted the interest in sociolinguistics, Pragmatics, Discourse analysis and Ethnography of speaking since the 1970s.

The social context described above forms the concept of 'context' in linguistics, andLyons (1977: 572) defines the term as:

> ... a theoretical construction in the postulation of which the linguist abstracts from the actual situation and establishes as contextual all the factors which, by virtue of their influence upon the participants in the language event, systematically determine the form and the appropriateness of the meaning of utterances.

Within the framework of this discussion, context is viewed from the pragmatic point in terms of knowledge of what both the speaker and hearer can assume to know and how that knowledge guides the use of language and the interpretation of utterances. It is therefore crucial to examine the relationship between language and society and how language use is influenced by the social context. This has prompted Dell Hymes (1974) in NOUN (2010: 30) to cite the following as the major goals of this kind of contextual study. They are to:

(1) Involve language in practical issues such as education, minority groups and language policy

(2) Show how social function gives form to the ways in which linguistic features are encountered in actual life
(3) Identify social functions and discover ways in which linguistic features are selected and grouped to serve them (sharing a concern with social realism and validity)
(4) Show that socially constituted linguistics is concerned with social as well as referential meaning and with language as part of communicative conduct and social action.

Generally, context refers to the situation, in which language is used. Such situations may be: physical/environmental, social, institutional situations which may include events, time, culture or any social convention that has direct bearing on the use of language. NOUN (2010: 30)attributes the first use of the term "context of situation" to Malinowski, a social anthropologist, who in his study of language behaviours among some native Indians drew the conclusion that language is a "mode of action" and as social behaviour is closely tied to the relevant social situation in which it is used. This implies that the use of words in any communicative situation is not just limited to the sounds uttered by the speaker at the grammatical level but also includes basically the pragmatic context in which such words are uttered as well.

Lyons (1996:242) examines the concept of context alongside language and concludes that the two are related because language use is sensitive to context. He buttresses this using the following illustrations:

Let us suppose that John says "I'll meet you at the bank" and Mary says "I will meet you at the bank".

In each instance, they have said the same thing i.e. produced the same utterance – inscription. But have they both uttered the same sentence? It is important to realize that we cannot answer this question without knowing not only what forms have been uttered, but also of what expressions they are forms. If 'bank' in John's utterance is a form of financial institution, and 'bank' in Mary's is a form of slopping side of a river, they have uttered different sentences.

This therefore demonstrates the fact that in one context a word may mean one thing but giving another context, the same word may assume an entirely different meaning as stressed by Malinowski (1946) quoted in Chukwuma (2001: 11 – 12):

> ...the conception of meaning as contained in utterance is false and futile. A statement spoken in real life is never detached from the situation in which

it has been uttered. A word without linguistic context is a mere figment and stands for nothing by itself...

Malinowski then concludes that language is a means of social activity and cooperation. The meaning of an utterance in a particular set of circumstance is to be seen in its effect on the environment, which speech seeks to preserve or alter. We have therefore stated the meaning of an utterance whether written or spoken, be it a proverb, joke, lecture or preaching when we have put it into its context of situation and we see what it does.

In the same vein, J.R. Firth asserts that context is the bedrock of any linguistic enterprise because "normal linguistic behaviour as a whole is meaning effort, directed towards the maintenance of appropriate patterns of life", (Firth 1957: 223). Since every utterance occurs within what NOUN (2010) describes as "a culturally determined context of situation", the meaning of what the speaker says is tied to that context not only about himself and the ways he perceives himself, but equally his roles as well as relationship with other members of the society.

Within the purview of Pragmatics and Discourse Analysis, it is commonly believed that linguistic codes are actually selected and used according to some social sets of standards. This is why the two fields give prominence to the investigation of context-based meaning thereby lending credence to the fact that it will be impossible to talk about the two fields without reference to the context in which utterances are made. In order to appreciate the functions and features of context, this chapter proceeds to examine the types of context in Pragmatics and Discourse Analysis.

Types of Context
2.1 Linguistic/Non-Linguistic context
Nunan (1993) identifies two types of context: the linguistic and non-linguistic. Linguistic context refers to the language that surrounds or accompanies the piece of discourse under examination. NOUN (2010:32) defines the term as referring to the set of words in the same sentence or utterance which forms the linguistic environment that determines the sense of the words in the context. For example:

> ...if the word 'shoot' appears as in a linguistic context along with other words like 'dribble', 'penalty', 'goal', or 'over the bar', we immediately understand what the word 'shoot' meant. If on the other hand, the same

word appears with words like 'soldier', artillery' or 'war', the meaning is immediately known.

The linguistic context of a word or words therefore has a strong effect on what we think they mean. Words therefore generally co-occur together to give us an insight into what they mean. According to Adegbija (1999: 192), in order to fully understand the linguistic context, there is need to examine questions such as: what are the other words appearing in the environment of a particular word used? What do they mean? What do they imply within the physical and socio-cultural setting? As can be observed in the quotation above, the words 'dribble', 'penalty', 'goal' and 'over the bar' as surrounding words with 'shoot' in the first instance suggest to the reader that the context of discourse is football while 'soldier', artillery' or 'war' as surrounding words to the same word 'shoot' gives the image of the military.

The non-linguistic context on the other hand includes the type of communication event that is taking place at the particular time, be it a joke, story, proverb or preaching which are expressed through the topic, the setting, physical situation, the participants as well as the relationship between them and the background knowledge and assumptions underlying the communication event as illustrated below.

In our daily conversations, both the linguistic and non-linguistic contexts feature prominently for an effective use and understanding in whatever social context we find ourselves. This can be amply demonstrated in the sphere of proverb usage and understanding where both the speaker and listener need to possess the knowledge of the two contexts. To this, any user of the Jukun proverb *Angwu hi bye dihimba* (A young partridge follows the crafty steps of the mother) must be aware of the fact that at the linguistic level, "Young partridge" personifies a young man while 'the mother partridge' is the personification of such young man's parents. At the non-linguistic context, the speaker and listener need to look at the physical environment before the uttering as well as interpreting the saying since in one context it can be taken as praise while in another context it can be an insult. For instance, in an event that a young man has distinguished himself, the utterance of this saying is praising him in relation to the good examples set by his parents for him to emulate in which case, the proverb is used positively. Conversely, if the young man in question has conducted himself in a disappointing or disgraceful manner, the uttering of the saying is a condemnation of the act in relation to the bad examples set by the parents, in which case the context of usage is negative.

2.2 Physical/Environmental context
Besides the linguistic and non-linguistic context, we can also know what words mean on the basis of the physical or environmental context as they influence how we interpret such words. Our understanding of certain words or expressions is therefore tied to their physical context especially with regard to the time and place being referred to in the expression. NOUN (2010: 33) identifies other features of the physical context to include:
(i) Participants, e.g. boys, girls, men, traders
(ii) Ongoing activity, e.g. playing, chatting, debating
(iii) The place, e.g. church, class, stadium, dining table
(iv) The time, e.g. time of the day or season.

Similarly, Hymes (1972) identifies the following as general features of the physical context:
(i) Participants, i.e. people involved, e.g. husband and wife, neighbours, colleagues, teachers and students etc.
(ii) Topic, i.e. what the discourse is about, e.g. politics, religion, race, health, etc.
(iii) Setting, i.e. where the event takes place, e.g. at home, at work, at school, etc.
(iv) Channel, e.g. medium- speech, writing, non-verbal
(v) Code (dialect/style)
(vi) Message form (debate, chat, etc.)

As observed by NOUN, all of the above features may not rigidly be ascribed to the physical context. Citing the instance of the channel/medium or code through which the piece of discourse is carried out, one can observe that they are determined by other variables such as education, age, status or class which may well be described as some features of the socio-cultural context.

However, Edward (1976) reviewed Hymes' categories, modified and came out with a reduced version of speech situations to include: Setting, participants and topic.
(i) Setting: this refers to the locale, rather than the action.
(ii) Participants: they are important because they give the discourse a clearly defined status, controlling what can be said by whom and how.

A notable example of how the physical environment can serve as a control mechanism on what the participant says according to Butari (2006: 20) is in the usage of proverbs in Jukun land. According to him:

> Men (the grown up) can use proverbs in whatever situation and to anybody unlike the women and children whose proverbs usage is restricted. They can only seek permission during a general gathering to 'quote the elders' and such permission must be granted.

(iii) Topic – This is what the speech is all about. The seriousness and sensitivity of a topic depends very much on the appropriate language in any given speech event. In a typical African society, proverbs are usually employed to garnish an utterance to show its seriousness in order to reprimand, caution, advise or even give judgment by the elders. For instance, Yamusa (1983:51) cites an example of a judgment delivered by the AkuUka (the king of the Jukun) in a quarrel between a man and the wife to show the futility of the wife's action to abandon her matrimonial home because:

> Even her stay in her father's house cannot prevent mis-understanding. If one observes the teeth and the tongue, he needs to think twice. In spite of their closeness, the teeth sometimes bite the tongue. Misunderstanding is inevitable. It is a visitor. It comes and goes...

Osisanwo (2008:79) observes that the following are issues involved when discussing the concept of physical context in Pragmatics:

(i) Participants: in any communicative situation, the sex, class and social status of the participants are important factors as they affect what they say, and how they say them. For instance, in an academic gathering, the importance attached to the participants will be determined by their levels of education. Here, a professor will naturally be given more respect and attention than any other person present.

(ii) Activities: in any physical context, the physical activity that is going on in the situation has a very important role to play in understanding the message. The physical activity therefore calls for the type of language that is used. For instance, during a football match, language is usually tailored to describe the various actions going on, so also with party and lectures.

(iii) Place: language use in any physical context is also reflected in the type of place in which such activity is going on. For instance, is the speech act going on in a school between the teacher and students, market between trader and customer, or hospital between the doctor and the patient? For instance, the following utterances made by a teacher and a doctor to their clients as adopted from Osasinwo (2008: 80) give an insight into what transpired in the two places:

Patient: That is just the problem.
Doctor: Well, I'll try my best for you.
Pupil: That is just the problem sir.
Teacher: Well I'll try my best for you.

In the above conversations, the physical settings, that is the place; hospital and school are clues which offer us the opportunity to infer the type of problems being talked about: one medical and the other academic.

(iv) Time: the time in which a speech occurs is a determining factor in language use. For instance, the expression 'good morning' is prevalent in the morning. Similarly, activities during the raining season are also reflected in the use of language.

2.3 Socio-cultural context

This type of context mainly centres on socio-cultural considerations such as: beliefs, value system, religion, conventions that control individuals' behaviour and relationship with others. The pertinent questions under the socio-cultural context include: what are the beliefs, habits, value systems, or cultures of those involved? Are they Nigerians, Ghanaians, Cameroonians? What these questions imply is that people from different cultural backgrounds are likely to have different beliefs, cultural heritage and religion. The socio-cultural 'rules' of behaviour therefore guide them in order to communicate effectively with one another. For instance, while 419 to an average Ghanaian or Cameroonian is just a figure in between 418 and 420, within the Nigerian socio-cultural context, it has an additional meaning of someone who obtains by fraud. To this, within the Nigerian context therefore to address one as 419 without any evidence is tantamount to saying that he is a fraudster, an allegation which is very serious.

Based on such peculiarity in the belief systems of people, one needs to consider the differences in the various speech acts, forms of address, expression of politeness during ceremonies and other significant activities between one culture and another. It is only by so doing that one can appreciate the importance of context of culture in shaping meanings,

(Onyemelukwu 2004). Context of culture therefore has to do with socio-cultural nuances which underlie the use of language.

The knowledge of socio-cultural rules of behaviours is the central focus of Dell Hymes' (1972) "communicative competence" which is the ability of the speaker to know when to speak, where, and in what manner.

Lawal *et al.* (1995) describe context and competence as the core and the most significant factor in any socio-cultural speech situation since it is "meaning" that unites the lexical, syntactic and phonological levels. In order to buttress their point, they identify two levels of semantic meaning in the use of proverbs in any given society at either the lexical or semantic level: the primary or literal level and the secondary or idiomatic/figurative level. The primary lower level feeds the secondary higher level through what would seem a fundamental and tacit assumption by all competent users that the use of every proverb is an idiom of a sort, a tightly condensed representation of a fairly comparable and rather large group of possibilities of socio-cultural experience. "Linguistic meaning" is thus transferred in part to "Pragmatic meaning" through the use of such figurative devices as metaphor, metonymy, synecdoche and symbolism. This can be illustrated through the use of the Jukun proverb *Kazuzurisuandemba*– "A single bracelet does not make a clatter", in which the literal translation of *Kazuzu* is a single individual. But at the figurative level, a person is expected to be sensitive to the norms of his environment, since a person's individuality derives from his group. Hence, what is presented as the English version of the proverb is not literal but idiomatic equipment, at which every competent user of the Jukun language is expected to arrive as the first major signpost to a pragmatic interpretation.

Hymes (1971) emphasizes the importance of communicative competence to include one's knowledge and ability to use all the semiotic systems available to one as a member of a given socio-cultural community as explained in the use of the proverb above.

Besides one's knowledge and ability to use the systems in the community, there is an understanding of certain universal logical principles and the general conditions of appropriateness that Grice (1975) has called "Conversational Implicatures" and to which Leech (1983) refers as "The cooperative principle and politeness principle".

According to Bahago (1999:45), six different kinds of communicative competence form part of the speaker's knowledge of the socio-cultural rules within the society. They include:

(a) The participants involved in the conversation must know their "role" and "status".
(b) The categorization of the situation in terms of its degrees of formality by the participant.
(c) The participants must know how to make their utterances appropriate to the subject matter.
(d) The participants must know how to make their utterances appropriate to the domain to which the situation belongs.
(e) Participants must know where they are in space and time.

In her own contribution, Onyemelukwe (2004) is of the opinion that the combination of context of culture and context of situation gives rise to the disparities and resemblances found between one language and another. According to her, context of culture should aim at addressing certain questions such as:
(i) What Socio-cultural factors determine the interpretation under immediate context?
(ii) What moral lesson can be derived from the utterance?
(iii) What ideology or philosophy is the author advocating?
(iv) How does the utterance relate to the themes and/or values reflected in the creative work?

It is on the basis of the above that she draws the conclusion that in analysing any given language, attention should always be paid to the people's culture.

Socio-cultural context is not tied down to the issue of mother tongue alone because if a language spreads out to different socio-cultural areas across the world, it is likely to be exposed to different ethnic groups .Under such situation, the religious or cultural belief of the people who use the language as their second language can still be expressed in the new language. English and French are good examples. As it is with Nigeria, different ethnic groups use English to express their religious belief. For instance, the language is used in churches and mosques to preach on Sundays and Fridays in spite of the fact that the worshippers have their own languages.

2.4 Interpersonal context

The state of mind of the speaker or writer influences how he or she interacts with others, and this in most instances is expressed through the use of language. The emotional predisposition of the language user as observed by Coulthard (1993:50) is instrumental in shedding light on the psychological setting as:

> This affects his choice of idiosyncratic forms. At the same time, it influences his degree of deviation from the standard/conventional forms in his attempt to paint a picture of his emotion within the limits of the language text he selects.

Interpersonal context therefore focuses on psychological considerations that influence the way a speaker expresses himself or herself either through writing or speaking. Fundamentally, the pertinent question to be considered here is 'what is the state of the mind of those involved in any given discourse? For instance, as observed by Adegbija (1999: 192), if one is mourning the death of a loved one and with that frame of mind cries out 'put me into the grave with him', the utterance will be interpreted based on the psychological state of his mind. As a result of this, the listeners are not likely going to grant his request.

The above picture points to the fact that the inputs and reactions of a speaker can largely be predicted if he is sad, happy, excited or bored. However, the critics of pragmatics according to Lavendra (1988) have argued that:

> the understanding of text and talk is not dependent on elements rooted in psychology rather, on social factors such as power, and status and how they are distributed and maintained in the society.

While agreeing to the fact that utterances made may not easily reflect the state of the mind on the surface, it can however be added that where one is able to succeed in discovering the exact state of the mind of the speaker, a step would have been taken forward at getting the message right. The fact still remains that an individual speaker or writer is prone to make linguistic choices and decide what to say and how to say it. Therefore, factors that place constraint on their ability to do so like the state of the mind are of interest to pragmatic analysts.

2.5 Institutional context

At the surface realisation, institutional context shares a lot with socio-cultural context but there are certain elements of the context which are in some specialised kinds of setting like educational institutions, which have a lot of restrictions in language use. This is because there are peculiar manner of expressions that help to identify the individuals and the institutions that they are associated with. There are ways people must greet one another to show their membership of certain religious or socio-cultural organizations. For instance, while the expression such as 'bless you' indicates strongly that the speaker is a Christian, '*aslamualeikum*' on the other hand is a pointer that the speaker belongs to the Islamic religion. In fact such expressions have become almost institutionalised that people are made to believe that unless they greet each other that way they may never enjoy certain privileges, (NOUN 2008:35).

According to Fairclough, (1989), such bodies that have tremendous influence on the way members behave are institutional because they 'determine social behaviour and individuals simply imbibe as natural and unchanging.'

3.0 Components of discourse context

M. A. K. Holiday (1976) has identified three components of discourse context which can be represented as complex dimensions such as: Field (the ongoing activities), Tenor (the role relationships), and Mode (the symbolic channel).

Field

This is the ongoing activity or the total event in which the text is functioning together with the activity of the speaker or writer. As the primary aim of the discourse, it represents what subject matter the interactants must explore. This could in another way be referred to as the topic or subject matter of a discourse. Hudson (1980) describes this as the 'what about', 'the why' of discourse which could be: political, religious, academic, health, marriage, etc., in most instances an individual's language use is governed by the field of discourse.

Tenor

This involves relevant social relations, permanent or temporary, among the participants involved, such roles as parent-child, friend-friend, superior – inferior, etc. These are the possible roles one finds in a speech event depending on the situation or context. Tenor also indicates role interaction, i.e. how interactants take turns and what influences it and how temporal or permanent such relationships are. It also mirrors the identities of the people involved. Some social variables such as age, status, education, etc. influence how individuals assign roles to one another in conversations, (NOUN 2088:36).

Mode

This is the function of the text/discourse in the speech event. This could either be spoken or written. Hudson calls it 'the how' of discourse. Basically, both the subject matter of a discourse and the relationship that exists among the interactants determine the appropriate mode of expressing the text, either written or verbally. For instance, while legal documents could be better written, interpersonal communication could be more appropriately done through verbal means. The spoken channel elicits instant feedback between interactants because it offers them the opportunity to chat face to face. In the written mode, there is no visual contact and thus, immediate feedback is not possible.

4.0 Mutual Context in Discourse

In every discourse, there is basic information that the interactants are expected to share in order to understand each other. In pragmatics, such information is known as "Mutual Contextual Belief" and it has as its major thrust the fact that in any speech event, a speaker has an intention and the listener or hearer will make some inference in which both of them will base their role on certain basic facts shared by them. Bach and Harnish (1979: 4) propose that in general, the inference made by the hearer and the inference he takes himself to be intended to make is based not just on what the speaker says but also on mutual contextual beliefs (MCBs), salient information from the context known to both speaker and hearer. They further state that:

> ...speakers' intention and hearers' inferences must be mutual if communication is to take place. In inferring what S is saying, H also relies on the 'presumption of literalness (PL)'that is if S could (under the circumstances) be speaking literally, then S is speaking literally. Conversely, if it is evident to H that S could not be speaking literally, S supposes H to be seeking non-literally and therefore seeks to identify what the non-literal illocutionary act is.

The theory further makes a distinction between conventional illocutionary acts and communicative illocutionary acts. The former, accordingly needs no communicative intentions, as success in the communication transaction is a matter of convention, and not intention. In communicative illocutionary acts, however, the speaker's intentions accompany the acts, and the recognition of such intention by the hearer is pivotal to the success of the act.

At the level of language, meaningful communication can only take place when the interactants have access to the language of communication while at the level of situation, the life experience of the interactants including shared code, linguistic or non-linguistic come to play. Hudson (1983:77) identifies three kinds of knowledge which interactants need to share in any given situation:

(i) Cultural knowledge: This is learned from other people whom we create because we see that other people around us make use of them in their thinking.
(ii) Shared non-cultural knowledge: This on the other hand is shared by people within the same community or the world over, but is not learned from each other (this is built without reference to other people as a convenient way of interpreting our experience).
(iii) Non-shared non-cultural knowledge: This is unique to the individual.

For instance, in a verbal discourse involving the Jukun proverb: *Gbaweajimjim she kurumba* (the slippery road does not have respect for even the king); the interactants need to depend on certain background knowledge. To this, if someone utters the saying to a friend (perceived to be advanced in age or in social status) who had earlier on complained of hunger, "Hunger" therefore forms the background knowledge needed for the interpretation. However, if the listener rather has reported the death of an important person and the co-interactant uttered the same saying, 'death' here becomes the background knowledge. The idea behind this saying is borne out of the belief in Jukun society that in spite of the king's status, he must succumb to nature's call like hunger and death. One important thing to note here is that knowing the proverb is not enough to interpret it but one needs to have the background knowledge of an issue before one can appropriately interpret it.

5.0 Text and context in Pragmatics and Discourse Analysis

Both Pragmatics and Discourse Analysis emphasize utterance, text and talk rather than the sentence because it is an utterance or passage spoken or written of any length that forms a unified whole, (Halliday and Hasan 1976). This therefore implies that a text here is considered based on its meaningfulness rather than in terms of its grammaticality. This is because the meaning associated with any given text can be realised in a context. What we mean by 'text' here is a piece of discourse or utterance which depends on a given context for its meaning. The Discourse analyst therefore is concerned with how speakers implore language and not the formal properties of language per say.

Context therefore is sustained both in spoken and written discourses if the participants must get along while interacting. We shall demonstrate this using a written discourse *The Lottery Ticket* by Ahmed Yerima and sample of two proverbs to represent the verbal form of discourse.

When examined from the Nigerian context, Ahmed Yerima's play *The Lottery Ticket* deals with many serious issues bedevilling the society such as the impermanence of human existence and the will to survive in an almost impossible scenario. The play specifically focuses on three major areas that have posed major challenges to the society in its present form which are: bribery and corruption, greed as well as quest for materialism. For instance, in order to cover up the case of the murder of Danger (one of the participants who was killed as a result of the commotion for the ticket)and the 'death' of Baba Tailor, another participant(the winner of the lottery ticket who was shocked and fainted and was thought to have been dead), a police sergeant who came into the scene in the Nigerian fashion demands for gratification and the conversation goes as follows:

    Landlord: Oga Sajent, how much you want?
    Sajent: Good una get sense. Each dead body na three hundred naira.
        (46)

The above conversation between the Landlord and the police sergeant demonstrates a typical Nigerian context where the law enforcement agents accept money from culprits in order to be set free. No wonder therefore that the Landlord's question is described by the officer as not only a 'good' one but also a mark of intelligence, hence 'una get sense'.

In order to explicate the theme of greed as one of the cankerworms bedevilling the Nigerian context, all the characters in the play are only interested in taking forceful possession of the ticket won by Baba Tailor without minding his health condition even when he was in a state of comma. The play portrays the idea of the quest for crass materialism as a canker warm that has eaten deep into the fabrics of the society. Right from the onset, every character in the play is schemes to win the lottery ticket for the prize of one million naira. In their desperation, customers who have come to eat in Mama Lizi's restaurant would rather prefer to buy Tuba cola (a brand of soft drinks to be qualified to enter for the raffle draw) than food as depicted below:

Mama Lizi: one man come here yesterday say he want one spoon of beans and two bottle of tuba cola.

The socio-cultural context of the play is amply demonstrated right from the opening discourse of the play. First and foremost, the language use is the Nigerian pidgin which situates the play within the Nigerian context thereby depicting the class of participants that are involved in the conversation which portrays them as low class and illiterates who cannot effectively communicate in the standard Nigerian English. Within the Nigerian setting, petty traders, food vendors, artisans and roadside mechanics belong to the low class and one of their attributes is the use of the Nigerian pidgin since many of them are either complete illiterates or school drop outs who cannot express themselves in the Standard English. The activities in the play centred among them hence the playwright's choice of this brand of English.

From the physical/environmental context, the speaker-addressee pattern of talk can be seen as it is sustained all through the play. As a play where conversations are carried out, there are prototypical participants who are engaged in the conversations. In the play, there is a total of eight participants whose appearance occurs in the following order: Mama Lizi, Lizi, Landlord, Danger, Yellow Fever, Baba Tailor, Blindman and Sajent respectively. While Mama Lizi, Lizi, and Landlord are the first participants, the others come much later in the play. For instance, Baba Tailor makes his first appearance in page 15, Danger on page 21, Yellow Fever on page 30 and Sajent on page 42 respectively.

The participants order of appearance shows the relevance and role of each of them in the play. From this, it can be established therefore that while Mama Lizi, Lizi and the Landlord play the major roles as major characters, Danger, Yellow Fever, Baba Tailor, Blindman and Sajent play minor roles hence, minor characters. This is glaring as depicted from the play. Mama Lizi participates for a total of 145 times, the Landlord 132, while Lizi 91 times. On the other hand, while Danger participates for 78 times, Baba Tailor 51 times, Yellow Fever 36 times, Sajent 26 times and Blindman just once. By appearing only once, the Blindman can be described as a passive participant because of his disability as the issue discussed in the play has to do with the sense of sight- the lottery ticket promo.

Form the psychological context, the discourse of the play closes with all the participants being shocked by the 'resurrection' of Baba Tailor, the winner of the lottery who fainted earlier as a result of shock. This discourse closing underscores the power of greed over the human soul as it rids the human soul of value for the life of his fellow man. This is amply demonstrated through the participants' lack of concern for the life of BabaTailor who instead of mourning his 'death' and thinking of how to assist his family out of poverty with the money he has won, prefers to jettison his dead body and went after the lottery ticket he won. With their frame of mind, Baba Tailor's death does not come to them as a surprise so also his 'resurrection'. It is in the light of this that they all yell out at the close of the text:

ALL: Baba Tailor!

From oral discourse, context plays important role in the use of proverbs as demonstrated in the two Jukun proverbs below:

Soana ma ndo u ra, ukatejirayayakaramba (Load is heavy for you, you don't blame head pad) meaning: If the load is too heavy for you, don't pass the blame on the head pad.

In order to fully bring out the complete meaning of the saying, there is need to examine it along the following Contexts/Competencies:

Linguistic: Here, there is a fundamental semantic requirement of understanding that *soana* (load) and *yakara* (the head pad) are metonyms for the condition in which one finds himself.

Situational: A person finds himself in a situation which he feels he couldn't withstand. Instead of admitting his inability he turns round to blame someone else.

Psychological: The speaker disapproves of the person's attitude of blaming someone else for his problem and the person is expected to know this.

Social: no special relationship is required between the interlocutors.

Sociological: Awareness of the fact that one must carry out one's responsibility. Where one cannot withstand such, one must not blame another person or situation.

Cosmological: Knowledge of the Jukun traditional disapproval of shifting blame on someone else.

The theme of the above saying is 'condition'. One is expected to live up to expectation no matter the condition one finds himself. However, there are situations that the human weakness could manifest. Under such situation, sincerity is expected. This implies that the Jukun society recognises human limitations and at the same time condemns shifting of blames.

Kazuzurisuandemba (Bracelet one make noise not) - meaning a single bracelet does not make a clatter.
Contexts/Competencies:
Linguistic: At the linguistic level, on must understand the personification of ka (bracelet) and nde (clatter) as representing a single individual and his worth in the society respectively.
Situational: A single individual over-estimates his worth, strength and independence within a group.
Psychological: The speaker frowns at this and wants the listener to know this.
Social: No special relationship is required here as the interlocutors could be friends, parent-child or husband-wife.
Sociological: The Jukun traditional expectation of personal modesty and humility irrespective of one's worth.
Cosmological: knowledge of the need for a person to be sensitive to norms of his environment, since a person's individuality derives from his group.

This saying can be seen as dealing with the issue of oneness in the society. An individual no matter his strength cannot isolate himself from other people in the society. This is because one is not an island. His individuality is derived from his group.

Conclusion

This chapter has been able to demonstrate that for proper use and understanding of any discourse (whether written or spoken), the context is vital. In order to justify this, the chapter examined the concept of context from the perspectives of pragmatic and discourse analysis and discovered four types: Linguistic/non-linguistic, physical/environmental, socio-cultural as well as institutional.

The chapter also discussed M. A. K. Halliday's components of discourse context which include: Field (the ongoing activities), Tenor (the role relationships), and Mode (the symbolic channel). Equally examined is the importance of background information between a speaker/writer and listener/reader commonly known as mutual contextual beliefs in pragmatics and finally, while Ahmed Yerima's text *The Lottery Ticket* was sampled to show the importance of context in the written text, two Jukun proverbs were equally cited to show the importance of context to verbal discourse.

Works cited

Bach, M. andHarnish, M. Linguistic Communication and Speech Acts.Cambridge: M.I.T Press, 1979. Print.

Bahago, Shawai. " A Pragmatic Analysis of Language of Religion in Selected Sermons of William Kumuyi". M.A. Thesis Submitted to English Department, ABU Zaria, 1999.

Chukwuma, Ezirim.D. "A Sociolinguistic study of Context of Situation in the use of Igbo Proverbs" MA Thesis submitted to English Department, ABU Zaria, 2001.

Cook, Guy. *Discourse, Language Teaching: A Scheme for Teacher Education.* Oxford: Oxford UP, 1991. Print.

Coulthard, M. An Introduction to Discourse Analysis. London: Longman, 1993. Print.

Edwards, A.D. *Language in Culture and Class.*London: Heinemann Educational Books, 1976. Print.

Fairclough, N.*Language and Power.* London: Longman, 1989. Print.

Firth, J. R. *Papers in Linguistics.* London: Edward Arnold, 1957. Print.

Hymes, Dell. *Foundations Sociolinguistics: An Ethnographic Approach.* Philadelphia: University of Pennsylvanian Press, 1974. Print.

Halliday, Michael, Exploration in the Functions of Language. London: Arnold, 1975. Print.

Halliday, Michael and RuqaiyaHasan. *Cohesion in English.* Essex: Longman, 1976. Print.

Hudson, R. A. *Sociolinguistics.* Cambridge: CUP, 1980. Print.

Hymes, Dell. *On Communicative Competence.* Philadelphia: University of Pennsylvanian Press, 1972. Print.

Lavandera, B. "The study of language in its socio-cultural Context" *Linguistics: The Cambridge Survey.* Ed. Newmeyer. Vol. 4. Cambridge, pp. 1-13.

Lawal *et al.* "A Pragmatic Study of Selected Pairs of Yoruba Proverbs". *Journal of Pragmatics.* Elsevier Science B.V, 1995. Print.

National Open University of Nigeria. 2010, print.

Oloruntoba-Oju, Taiwo "Sociolinguistics: An Overview". *The English language and Literature in English: An Introductory Handbook.* Ed. Adegbija, Efurosinina. Ilorin: Department of Modern European Languages, 1999. Print.

Onyemelukwe, Ifeoma "Proverbial Text, Context and Meaning in Achebe's Things fall Apart". Conference of SYSFLAN of ABU Zaria from 1-8 August, 2004.

Osisanwo, Wale .*Introduction to Discourse Analysis and Pragmatics*. Lagos: Femolus-Fetop Publishers, 2008. Print.

Yamusa, Grace. *Clock of Justice*. Wukari: Amune Printing Press, 1983. Print.

Chapter 3

Conversational Analysis

- Solomon Oreoluwa Abraham

This chapter discusses conversation analysis and in doing so, considers it necessary to take a look at conversation itself in order to provide a firm basis for the topic. The discussion proceeds to provide some insights into conversation analysis and how it is carried out, since conversation is a deliberate act, an exercise that is carried out for specific purposes. It concludes with the significance of conversation analysis to the study of Discourse Analysis specifically and language generally.

Conversation

Conversation of talk-exchange is regarded as talk in interaction. Conversations are structured sequences of expressions by more than one single speaker. The participants in a conversation range from two to as many as is reasonably possible. Locutionary acts in conversations are governed by the principles of turn-taking. Acceptable conversation norm acknowledges certain social obligations such as greeting and leave-taking. Relevant contributions in the course of any conversation are guided by principles. According to Levinson (1985: 284) conversation may be taken to be that familiar predominant kind of talk in which two or more participants freely alternate in speaking, which generally occurs outside specific institutional settings like religious services, law courts, classrooms and the like.

Levinson points out that conversation is the outcome of the interaction of two or more independent, goal-directed individuals with often divergent interests. Conversation is characterised by local organisations, especially turn-taking. It has been observed that talks like courtroom or classroom interrogation which exhibit features of conversational activity like turn-taking are not conversations. This could be because of the formal restrictions and underpinnings of such types of conversation.

Furthermore, Ruiz Mayo (1990) posits that conversation is not only a human right; it is a duty. It is that conversation is inherently one unrestricted human activity in all human societies. This is because people engage in it freely and by choice. Conversation as an activity is conducted both in the palace and the prison. Conversation as a form of speech is one of the inalienable human rights enshrined in the United Nations Article of freedom of speech.

Similarly, Mey (2001) states that conversation is a way of using language socially, the linguistic interchanges between two or more people. It is what happens among people when we use language together. Conversation is a platform of doing things with words together with other persons, socially.

A conversation can be initiated in many ways. It could be by making use of attention-getters, vocatives or greeting. The opening of a conversation is then followed by turn-taking in which the conversation proper takes place. A normal conversation is brought to a close by shared agreement of the conversationalists who get involved in pre-closing turn-taking and then the closing proper. Conversations vary in degree of formality, informality and familiarity. Conversations are both social and linguistic acts and they vary from culture to culture.

According to Levinson (*op. cit.*), conversation is clearly the prototypical kind of language usage which every human being is first exposed to and this is the reason why pragmatic investigation looks to conversation for insight. In his words, conversation is the matrix for language acquisition.

Conversation has organised structure and the structure is determined by the norms governing it in any society. The participants in conversation are either consciously or unconsciously regulated by the norms except where they wish to subvert such norms. Furthermore, Mey (*op. cit.*: 114) opines that:

> Users are part of a world of usage: they are never alone in their use of language but use their language as members of a speech community that reflect the conditions of the community at large.

This is true as observed in some people's language use of slang and other forms of colloquial expressions that reflect certain conditions of the society. In contemporary Nigeria, language use such as: 'They *settled* the fuel attendant before he agreed to sell full tank for them' and 'The Ciroma Consensus Committee was the *tsunami* which swept away the general who resides in Minna' reflect some social and political occurrences in the country.

Adegbija (1999) views conversation as a string of at least two turns. One or more than a person may speak at a time. Transitions could occur between one turn and the next without a gap or overlap. According to him, turn allocation techniques vary from culture to culture and that turn-taking could be determined by speakers' roles. Speaker change is often introduced by grammatical, phonological or semantic clues.

The conversational structures presented by Levinson (*op. cit.*) and Mey (*op. cit.*) represent some of the structures that have been identified. Sacks (1995) remarks that the basic unit of conversation is the 'turn', that is, a shift in the direction of the speaking flow and it is a characteristic of normal conversation.

What Conversation Analysis Is

Conversation analysis describes the social interaction order that is both moral and institutional when participants in normal linguistic discourse engage each other, and according to Heritage (1998), both the moral and institutional orders are acquired early in life, even though complex and intricate. Heritage avers that the observance of the moral and institutional orders make social action and interaction mutual sense-making. Conversation analysis explains how interlocutors in normal conversation take their turns, the way interruptions overlap are managed, as well as the process of opening and closing conversation.

Heritage *(op. cit.)* says conversation analysis is a discipline which is interested in the relationship that exists between meaning and context in linguistic interaction by connecting meaning and context to the idea of sequence of utterance in any discourse. Furthermore, he sees in conversation analysis a body of theory which argues that sequences of actions, that is utterances or linguistic actions, form a significant part of what is known as context; the meaning of one utterance is 'heavily shaped by the sequences of ' utterance from which it 'emerges'. He explains the theory in a tri-dimensional way thus:

> Context-shaped, that is, participants in a discourse normally address themselves before it commences and 'the immediately preceding talk'.
> Participants usually create a context for the next interlocutor to talk.

By producing a next action, participants demonstrate an understanding of a prior act which occurs at a 'multiplicity of levels'.

According to him conversation analysis begins with the responsiveness to context by producing a 'next action that a prior action projected, the creation of context by the production of the next action, and showing the understanding by these means' form 'the products of a common set of socially shared and structured procedures.' Therefore, for him, conversation analysis is a simultaneous analysis of action, that is linguistic action, context management and inter-subjectivity; as they are the 'object' of the participants' actions.

Moreover, the procedures on which these activities are based are normative, consequently, participants are liable for non-adherence to them or the inferences which their use engenders

Moreover, Heritage (*op. cit.*) argues that conversation analysis' starting point is in the assumption that 'context is both a project and product of the participants' actions' as context is built, invoked and managed through interaction.

Woodruff and Paul M. Aoki view conversation analysis as a sociological discipline. The implication of this view is that conversation is a human behaviour in the society and as such a discipline which examines this behaviour cannot be but sociological. Furthermore, conversation analysis is said to focus on human to human interaction, citing Sacks, they identify conversation analysis as the most visible and influential form of ethno-methodological research which is concerned with describing the methods by which members of a culture engage in social interaction. For them, a fundamental role of conversation analysis is to investigate social interaction and demonstrate its organised patterns of actions by assuming that linguistic, social interaction is structurally organised. Conversation analysis not only examines how utterances are organised but it also describes how sequences of linguistic actions are organised in a context as well as identifying features which are peculiar to the context.

In explicating conversation analysis, Sidnell (2010:1) in Sert and Paul Seedhause (2011:1) states that the aim of conversation analysis is to 'describe, analyse, and understand talk as a basic and constitutive feature of human social life.' In addition, Seedhause (2005) in Sert and Paul Seedhause (*op. cit.*) asserts that the basic principles of conversation analysis are four which are:

Order exists at every point of interaction, meaning that talk-exchanges, talk in-interaction or conversation is 'systemically organized and deeply ordered and methodic.'

Contributions to interaction are context-shaped and context-renewing, by this, contributions to conversation can be adequately understood only when reference is made to the sequential environment in which they occur, as the participants' determine them, forming part of the sequential environment for the subsequent contribution.

Any order of detail cannot be dismissed a priori as disorderly, incidental, or irrelevant.

Analysis is carried out bottom-up and data-driven which require absolute objectivity that takes cognisance of values and norms which interlocutors orient to.

Conversation analysis provides a comprehensive description of the nature of conversation (Suzanne E. and Diana S., 1997). The import of this is that conversation analysis is a linguistic endeavour that presents a description of the nature or constituent of conversation in a comprehensive detail. Mazeland (2006) states that conversation analysis studies the methods that 'participants orient to when they organise social action through talk.' He acknowledges that conversation analysis has its origin in American sociology; the sociologists Erving Goffman and Harold Garfinkel are the foremost scholars. Also, he says that conversation analysis is a sub-field of Pragmatics which discusses analysis or interactional sociolinguistics.

The Practice of Conversation Analysis

Turn- takings, adjacency pairs, repair and preference are some common features of conversation that are significant to conversation analysis. Conversation analysis is done by collecting linguistic interactive exchanges between some interlocutors for analysis. Then 'a moment by moment, turn by turn transcript' of the conversation in each sequence is done. This is followed by conducting an examination of the linguistic exchanges 'individually' and 'comparatively so as to observe a characteristic general orderliness. Similarly, Mazeland affirms that conversation analysis is carried out by recording real -life interactions with the aim of investigating the rules and practices from an interactional perspective and studying them.

The natural linguistic exchanges of interlocutors are carefully audio or video recorded and afterward, transcribed. Jefferson in Mazeland (*op.*

cit.) has developed 'specific conventions' known as CA transcription notation to give a detail account of the 'intelligibility and organisation of talk' that retain the prosodic features and turn- takings. A conversation analysis is readable to non-expert. Mazeland says the transcript is an empirical 'reliable approximation of the interpretative assemblies that participants in talk are working with' and that it is a combination of carefully listening to how and where utterances are produced as well as the interpretative work of the transcriber who should be a competent member of the culture being investigated.

It is important to take note of the significance of culture to conversation analysis as conversation is domiciled in 'a particular culture' within any social interaction. An understanding of the culture within which a conversation occurs sheds much light on the conduct of the conversation, the turn-takings, deference and face, among other variables.

For instance, a conversation between a very older person and a youth among the Ijesha people of Yorubaland in the southwest of Nigeria, differs from that engaged in by youth of the same age, even where the topic or issue is the same. The culture demands the youth to demonstrate his or her fine up-bringing as a cultured Ijesha youth in conversing with the elderly. It is a social norm enshrined in the Ijesha concept of '*Omoluabi*'. An accurate analysis of such a conversation should bear in mind this concept. Culture is both universal and specific. A good conversation analysis seeks to understand these aspects of culture and factor them into the analysis objectively.

Furthermore, taboo words exist in some culture and interlocutors are restrained by a shared social norm from uttering them. Similarly, some acts are forbidden by social norms in some cultures. The Yoruba culture restrains the youth to make proverbial constatives before the elderly without any deference because it is believed that proverbs are the exclusive constatives of elders. (It is said that proverbs are ripe only at the mouth of the elderly), '*enu agba lobi tii gbo*'. A youth who needs to make proverbial constative must do so deferentially with: 'It is the elders that say....'(the proverb then follows) and the elder present replies with: '*Oo pa 'mi si*' meaning : you will make another or this shall not be your last proverb. Culture is crucial; it affects conversation, so a good understanding of the culture within which an interaction takes place, or which interlocutors bring to bear upon a conversation is imperative to its adequate analysis.

Conversation analysis has been employed to investigate talk in-interactions in many human activities which include: CA-for-SLA to analyse second language interactions for the promotion of second language learning (Markee and Kasper 2004), Jenks (2010). An attempt is provided below to illustrate how conversation analysis is carried out. It is an adaptation of the Conversation Analytic Methodology offered by Mazeland (*op. cit.*)

Method of Conducting Conversation Analysis

One needs to understand that conversation analysis is data-driven and as such, reliable and valid data should be gathered for the exercise. Thereafter, the approach to be adopted is worth the analyst's consideration. The method proposed in this chapter rests on the assumption that participants in conversation operate on the basis of their contextual awareness of their involvement in a situated interactional reasoning. A convergence of the reasoning of the participants and the analyst is important to this approach as the analyst needs to provide in-built evidence that the analysis is a true reflection of the methods to which they orient themselves.

Data
Data for conversation analysis need to be ecologically valid: data that are a string of naturally occurring conversation will serve the best purpose. Such data are reliably, carefully recorded and transcribed using the appropriate conventions. One importance of the transcription is that it provides information about how participants in conversation conduct themselves during conversation as well as how they communicate. Also, researchers can make their transcripts available to others to do some work on them.

Analysis of Data
The data that has been transcribed can be analysed as a single case analysis in which the researcher conducts the analysis of the linguistic interaction in a single episode, bearing in mind some interesting aspects. Single case analysis is used to generate ideas that can be used in a collection study, testing and applying the results to collection studies or exploring the constellations of practices in episodes of conversation. The second type of analysis is called the collection study. In this, the analyst generalises the results of cumulative series of single case analyses of specific aspects and all the cases are then compared on the basis of certain

features which describe how, and also the degrees to which they are the same, similar or different.

Contribution of Conversation Analysis

Language is primarily a spoken code of human communication and this code is significant to the society because it is the representation of humanity. The main preoccupation of conversational analysis with the performance of utterance in live interaction underscores the point that human speech as the expression of language is a science of form and prosody which is observable, recordable and can be rated on time -scale. Conversation analysis, which is a study of speech that gives its full description in performance, elevates the study of language beyond abstraction. It is the study of language in its real world as the first obligation of the linguist to language.

References

Adegbija (1999) Adegbija, E. (ed.) (1999) *The English Language and Literature in English: An Introductory Handbook* Ilorin: Ilorin University.

Suzanne E. and Diana S. (1997) ' Analysing Casual Conversation.' London: Cassell. Online:
home.alleganycountylibrary.info/...MLA%20Style%20City%20Sources. Accessed 13/2/2015 7.56pm

Jenks, C. (2010). In Sert, O., and Seedhause, P., (2011) 'Introduction: Conversational Analysis and Applied Linguistics' Novista –Royal (Research on Youth and Language), (2011) 5,(1), 1-14. Online. Accessed 13/2/2015 6.30pm

Heritage, J. (1998) "conversational analysis and institutional talk Analysing data." In Proceedings of the 6th International Congress of IADA Tubingen: Niemeyer (pp. 3-17).Online:
www.sscnet.ulca.edu/soc/faculty/heritage/site/publication.../PRAGUE pdf. Accessed 13/2 /2015 7.59pm

Levinson, S. (1985) *Pragmatics*, New York: Cambridge Univ. Press.

Markee, N. and Kasper, G. (2004) 'Classroom talks. An Introduction'. *The Modern Language Journal.* 88, 491-500. In Allison Woodruff &Paul M. Aoki: 'Conversation Analysis and the User Experience'. Online. Accessed 13/2/2015. 6pm

Ruiz Mayo, J. 'The Pragmatic of a Civil Liberty,' *Journal of Pragmatics* 13 (6) (1990): 1009-12.

Mazeland H. (2006) 'Conversation Analysis'. University of Groningen, Groningen, The Netherlands. Online. Accessed 13/2/2015, 7.59 pm

Mey, J. (2001) *Pragmatics: An Introduction*, Oxford: Blackwell Publishing.

Sacks, H. (1974) 'An Analysis of the Course of a Joke's Telling in Conversation,' in Bauman, R. and Shazer, J. (eds) *Explorations in the Ethnography of Speaking*. CUP, Cambridge. In Allison Woodruff &Paul M. Aoki: 'Conversation Analysis and the User Experience'. Online. Accessed 13/2/2015. 6pm

Sacks, H. (1995) Lectures on Conversation Vol. 1-11 Oxford: Blackwell.

Seedhause (2005).In Sert, O., and Seedhause, P., (2011) 'Introduction: Conversational Analysis and Applied Linguistics' Novista –Royal (Research on Youth and Language), 2011 5,(1), 1-14. Online. Accessed 7.59pm

Sidnell (2010:1) In Sert, O., and Seedhause, P., (2011) 'Introduction: Conversational Analysis and Applied Linguistics' Novista –Royal (Research on Youth and Language), 2011 5(1), 1-14. Online. Accessed 7.59pm

Chapter 4

History and Scope of Pragmatics

- Rita Bossan

Introduction

The first use of the word pragmatics is credited to the philosopher Charles Morris. As noted by Levinson (6), Morris was concerned with a general shape of science of signs, or semiotics. Morris, in his inquiry, distinguished three distinct branches of semiotics (or syntax), semantics. To Morris, pragmatics is defined as the study of the relation of signs for users.

Between 1950 and 1960, linguistic pragmatics emerged under the leadership of two Oxford professors of philosophy in the Oxford University, J.L. Austin and H.P Grice. Other great thinkers of the school included Peter Strawson, John Searle and Ludwig Wittgenstein (Huang 7). In the 1960s and early 1970s, generative semanticists such as Jerry Katz, J.R. Ross and George Lakoff were attracted by the works of J.L. Austin and others and so launched a campaign against Noam Chomky's treatment of language as an abstract, mental device divorced from the uses and functions of language. As a result, a great deal of important research was done in the 1970s to bring some order into the content of pragmatics. Levinson (6) posits that pragmatics is the first major efforts at distinctly defining the field of pragmatics.

Kasher (568) explains that "the scope of what is called "pragmatics" depends on one's view of the nature of pragmatics." No doubt, pragmatics as a distinct discipline now has several sub field: discursive pragmatics, cognitive pragmatics, clinical pragmatics, intercultural pragmatics, multimodal pragmatics etc. Commenting on the new development in the field of pragmatics, Kecskes and Horn (1) write:

> The development of new perspective on pragmatics has been prompted by several Factors. Recent theoretical work on the Semantics/ pragmatics

interface, serious of language, and empirical work within cognitive and developmental psychology and Intercultural communication has direct attention to issues that warrant re-examination and revision of some of the central tenets and claims of the field.

The assertion above only attests to the growing development in pragmatics which makes it a viable discipline in the study of human communication in general.

The Goals of Pragmatic Enquiry

The purview of pragmatics revolves around how language is used in relation to social context. To put it another way, it is concerned with how language is manipulated in the social dynamics of interaction. In any pragmatic enquiry, the aim, prima facie is to treat the text as a series of communicative acts, not just as a configuration of phonetic, syntactic and lexical patterns. According to Mey (59-60), "the true concern of pragmatics is not to what extent the rules of grammar have been observed but whether the rules serve to veil or reveal the conditions that govern their use". Leech (13) in an attempt to distinguish pragmatics from the study of semantics made reference to one or more of the following aspects of the speech situation as the foci of pragmatics:
a) Addressers or addressees
b) The context of an utterance
c) The goals of an utterance
d) The utterance as a form of act or activity: a speech act
e) The utterance as a product of a verbal act.
(Leech,13-14)

In relation to the aforementioned, Adegbija (198) however identifies the following as the goals of pragmatic enquiry:
a) To explain how utterances convey meaning in context;
b) To explain how meaning is decoded from utterances in context in particular situation.
c) To explain how context contribute to the encoding and decoding of meaning
d) To explain how speakers and hearers of utterances perceive them as conveying the meaning they are considered as conveying in particular utterances.
e) To explain how speakers can say one thing and mean something else

f) To explain how deductions are made in context with respect to what meaning has been decoded in a particular utterance.

Definitions of Pragmatics

Pragmatics, the study of language in use, is closely associated with Systemic Functional Linguistics, O'Donnell (7). In fact, the idea of emphasising language use and function, which is the major preoccupation of pragmatics was first championed and popularised by SFL. Pragmatics has three components: ideational pragmatics; interpersonal pragmatics; and textual pragmatics. Ideational pragmatics relates to the propositional contents of linguistic structures (words, phrases, sentences, etc.) Interpersonal pragmatics is concerned with actual (pragmatic) language function, exchange structure, expression of attitude, intention and convention of interpersonal communication. It also deals with the functional choices that encoders make in various discourses, the constraints they encounter in making such choices in verbal communication, and the effects their choices have on the audience in a way that both the encoder and decoders are protected. Textual pragmatics deals with the ways by which the various principles of textual rhetoric (economy, clarity, expressivity, and processibility) help in structuring a written text as a comprehensible and acceptable message Leech (8).

Allot (1) notes that "Pragmatics is not the same for all its practitioners." Pragmatics as a distinct field of linguistic inquiry, just like any other academic discipline, is approached and defined differently by its many scholars. The varied definitions are predicated on the fact that the central focus of the subject, as the study of meaning, gives an impression that it cannot be adequately streamlined. But this presumption is misleading. A review of some definitions of pragmatics in the literature will suffice in throwing more light on the subject and also put in a proper perspective of what a pragmatic study entails.

Leech (15) defines pragmatics as "the study of how utterances have meaning in situation." Leech sees communication as a problem solving task for both the speaker and the hearer. The speaker has the best way to accomplish his conversational aim through his/her use of language. On the other hand, the hearer has to work out the most likely reason for the speaker's utterance. In this view, pragmatics is essentially goal directed and evaluative.

Developing this further, Levinson (21) defines pragmatics as "the study of the relations between language and context that are basic to an account of language understanding." In the words of Levinson (38), "Pragmatics provided spaces to account for hints, implicit purposes, assumptions, social attitudes and so on which are effectively communicated by the use of language." Explaining further, Levinson says that understanding an utterance involves making inferences that will connect what is said to what is mutually assumed or what has been said before. He reiterates the importance of inference as one of the key elements in utterance interpretation, and this idea is shown better in Grice's conversional implicature, which will be discussed shortly.

In line with Levinson, Yule (127) holds that "pragmatics is the study of invisible meaning or how we recognize what is meant even when it is not actually said (or written)." This means that for meaning to be derived from an utterance, the speaker and hearer must be able to depend on a lot of shared assumptions. Yule's idea is a further development of Grice's concept of implicature. In Gricean's framework (particularly with respect to the cooperative principle), participants must of necessity operate on several shared assumptions.

To Verschueren, (9) linguistic pragmatics is the study of people's use of language. He emphasises the multi-disciplinary approach of pragmatics by defining pragmatics as "a general cognitive, social, and cultural perspective on linguistic phenomena in relation to their usage in forms of behaviour "According to him, the function of pragmatics is to provide information on how language functions in the lives of human beings. Although this definition captures the relevance of pragmatics to all human activities, it is too general in scope and may be difficult in delimiting the scope of pragmatics from other linguistic studies.

Grundy (13) defines pragmatics as "the study of the relations between language and context that are basic to an account of language understanding." He explains that understanding an utterance involves making inferences that will connect what is said to what is mutually assumed or what has been said before. To him, pragmatic meaning depends so much on inference, which is not a directly observable phenomenon. The importance of deriving inference from propositions used by speakers and hearers is also brought to bear in Grundy's definition.

While supporting this, Mey (23) says "pragmatics studies the use of language in human communication as determined by the conditions of society". The problem with this definition, as highlighted in Ariel (11), is that it is too extremely general. The definition makes it hard for one to know what is excluded from a pragmatic study.

Ariel (249) explains that "pragmatics is responsible for inferences which are based on the linguistic strings expressed when contextual assumptions are taken into account". Such interpretations are guided by pragmatic theory. A theory of pragmatics, according to Ariel (11), is a theory about pragmatic inferencing in the service of linguistic communication. Some of these pragmatic theories are: Grice' pragmatics (1975), Neo-Gricean pragmatics (Horn, 1984, Levinson, 2004). Relevance theory (Speber & Wilson, 1986, 1995), Speech Acts (Austin, 1962; Searle, 1969), Pragmatic Act theory (Mey 2001), Activity type (Levinson 1979), Contextual beliefs model Odebunmi (6)etc.

As reflected in the foregoing paragraphs, the areas of interest of a pragmatic analysis are as diverse as its practitioners. This study aligns with Mey's (23) definition of pragmatics as that which studies users, their use of language, conditions for communication and the ability of language users to use the language in such a way that will allow them to achieve their conversational goals.

Pragmatics explores questions such as:
1. How do people communicate more than what the words or phrases of their utterances might mean by themselves and how do people make these interpretations?
2. Why do people choose to say and/or interpret something in one way rather than another?
3. How do people's perception of contextual factors like interlocutors and relationship influence the process of producing and interpreting language? (Schmitt 475).

A focal point of the definitions above is context. In addition to this, the message being communicated, the participants involved, their intention and knowledge of the world are also taken into consideration in any pragmatic study.

The growing interest of scholars in pragmatics and pragmatic problems has led to the emergence of different theories of pragmatics. Some of these theories include: speech act theory, cooperative and politeness principle, deixis, implicature, presupposition, hedging, etc.

Theories of Pragmatics

Speech Act

Language in use is liable to illocutionary indeterminacy, Leech (3): it is not always plausible for a hearer to easily come to conclusion about what a speaker means. So to account for the correct inherent meaning or the likely inherent meaning in an utterance of a speaker several theories were put forward by pragmaticians. Prima-facie among these theories is the speech act theory.

The British philosopher J.L Austin (1911-60) was the first to draw attention to the many functions performed by utterances as part of interpersonal communication. Specifically, he pointed out that many utterances do not communicate information but are equivalent to action. One can use language to do things. Language can be used to make promises, lay bets, issue warnings, christen children, offer congratulations and swear testimony.

Mey says that speech acts are verbal actions happening in the world (94). He further states that by uttering a speech act, one does something with his words (94). Speech acts are communicative acts performed with the use of oral or written language in order to bring about a change of affairs in the world. Verscheuren posits that Austin broadly classifies acts into two which are 'constative and performatives' (22).Constatives are utterances which can be either true or false and performatives are utterances used to perform actions which can be either felicitous or infelicitous. Austin further classifies 'performatives into explicit (e.g. I name this child Sandra) and implicit (e.g. Go out!). The action naming is stated in the word 'name' while the action of ordering is implied in 'go out'.

As the foremost proponent of speech act theory, Austin (1962) postulates that engaging in speech act means performing the complementary acts of locution, illocution, and perlocution.

Locutionary Speech Act

A locutionary act is an expression used with a determinate sense or reference. In other words, a locutionary act refers to the actual words uttered (Thomas 49). Yule says that to produce a meaningful linguistic expression is to perform a locutionary act (48). It refers to utterances being uttered that are well organized in grammar. Locutions are acts of saying something or producing an utterance; they are equivalent to utterances.

Illocutionary Speech Act

An illocutionary act is an act performed through an expression. It can also be said to be the intention of the speaker. Illocutionary acts include commanding, informing, warning, threatening, deterring, promising, directing, appreciating, congratulating etc and can be performed through performatives, whether or not they contain performative verbs.

Austin Postulates five categories of illocutionary acts which are
- **Exercitives:** These are acts that connote order, request or advice with the use of verbs like command, order, plead, beg etc.
- **Verdictives**: Verdictives are acts of making judgments or decisions with the use of verbs such as acquit, hold, calculate, analyse.
- **Commisives**: These are used to make promises, pledge, contract etc.
- **Expositives**: They are acts that expand views, make illustrations and give responses with verbs such as affirm, deny, illustrate, answer, describe etc.
- **Behavitives**: Are acts that express the mental state of speaker with verbs such as apologize, thank, commiserate, congratulate etc.

Perlocutionary Speech Acts

Lawal (5) explains that a perlocutionary act results from the encoder's use of representational resources and it is the intended or unintended consequence of or reaction to what is represented. In other words, perlocutionary speech act is the effect of an utterance. This means that when an utterance is uttered, it has certain effects on the hearer; it makes the hearer to behave in a certain way. Perlocutionary act therefore refers to what is being done by saying something. For example an utterance may make the hearer laugh, cry, leave a place, become dejected, become hopeful stand or sit.

Kempson places the three acts thus:

> ...speaker utters sentences with a particular meaning (locutionary act) and with a particular force (illocutionary) in order to achieve a certain effect (perlocutionary act) on the hearer (51).

Direct and Indirect Speech Act

Yule distinguishes between direct speech act and indirect speech act (133). Direct speech acts are straight forward and in most cases contain performative verbs. Direct speech act shows a clear relationship between the form (structure) and the meaning of an utterance. If there is a correlation between the structure and the function the structure is performing, then the speech act is direct. Functionally, the directive sentence is expected to make a statement; the interrogative should ask a question; while the imperative should give a command or make a request. Ideally when this happens, the speech act is direct (Osisanwo 69).

On the other hand, indirect speech acts require inferences on the part of the hearer or reader. Searle says that an indirect speech act is one performed by a 'means of another speech' (cited in Thomas 93). Mey views indirect speech act as a combination of two acts, 'a primary illocutionary act and a secondary one, where the primary act operates through and enforce the secondary one' (113). Indirect speech acts result if there is no correlation between a structure and the function the structure is performing. For example:

Could you dress the baby?

The above sentence is a question, but it is also understood as a request; hence an indirect speech act because the structure (interrogative) is different from the function (which is a 'request'). Indirect speech acts besides asking and answering questions and criticizing others add humour and sometimes show politeness.

Searle's Model of Speech Act

Unfortunately, Austin did not live long enough to modify his embryonic ideas or to answer critics who found his theory discursively unwieldy. One of his notable critics is John Searle. Searle (1969) while maintaining Austin's threefold classification of speech acts streamlined and modified the types of illocutionary acts.

Searle initially put together a similar speech act classification but dissociated himself from Austin's assumption of such a correspondence between verbs and speech acts. Searle gave some criteria as forming the foundations for a better classification of speech acts. Such criteria include illocutionary point (the force there in), direction to fit (the way the speech act fits the world, and /or the world fits the speech act), expressed psychological state (of speaker: a belief may be expressed as a statement, an assertion, or remark)., content (what the speech act is about: a promise, or refusal to pay certain amount), reference (to both speaker and hearer), and the contextual conditions of speech acting (societal framework in which a speech act has to be performed in order to be valid). Based on their essential conditions and the intention of the speakers, he came up with five distinct typologies: Assertives, Expressives, Directives, Commissives and Declaratives. They are explained next:

- ***Representatives***: The speaker is committed, in varying degrees, to the truth of proposition e.g affirm, believe, deny, conclude, report.
- ***Directives***: The speaker tries to get the hearer to do something, e.g.ask, challenge, command, insist, request.
- ***Commissives***: the speaker is committed to varying degrees, to a certain course of action e.g guarantee, pledge, promise, swear, vow.
- ***Expressives***: The speaker expresses an attitude about a state of affairs eg. apologize, deplore, congratulate, thank, welcome.
- ***Declarations***: The speaker alerts the external status or condition of an object or situation solely by making the utterances, e.g. I resign, I baptized, you're fired, war is hereby declared.

Felicity Conditions
Speech acts can only be successful if they satisfy several criteria known as 'felicity conditions'. The first is the preparatory condition. Crystal explains that the preparatory conditions have to be right: the person performing the speech act has the authority to do so (121). This does not matter with verbs such as apologize, promise, or thank, but it is an important constraint on the use of such verbs as fine, baptize, arrest etc. Here only certain individuals are qualified to use these utterances.

The second felicity condition is the executive condition. In most cases, there is usually a procedure to be followed exactly and completely e.g. marriage. In other instances certain expectations have to be met.

In addition, the 'sincerity' conditions have to be met. The speech act must be performed in a sincere manner, devoid of deceit. Verbs such as apologize, guarantee and swear are only effective if speakers mean what they say; believing and affirming are realistic only if the speakers are not lying. When these conditions are met, then an illocutionary act is said to be felicitous (Crystal 121, Osisanwo 65).

Pragmatic Act Theory

Several criticisms were made at the speech act theory after Austin (1962) propounded it. In Austin's defence, he did not live long enough to expand his original thoughts. In fact his lecture notes were actually concatenated, posthumously, by J. O. Urmson, who was one of his students at Harvard University, to produce the premier book on speech act: *How to Do Things with Words*. These criticisms however did not wither after scholars such as Searle, Bach and Harnish, etc., modified Austin's original idea to what they believed to be more coherent, cohesive and comprehensive models. Now, one of the main criticisms according to Mey (221) is that the speech act theory concentrates on 'speech' to the exclusion of other phenomena such as writing (and language, as noted earlier, manifests both in the written and spoken forms). Mey is of the opinion that as a result of this critique, some linguists have suggested that the term 'speech act' be replaced by a more 'general' one, such as 'act of language'. Was Mey just interested in mere *terminological quibble*? No. In fact he was more interested in seeing language in use manifesting as situation-bound-dependent phenomenon. Thus, he concludes that the typical way of looking at people using language is to see them as performing pragmatic acts.

The progenitor of Pragmatic Act Theory (PAT) is Jacob Lee Mey (212). Mey propounded this theory to fill what he believes to be a lacuna in the speech act theory. He affirms that: "the speech act theory is individual oriented rather than societal-centred" (Mey 214). This view is further reiterated by Fairclough who opines that the speech act theory "is thought of atomistically, as wholly emanating from the individual" (Mey, 214). In the pragmatic act theory, Mey believes that emphasis should be placed on the importance of the situation, environment and extra-linguistic factors in meaning construction and comprehension. He argues that human activity is not the privilege of the individual; rather the individual is situated in a social context, which means that s/he is empowered, as well as limited, by the conditions of his/her social life.

To Mey, a speech act never comes alone but carries always with it a bevy of other acts on which it essentially depends for its success. These inclusive acts include a conglomeration of the member resources of the activity part and the textual part of a *pragmeme* and they are known as pragmatic act. In other respects, if speech, by itself, is not necessarily performing an action, then in a technical way there are no speech acts, but only situated speech acts, or rather what Mey calls *instantiated pragmatic acts*. This is because speech acts, in order to be feasible, have to be situated in a particular context of situation, as no speech act, or any conversational contribution in general, can be understood properly unless it is situated within the environment in which it was meant to be understood. The environment, so to speak, creates the 'affordances' by which language users oriented towards a correct interpretation of what they say as well as what they hear. The setting's affordances are also the affordances of our actions. So our activity is predicated on what the setting can afford as well as by what we can afford in that context. The implication of this is that emphasis is no longer on describing straitjacket speech acts (just like Austin, Searle et al) but on figuring out how a particular act of language came to be used in a particular context and with what effect.

Therefore, pragmatic acts are situation-derived and situation-constrained. It does not explain human language use by starting from the words uttered by speaker. Instead, it focuses on the interactional situation in which language users realise their aims. The explanatory movement is from the outside in,

> the focus is on the environment in which both speaker and hearer find their affordances, such that the entire situation is brought to bear on what can be said in the situation, as well as on what is actually being said (Mey 221).

That is, from the environment, rather than from the inside out. Consequently, instead of starting with what is said, and looking for what the words could mean, the situation in which the words fit is invoked to explain what can be (and is actually being) said. The importance of contextual aspects of speech acts was echoed by Short (23) who said that "we can use this context-boundness to infer important unstated aspects of context, including social relations between characters, when we read literary texts... Most ordinary *spoken* language behaviour takes place in a firmly grounded situational context" So instead of speech acting, people using language can be viewed as *practing* or performing pragmatic acts.

Pragmemes, Practs and Allopract
Pragmatic acts theory is an attempt to explain the way pragmemes are represented in pragmatic acts in relation to speech situations. The emphasis is not on conditions and rules for an individual speech act, but on characterising a general situational prototype i.e. a pragmeme that can be executed in the situation. Following the tradition of adopting familiar linguistic terminology terms such as phoneme, morpheme. etc., Mey coined the term *pragmeme*. A particular pragmeme can be substantiated and realised through individual pragmatic acts. For Mey it is the activity (interactants) and the textual part (co(n)text) of the pragmeme that defines a pragmatic act. Pragmemes, to be more precise, represent situational prototypes to which there may be several pragmatic access routes (practs). For instance, the pragmeme of requesting a pen can be realised through the following practs:
(1) Can you loan me your pen?

(2) Please my pen is bad, kindly lend me yours.
(3) I don't suppose you'll be able to do this, but could you lend me your pen, please? etc.

These are some of the kind of practs through which this pragmeme can be realised.

So **pract** refers to a particular pragmeme in its realisations. When we study practs or ipras(short form of instantiated pragmatic acts), we aren't concerned with matters of grammatical correctness or the strict observance of rules (Mey, 214). What counts as a pract is determined exclusively by the understanding of the given context. Hence, a pragmatic act is instantiated through a pract which realises a pragmeme. Just like a variant of a particular phoneme is an allophone, every pract is at the same time an **allopract,** that is, a concrete instantiation of a particular pragmeme (Mey, 216). Since no acts ever will be completely identical, every pract is also an 'allopract' – that is, a different realisation of a particular pragmeme. To further buttress this model, Mey came up with the schema below:

PRAGMEME

ACTIVITY PART PART (INTERACTANCTS)	TEXTUAL
SPEECH ACT MPH 'M'...	CO(N)TEXT INF REF REL VCE SSK
Indirect Speech Act	
Conversational ('Dialogue') Acts	
Psychological Act (Emotions)	
Prosody (Intonation, Stress...)	
Physical **(Non-Verbal)** Act:	
Body Moves (Incl. Gestures)	
Physiognomy (Facial Expressions	
Bodily Expressions Of) Emotions	
...	
∽ NULL	

PRACT
ALLOPRACT
PRAGMEME, PRACT, ALLOPRACT
A Model of Pragmatic Acts (Mey 222), (the emphasis in bold is mine)

From the model above, a pragmeme comprises two parts: activity and the textual parts. The activity part is meant for interactants, i.e. participants in a discourse, while the textual part describes the context within which the pragmeme operates. Now, in an interaction between two or more persons, the interactants draw on such speech act types direct or indirect speech acts, conversational ('dialogue') acts, psychological acts, prosodic acts and physical acts which consists of all forms of non-verbal language. These are engaged in contexts, which include INF representing "inference"; REF for "reference"; REL for "relevance"; VCE for "voice"; SSK for "shared situation knowledge"; MPH for "metaphor"; and M "metapragramatic joker". The interactions between the activity part and the textual part of a pragmeme results in a pract or an allopract. Thus, they are synergised (not necessarily all) to project the intended meaning of the language user.

Principles of Pragmatics

A concept like grammar is rule governed; hence we talk about rules of grammar, but in pragmatics, we are interested in the principles of pragmatics; ergo, principles of pragmatics. According to Leech (16) the rules of grammar are fundamentally conventional; the principles of pragmatics are fundamentally non-conventional, they are motivated in terms of conversational goals. The speech act theory as well as the pragmatic act theory has relatively proven to be a useful theory in the analysis of language in use. Nevertheless, some principles of pragmatics have also evolved to complement them for an even more in-depth analysis of language in use. Some of these principles of pragmatics include politeness principle (see Leech, 1983 and Brown and Levinson, 1983), Irony and Banter principle, Interest principle, Pollyanna principle (see Leech 17), Economy principle (see Sperber and Wilson 34) Communicative principle, Efficiency principle (see Mey, 321), cooperative principles (Grice,1975), etc.

i. Politeness Principle
Except otherwise, people invariably prefer to express polite rather than impolite views.
In daily interactions, people have expectations as to how they should be addressed by the other people they meet in the various contexts in which they meet them. Except otherwise, the aim of every interaction is to ensure smooth communication. Even in discourses where there are potentially aggressive parties, some strategies are deployed to make communication

seamless and less complicated. Politeness is a strategy or series of strategies employed by a speaker to achieve a variety of goals such as promoting or maintaining harmonious relations. Pizziconi pointed out that:

> In ordinary, daily contexts of use, members of speech communities possess clear metalinguistic beliefs about, and are capable of, immediate and intuitive assessments of what constitutes polite versus rude, tactful versus offensive behaviour. Politeness in this sense is equivalent to a normative notion of appropriateness (706).

Hence, the principles of politeness were developed to account for face to face interaction. Thomas (23) observes that these strategies may not only include strategic use of the conventional politeness strategies e.g. rapport, deference, courtesy etc. but also include a range of other strategies including many forms of conventional and non-conventional indirectness. Nevertheless, the linguistic realisations of politeness are inextricably linked to the respective cultural context of usage.

Generally, politeness involves two entities: *self and other*. *Self* is the speaker, the encoder, the addresser or the sender while *other* is the decoder, the addressee, the receiver or any other participant, covert or overt. The theory that undergirds the principles of politeness, especially Brown and Levinson's (1978 and 1987) *Face Saving* and *Face ThreateningActs* is Goffman (1967) *Theory of Face*. However, it was in fact Robin Lakoff who provided pioneering work by linking Politeness with its three rules:

1. 'Don't impose'
2. 'Give options'
3. 'Make the other person feel good', 'be friendly' by sometimes being indirect.

Thomas (23) identifies four theories under the principle of politeness:
I. The conversational maxim view (Leech)
II. The face management view (Brown and Levinson)
III. Conversational contract view (Fraser)
IV. Pragmatic scales view (Spencer-Oatey)

Focus will however be on the first two with the second undergirding this study.

a. Leech's Conversational Maxim View

Leech's conversational maxim addressed the issue of "why people are often so indirect in conveying what they mean" (80). He postulated that deviations from the Gricean conversational maxims are motivated by interactional goals and posits a parallel politeness principle articulated in a number of maxims. He therefore explores politeness principles in relation to the Gricean maxims of quantity, quality, relevance and manner. In that faith, he first came up with four rhetorical maxims:

i. Tact maxim: minimise (other things being equal) the expression of beliefs which express or imply cost to other; maximise (other things being equal) the expression of beliefs which express or imply benefit to other. In this maxim, speakers are expected to bias the illocution towards a positive outcome, by restricting hearer's opportunity of saying "No". Hence, avoid imposition, give options and if possible be indirect. For example:

(a) Let me carry those bags for you.
(b) I need to drop off Juliana. Can you loan me your car?

ii. Generosity maxim

Minimise (other things being equal) the expression of beliefs which express or imply benefit to self; maximise (other things being equal) the expression of beliefs which express or imply cost to self. This is generally observed in playing down of speaker's beneficent role. For instance,

(a) *My phone is short of juice. Could I borrow yours?*
(b) *I wouldn't mind a plate of pounded yam.*

If the two examples above are observed in a technical way, the illocutionary force inherent in them appear more polite because it seems that the offerer makes no sacrifice, so that in turn it can become less impolite to accept the offer.

iii. Approbation maxim

Minimise (other things being equal) the expression of beliefs which express or imply dispraise to other; maximise (other things being equal) the expression of beliefs which express or imply praise to other. This is mostly observed in flattery. The emphasis here is to avoid saying unpleasant things about the addressee. For instance, one can say:

(a) What a gorgeous suit you are wearing. √

But not:

(b) What an awful suit you are wearing. **X**

In extreme cases, especially where the situation is bad, we can have an understatement like:

(c) Your suit is not (that) bad.

In sum, we prefer to praise others and if we cannot do so, we have to sidestep the issue to give some sort of minimal response (like (c) above). Alternatively, the speaker can choose to remain silent. For instance, it is not wrong to say *I enjoyed your food*, while if I did not enjoy it, I will either keep quiet about or convey my point more indirectly. An example of using indirect strategy to mitigate the effect of criticism is that of Professor Okoye who writes a referee for a student, Mr Ikemefuna, applying for a philosophy job (this is actually a recast of Grice 152 example):

> 'Dear Sir, Mr Ikemefuna's command of English is excellent, and his attendance at lectures has been regular. Yours, etc.'

Now, professor Okoye must be wishing to impart information that he is reluctant to write down. This deduction is plausible only on the assumption that professor Okoye thinks Mr Ikemefuna is no good at philosophy. So this reluctance to declare his opinion directly is due to the adherence to the approbation maxim.

iv. Modesty maxim
Minimise (other things being equal) the expression of beliefs which express or imply praise to self; maximise (other things being equal) the expression of beliefs which express or imply dispraise to self. Do not brag; do not commit the social transgression of boasting (Leech, 32). Adhering to this maxim, if a speaker is presenting let us a car to the hearer, he can use an expression like: *Please accept this little token* to minimise the expression of praise.

Leech however added the following two maxims and a principle:

v. Agreement maxim
Minimise (other things being equal) the expression of disagreement between self and other; maximise the expression of agreement between self and other. Even when you are on the other side of the pole, an expression with an illocutionary force of partial disagreement is often preferable to complete disagreement. To illustrate:

> Chioma: Half of a yellow sun is a very good novel.
> Nnenna: Yes, well written as a whole but there are some improbable scenario that makes it rather too fictious.

vi. Sympathy maxim
Minimise (other things being equal) the expression of beliefs which express or imply apathy to other; maximise the expression of beliefs which

express or imply empathy to other. This maxim encourages speakers to use pragmatic acts whose illocutionary forces are congratulatory and condolence. This is because they are perceived as pleasant and courteous to the hearer:
    (a) I rejoice with you today as you clock one year.
    (b) I'm terribly sorry to hear that you lost your iPhone.

Pollyanna Principle
According to Leech, participants in a conversation will prefer pleasant topics of conversation to unpleasant ones. This was the idea behind the Pollyanna principle which in a technical sense is not one of Leech's maxims. (Remarkably, some scholar identified it as one of Leech's maxim of politeness [Thomas, 160]). Pollyanna was actually the eponymous character of Eleanor H. Porter's 1913 novel, *Pollyanna*. She is perceived to be an "appallingly saccharine child who always looked on the bright side of life" Thomas, (160). So the observance of this principle makes us to put the best possible gloss on what we have to say (Thomas, 160). Put differently, it is the tendency to understate the degree of which things are bad.

    So in relation to communication, the principle postulates that participants in a conversation will want pleasant topics of conversation rather than unpleasant ones. To avoid the latter, interlocutors use euphemisms, litotes and hyperbole. For instance, two students, male and female, were alleged to be living couple's life off campus (they were unmarried [with no intention whatsoever to marry] but were living together like married couple). Despite the seeming atrocity of the act, someone made striking but remarkable conclusion about them:
    Thank God they are not gay.
Kayode was once caught stealing tubers of yam. He was mobbed. Some passers-by pleaded on his behalf, reiterating that:
    At least he did not kill anyone, he only stole some yams.

    Leech's politeness model as explicated above is essentially a scalar phenomenon: the degree of imposition on the hearer will normally condition the degree of indirectness, mitigation or other politeness marker from the speaker.

b. Brown and Levinson (1978, 1987): Face Management Act View
As stated earlier on, Brown and Levinson's face management act view is built on Goffman (1967) theory of face (Grice's theory of implicature is

also remotely axiomatic here). Actually, Goffman sees face as an image of the self, delineated in terms of approved social attributes. Brown and Levinson then borrowed the notion of face from Goffman and redefine it as the public self-image that every member of society wants to claim for himself.

Brown and Levinson see politeness as a cogent and rule-governed aspect of communication, aimed predominantly at maintaining social cohesion via the maintenance of individuals' public face. Thus, they identify two types of face: positive face and negative face. Positive face is observed by the individual need to be appreciated and respected by others as well as to maintain positive self-image. To put it another way, positive face has to do with a person's wish to be thought of; the desire to be understood by others, and the desire to be treated as a friend and confident. Negative face on the other hand involves the freedom of action and the freedom from imposition. That is to say, it has to do with our wish not to be imposed on by others and to be allowed to go about our business unimpeded and with our rights to free and self-determined action intact. Hence in dealing with each other, our utterances may be oriented to the positive or to the negative face of those we interact with.

In corollary to that, they identify two types of face act: face threatening act (FTA henceforth) and face saving act (FSA henceforth). FTA occurs when one participant say something that represents a threat to another person's self-image. FSA on the other hand is the opposite of FTA. It ensues whenever one of the participants in a discourse says something that lessens the possible threat to another's face.

There are three superordinate and one opting out strategies of performing an FTAs:

a. **Performing FTA without redress**: do the act bald-on-record. This is observed in speaking directly or very directly, in the most direct, clear, unambiguous and concise way possible without any attempt whatsoever to mitigate the illocutionary force inherent in an act, regardless of the rating of the imposition. By implication, the act will be in full conformity with the Gricean maxims: quantity, quality, manner and relation. For example, an utterance like *Leave the house* does not say more or less than is required *(quantity)*, is maximally efficient in so far as it is non-spurious *(quality)*, it is relevant *(relation)* and it avoids ambiguity and obscurity *(manner)*.

It is also significant that in performing such an act, a speaker shows little concern for the hearer's *face*. This is because the speaker in this context will highly likely to focus on the propositional content of the message; thereby provide no effort to reduce the impact of the FTAs, and are likely to shock the addressee, embarrass them, or make them feel uncomfortable. Examples of this strategy is abound where the power differential or role relation is asymmetrical, e.g. military setting, law court, and so on. It is also observed in a discourse where the speaker holds high relative power and fears no threat to his own face from the addressee.

b. *Performing FTA with redress*: this is when the act is performed with no threat to the addressee's face intended. This can be done in two ways: *performing FTA with redress using positive politeness strategy* and *performing FTA with redress using negative politeness strategy*. Performing FTA with redress using positive politeness strategy is observed when a speaker orient himself/herself towards the addressee's positive face by using positive politeness strategy (which appeals to the addressee's desire to be liked and approved of). It is frequently employed in groups of friends, or where people in the given social situation know each other fairly well. They usually attempt to minimise the distance between interlocutors by expressing friendliness and solid interest in the hearer's need to be respected, in other words to minimise the FTA. For example, *You look nice today. What an elegant suit you are putting. It was a fantastic presentation you gave only a little bit of details is lacking.* Other manifestations include where a speaker avoids disagreement, is optimistic, extend praise, give sympathy, hedge opinion, etc.

In other respects, performing an FTA with redress using negative politeness is obvious when a speaker aims to orient him/herself towards a hearer's negative face — which appeals to the hearer's desire not to be impeded or put upon, to be left free to act as he or she chooses. Generally, negative politeness manifests in the use of conventional politeness markers, deference markers, minimising imposition, being indirect etc. However, Simpson (1989) modifying Brown and Levinson's (25) taxonomy, identifies seven major strategies of using negative politeness:

i. Hedge e.g. *I'm sorry but I must ask you to leave my office.*
ii. Indicate pessimism e.g. *The situation in the country is harsh. I will understand if you could not lend me #5,000.*

iii. Minimise imposition, e.g. *I need a little favour from you.*
iv. Indicate deference, e.g. *I am ashamed but to have to ask you this favour;*
v. Apologise e.g. *I don't mean to bother you.*
vi. Impersonalise, e.g. *We regret to inform you.*
vii. Acknowledge the debt, e.g. *I would be eternally grateful if.*
(Simpson, 174-176)

c. ***Performing FTA using off-record politeness***: this is observed when an FTA is done off-record by giving hints, using metaphor, being ambiguous or vague, sarcastic or jocular. In this case, the utterance bears an implicature that evades clarity and thus can be immediately dismissed because, theoretically, the speaker doesn't commit him/herself to a specific intent.

To illustrate, one might indirectly request an addressee to open the window, switch on the fan or the air-conditioner by saying: *It is hot in here.* This is an off-record strategy. The utterance takes the form of a declarative sentence containing no direct lexical link to the real request being made implicitly. So by selecting this particular declarative form, the speaker can appear not to be coercive and can thereby avoid the responsibility for a potentially face-damaging interpretation.

d. ***Do not perform FTA***: do not perform the act at all. This has to do with "saying nothing" i.e. "opting out". Since an option every communicator has is not to talk, not performing FTA is the strategy that can be most easily implemented because all a speaker has to do is resist or renounce his/her wish to make an utterance that risks being face-threatening. Silence they say is gold. Silence becomes even more priceless when something is potentially so face-threatening that one decides not to say it. This is especially observed in situations when a speaker decides to say nothing and genuinely wishes to let the matter drop; there are other occasions when an individual decides to say nothing (decides not to complain) but still wishes to achieve the effect which the speech act would have achieved had it been uttered. This stratagem can be best applied when considering all other options inefficient.

In sum, language serves many functions; expressing linguistic politeness is only one of them. Brown and Levinson's linguistic strategies as well as Leech's maxims are relatively available in all human languages; however, there are local cultural differences in what triggers their use while some factors such as social distance, power differential and ratio of imposition determine which of these FTAs strategies to be used in a language like English. The principle of politeness is one of the core principles of pragmatics because it sets out to describe the quality of social relationships between individuals which specifically sets out to integrate a description of language use with an account of the social relations of the interactants. Unlike cooperative principle, the principle of politeness also helps to explain why people are often so indirect in conveying what they say. And according to Leech (80) "it is interested in a broader, socially and psychologically oriented application of pragmatic principles."

ii. Cooperative Principle
There is the socio-anthropological need to overcome the fundamental impediment in the efficiency of human communication, occasioned no doubt by absolute **contextual** (physical, psychological, socio-cultural and linguistic) constraints on the language users.

Sometime in 1967, scholars presented papers on topical issues in linguistics in a William James Lectures at Harvard University. One of these scholars is Herbert Paul Grice. In his submission, Grice was concerned with the task of accounting for how human beings behave in normal conversation. Thus, to streamline conversational behaviours, he posited a general set of rules that interlocutors in ordinary conversation were generally expected to follow. This set of rules he named Cooperative Principle (CP), and formulated it as follows: *Make your conversational contribution such as is required, at the stage at which it occurs, by the accepted purpose or direction of the talk exchange in which you are engaged* (Grice 26, cited in Lindblom, 152).

A scrupulous evaluation indicates that Grice's Cooperative Principle may appear as an idealistic representation of actual human communication i.e. how human beings are expected to conduct when they are engaged in any language activity. So invariably, participants in a discourse must have some common immediate aim, and as such, their contributions dovetail and in other cases, are mutually dependent. Except otherwise, they try to be understood correctly, and avoid giving false impression. On this account, Grice came up with four set of rules or rather maxims in an attempt to further streamline his standpoint. These maxims, he claim, should form the guideline for an effective communication. They are:

i. *Maxim of Quality*: Do not say what you believe to be false: do not say that for which you lack adequate evidence.

ii. **Maxim of Quantity**: Make your contribution as informative as is required; do not make your contribution more informative than is required.
iii. **Maxim of Relevance**: Be relevant. Make your contribution in relation to the topical discourse.
iv. **Maxim of Manner**: Be perspicuous; do not be ambiguous; avoid obscurity of expression.

These maxims, according to Grice should be the prototype guideline in every human communication.

But do people always follow these maxims as they communicate? There answer is NO. A capital NO at that. The reason being that firstly, people (those who are aware of them) jettison these straitjacket maxims in order to manipulate their talks to suit their purposes. Secondly, if these maxims are invariably adhered to, communication apart from being too rigid and monotonous will be too dreary and lifeless as well as predictable. In fact the unpredictability of human communication is what makes it more unique and further distinguishes it from animal communication. Tannen (21) further shored up this view when she stated that the Gricean maxims of cooperative discourse can't apply to "real conversations" (Why?) because in conversation "we wouldn't want to simply blurt out what we mean, because we're judging the needs for involvement and independence" (cited in Lindblom 153). The need for involvement and independence is very important when one put into circumspect that the essence of every communicative act is that the receiver should understand the message as intended by the sender. If being ironical, providing more information, digressing or being ambiguous is germane to convey a message, the sender wouldn't hesitate to adopt any of these means as long as the illocutionary force inherent in his message is understood.

Therefore, interlocutors can fail to adhere to the maxims in a variety of ways, some mundane, some inadvertent (Lindblom, 9). According to Short (12), the Gricean maxims are not, however, as strongly regulative as grammatical rules, and are therefore broken quite often. Therefore, these maxims can be broken in the following ways:

a. **By Flouting:** this is when a speaker blatantly fails to observe a maxim at the level of what is said, with the deliberate intention of generating an implied meaning. Chioma and Emeka have courted for three years. But the former was sceptical Emeka would still marry her after they just discovered that Chioma was once intimate with Emeka's elder brother who is now married. Thus the following conversation ensued:

Chioma: Emeka, will you still marry me?
Emeka: Is the Pope a Catholic?
Emeka's reply overtly flouts the maxim of relevance. His utterance generates the implied meaning that his intent to marry Chioma is a certainty, not to be disputed.

b. By Violating: this is usually observed by saying pragmatically misleading utterances. To illustrate: Mrs Abah left some apples and oranges in the refrigerator in the morning. After a frazzling day at the office, she came back in the evening to make orange juice. To her chagrin, she discovers that her fruits are missing. She immediately questioned her daughter, Amaka, who happened to be the only person staying with her at that material moment.

Mrs Abah: Amaka did you take some apples and oranges in the refrigerator?
Amaka: Mummy, I... took some fruits.

Well, Amaka's answer interestingly violates three of the Gricean maxims: quantity, relevance and manner. Firstly, she subtlety gives more than enough information by saying she *took some fruits* instead of narrowing it down to whether she took *apples* and *oranges*. Secondly, she violates the maxim of relevance by digression from particulars *apples* and *oranges* which are kinds of (co-homonyms) of fruits to the general *fruit* which is hypernym of *apples* and *oranges*. Finally, Amaka also violates the maxim of manner by deliberately being ambiguous i.e. by claiming to have taken *some fruits*, that she took *some apples* and *oranges* could be either true or false.

c. By Opting out: when a speaker opts out of a maxim, he/she is actually indicating unwillingness to cooperate. One might opt out by making it clear that one refuses to cooperate in a conversation for some reason especially when one may not be legally bound to provide information. To illustrate, Chkuwuma and Daura are colleagues in the office. Nigeria's President has just assigned portfolios to some ministers. And Daura happens to be an ardent follower of the President.

Chukwu: What's your take on President Buhari's appointment of ministers and super ministers?
Daura: Well, I'll rather not comment on national politics.
Ahmed's decision not to cooperate with Daura is undergirded by the fact that he, Ahmed, is not obliged by any law, whatsoever, to do so.

d. By Infringing: this has to do with the failure to observe a maxim but usually not deliberate. Sometimes, it may be due to impairment or incompetence in the language.

In other respects, typical cases of implicature as regards the maxim Quantity is often observed in *tautology*. The maxim of Quality is not adhered to in cases were irony, metaphor, sarcasm are being used. For Relevance implicatures are generated due to thematic switch or digression. Elsewhere, the maxim of Manner is broken when there is obscurity, ambiguity or vagueness in an expression. To illustrate further, Leech and Thomas (1) opines that

> the observance of the maxim of Quality is a yes/no proposition, whereas the observance of the maxims of Manner and Quantity is usually a matter of degree. How well-ordered is 'orderly'? How prolix is 'prolixity'? How much information is 'enough information'?

Elements of Pragmatics

Implicature

The term 'implicatiure was coined by H. P Grice in his publication *Logic and Conversation* (1975).Implicature refers to 'propositional form communicated by an utterance whose content consists of wholly pragmatically inferred matter' (Carston10). It also relates to how meaning can be implicated rather than explicitly communicated. Yule states that implicature is a short version of conversational implicature which is defined as an additional unstated meaning in a situation whereby speakers mean more than what they literally express (131). It is what is implied but not stated in the proposition of an utterance. In practical terms, implicature refers to:

I. What is not literally said by the text encoder
II. What is inferred from what is coded.
III. What is defeasible, and
IV. What is meant in addition to what is encoded.

There are two main types of implicature: conventional implicature and conversational implicature. Osisanwo explains that conventional implicature is determined by the conventional meaning of words (93). Thomas states that conventional implicature refers to 'what is implied by the literal meaning of words (57). Yule observes that:

Conventional implicature are not based on the cooperative principle, don't have to occur in conversation, don't depend on special contexts for their interpretations, are associated with specific words and result in additional conveyed meanings when those words are used (46).

Conversational implicature on the other hand is based on the cooperative principle. Melchenko opines that:

The concept of conversational implicature explains how it is possible for speakers to mean and for hearers to understand more than is literally said. The hearer understands the speaker's intended meaning by generating conversational implicature (23).

Conversational implicature thrives when additional meaning is conveyed by the encoder in the way required by the maxim and involves locally derived inferences from specific context. The theory of cooperative principle could be traced to the work of Paul Grice (1975, 1989) who developed four pragmatic sub-principles of maxims.

The four aspects of cooperation which are descriptive rather than prescriptive are:

I. Quantity
a. Make your contribution as informative as is required (that is for the purpose of the on-going exchange).
b. Do not make your contribution more informative than necessary.
Your contribution should be based on truth.
a. Do not say what you believed to be false
b. Do not say that for which you lack adequate evidence
II. Relation
Be relevant
III. Manner
Try to be perspicuous (i.e. be clear)
a. Avoid obscurity of expression
b. Avoid ambiguity
c. Be brief (avoid unnecessary prolixity)
d. Be orderly (i.e. present your materials in the order in which they are required)

Odebunmi opines that a text encoder or speaker can flout the maxims either as a result of 'linguistic incompetence' or because of some institutional ideologies (85). What is paramount here is that because of the essentially cooperative nature of textual conversation, if one or more of these maxims are flouted, we still strive to interpret some meaning from what is encoded. Occasionally writers or speakers may not wish to cooperate with readers and may violate the maxim of quality for instance by telling lies or fantasying or deliberately obscuring the meaning - violating manner maxim (Bloor and Bloor n.p.).

Presupposition
Presupposition is an implicit assumption about the world or background belief relating to an utterance whose truth is taken for granted (Karttunen1). In written as well as spoken communication, the writer makes some basic assumptions about the reader or listener. Such assumptions are made without any challenge from the interlocutors since they are anchored on assumed common knowledge (Osisanwo 86). Any text is a combination of explicit meaning – what is overtly said an implicit meaning – what is left 'unsaid' but taken as a given, as presupposed (Faircough 106).
Yule (45) identifies six forms of presuppositions:

1. Existential presupposition:
This has to do with entities named by the speaker and assumed to be present. When we name an object, it is presupposed that the object exists. All nouns are presuppositions, e.g.
Simba's car is new.
This presupposes that Simbi exists and that she has a car.

2. Factive Presupposition
It is the assumption that something is true due to the presence of some verbs such as "know" and "realize". For example, when a teacher says that he didn't realize someone has failed the exam, we can suppose that someone has failed the exam.

3. Lexical Presupposition
It is the assumption that, in using one word, the speaker can act as if another meaning (word) will be understood. Example
- Clara stopped smoking (she used to smoke)
- You are pregnant again (you were pregnant before)

The use of the expressions "stop" and "again" are taken to presuppose another (unstated) concept.

4. Structural Presupposition
This is the assumption associated with the use of certain words and phrases. WH- questions in English (e.g. when and where) are

conventionally interpreted with the presupposition that the information after the Wh-form is already known to be the case. Examples
- When did she leave home? (She left)
- Where did you get the information? (you got the information)

5. Non- Factive presupposition
It is an assumption that something is not true. For example, verbs like "imagine", "pretend" and "dream" are used with the presupposition that what follows is not true.
- I dreamt that I got married (I am not married)
- We imagined that we were Americans (we are not Americans)

6. *Counterfactual presuppositions*
It is the assumption that what is presupposed is not only untrue, but is the opposite of what is true or contrary to facts.

Mutual Contextual Beliefs
Bach and Harnish (1979) Pragmatic theory is inference and intention based. Osisanwo in explaining Mutual Contextual Belief (henceforth MCB) state that the process of inferencing starts from the identification of the intention of the speaker based on mutual understanding between the speaker and the hearer (115). Bach and Harnish argue that 'for speakers to perform illocutionary acts, their hearers must understand what such acts mean; whether the acts are within or without the bands of literalness' (qtd. in Acheoah 40). They also posit that MCBs between S (speaker) and H (hearer) in addition to their world knowledge facilitate the inferential process since the inference made or is expected to be made by the hearer does not depend on what the speaker says but on the contextual knowledge shared commonly by the speaker and hearer in discourse.

Bach and Harnish terminology Speech Act Schemata (SAS) refers to an inevitable part of the inferential process in a communicative event. They argue that MCBS between a speaker and his hearer facilitate a streamlined inferential process, as the inference made by the hearer does not depend on what the speaker says but on the contextual knowledge shared commonly by the speaker and hearer in discourse.

Bach and Harnish further recognize linguistic presumption and communicative presumption as other beliefs shared by an entire linguistic community which the hearer relies or falls back on for his inferences.

i. **Linguistic Presumption**: This relates to what members of the same speech community share. Linguistic presumption in other words refers to the moral beliefs that the members of a linguistic community share on the particular language in question. Unless there is evidence to the contrary, the hearer is presumed capable of determining the meaning and the referents of the expression in the context of utterance.

ii. ***Communicative Presumption***: The communicative presumption is the presumption that when the author of an utterance is saying something to another party, 'he is doing it with some recognizable illocutionary intent (Botha 71). Osisanwo states that communicative presumption covers the illocutionary intent with which the speaker says something to another member (115). Unless there is clear evidence to the contrary, a speaker is assumed to be speaking with some identifiable communicative intent.

Hedging

Fraser traces the concept of hedging to Weinreich (16). According to him, Weinrich was the first person to write about hedging in the linguistic research literature where he discussed about "Metalinguistic operators". He argued that:

For every language "metalinguistic operators" such as (in) English *true, real, so-called, strictly speaking,* and the most powerful extrapolator of all, *like* function as instructions for the loose or strict interpretation of designata.

In 1972, Lakoff popularized the concept. According to Lakoff 'the most interesting questions are raised by the study of words whose meaning implicitly involves fuzziness-words whose job it is to make things fuzzier or less fuzzy' (195). Crystalis of the opinion that Hedging modify a proposition directly (qtd. in Hua 567). Yule (1996) also cited in Hua (2005) defined it as cautious, annotative expression of words. From the above definitions, there is no cut consensus on the concept of hedges.

Hedges are classified into two groups; approximators and shields.

i. Approximators: they refer to the expressions which can change the original meaning of a proposition or provide alternate meaning to the proposition according to different situations. Approximators can affect the original truth condition of the proposition, and sometimes can even change the meaning of the proposition. Approximators are divided into *Adaptors* and *Rounders*.

I ***Adaptors***: These are expressions which reveal the degree of truth of the original proposition. Occasionally, the proposition is correct or it is partially correct. Adaptors help to express the degree of correctness. Examples of adaptors are: sort of, kind of, somewhat, really, almost,

quite, entirely, a little bit, to some extent, more or less, etc. Example: *In view of her performance, she is sort of lazy.*
In the example above, the original degree of certainty has changed in accordance with the real situation through the use of "sort of".

ii. **Rounders**: Rounders are usually used when it comes to measuring, especially if the exact data is missing or precise information is unavailable. Examples of rounders are essentially, about, approximately, something between...and...roughly, etc. Example: *The number of unemployed youth in Nigeria is approximately two million.*
In the example above, the expression 'approximately' makes the original accurate data less precise.

B. Shields: Shields usually do not affect the truth condition but reflect the degree of speakers' commitments to the truth value of the whole proposition. In other words, shields indicate that speakers are not fully committed to the validity of the proposition they are conveying. Shields are divided into *Plausibility* and *Attribution* shields.

i. **Plausibility Shield**: Plausibility shields are used to show speakers' own attitude towards a proposition. Mostly, they express speakers' doubtful attitude or uncertainty of the truth value of propositions. Consequently, they usually include first person pronouns so as to show speakers that their statement is not absolutely right or true since it is just their own opinions. Examples of plausibility shields are: I guess, I believe, I am afraid, I assume, I suppose, as far as I'm concerned, seem, I think, etc.

i. **Attribution shields**: These are used to express the attitude of doubt or guess, but they attribute the degree of uncertainty toward a proposition to another party. Examples are: someone suggested that...the possibility will be, as is well known, according to, etc. (Hua 563-564)

Deixis

The word deixis comes from the Greek adjective *deiktikos* meaning 'pointing.' In linguistics, diexis refers to words and phrases that cannot be fully understood without additional contextual information. In other words, deixis is reference by means of an expression whose interpretation is relative to extra-linguistic context of the utterance, such as; who is speaking, the time or place of speaking, the gestures of the speaker or the current location in the discourse (Loos 2003).

Yule defines deixis as technical term for one of the most basic things we do with utterances (9). In addition, Cruse opines that deixis signifies different things to different people (319). Deixis relates to the ways in which language encode or grammaticalize features of the context of utterance or speech event, and thus relates to the ways in which the interpretation of utterance depends on the analysis of that context of utterance (Levinson 54). Also, Saeed states that deitic devices in a language commit a speaker to set up a frame of reference around himself (173).

Finegan states that deixis is the marking of the orientation or position of entities and events with respect to certain points of reference (193). Levinson (1983) highlights five types of deixis which are: person deixis, time deixis, discourse deixis, and social deixis

i. *Person deixis*
According to Levinson, person deixis deals with the predetermination of the role of participants in the speech event in which the utterance in question is uttered and it is reflected directly in the grammatical categories of person (3). Finegan calls this category of deixis personal deixis (193). The pronouns I, you, and we along with she, he, it and they are markers of personal deixis. Whenever we use these pronouns, we orient our utterance with respect to ourselves, our interlocutors and third parties (e.g. your majesty) and this (e.g. this girl) are also markers of personal deixis.

ii. *Time Deixis*
Time deixis is also referred to as temporal deixis. Time deixis is the orientation or position of the referent of actions and events in time (Finegan 195). In other words, time deixis is a reference to time relative to a temporal reference point and it is typically the moment of utterance. Markers of temporal deixis are the adjectives of time in the line...yesterday...now...tomorrow, and the verb tenses.

iii. *Place Deixis*
Place deixis is also known as spatial deixis. It has to do with the marking of the orientation or position in space of the referent of a linguistic expression. Demonstrators (this, that) and adverbs (here, there) are the words which are commonly used to express spatial deixis. Directional verbs 'go' and 'come' also carry deitic information (Finegan 193)

iv. *Social Deixis*
Social deixis concerns the encoding of social distinctions that are relative to participants- roles, particularly aspects of the social relationship holding between speaker and addressee(s) or speaker and some referent

(Dewi 2). Levinsnon explains that there will be different expressions between speaker and addressee or other referent, if they have different social relationship (63). Distinctions between relative ranks of speaker and addressee are systematically encoded throughout: morphological system and honorifics. In addition, such distinctions are regularly encoded in choice between pronoun, summons forms (vocatives) and titles of address in familiar language.

v. Discourse Deixis
Discourse deixis is known as textual deixis. It is concerned with the orientation of an utterance with respect to other utterances in a string of utterances. Discourse deixis looks at possible ways in which an utterance signals its relation to surrounding text, e.g.
> She served us canary pudding and jellof rice with salad. That was a special treat.

The demonstrative 'that' at the beginning of the second sentence refers not to a distinction in space or time but rather to something previously mentioned. It marks discourse deixis. Discourse deixis enables language users to indicate relationships across utterances.

Relationship between Semantics and Pragmatics

A comparison of semantics and pragmatics is a herculean task. Semantics and pragmatics are both related to the way meaning is derived from language. Semantics account for meaning. It studies the meaning that words and certain combinations of words hold for both the speaker and hearer. Pragmatics on the other hand deals with how the context in which words are used can dictate their true meaning at that given time. In other words the meaning of words can be understood from two different perspectives: the semantic perspective refers to the study of the relations of words to which they refer while the pragmatic perspective refers to the study of the relationship between words, the interlocutors and the context.

Semantics adopts a narrow scope to the study of meaning because it deals with only text and analyse the meaning of words and how they are combined to constitute meaningful sentences.

In contrast, pragmatics adopts a wider scope beyond the text itself. It examines the facts surrounding the utterance such as the contextual factors, knowledge of the word surrounding the context of the message; the speaker's intended meaning and the hearers' inferences so as to interpret the utterance. In semantics, the meaning of an utterance is not context-dependent, but it is context-dependent in pragmatics. (Alghamdi 2013)

I n addition, semantics is rule governed while pragmatics is principle governed (Leech 1980)

In conclusion, semantics and pragmatics both require knowledge of the language and knowledge of the world. It is important to note that semantics and pragmatics are not separable from each other; they are complementary disciplines.

Works cited

Austin, John L. *How to Do Things with Words*. Oxford: Clarendon, 1962.
Baarton, Ellen. *Non-Sentential Constituents: A Theory of Pragmatics and Grammatical Structure*. New York: John Benjamin, 1990.
Bloor, Meriel and Bloor, Thomas. *The Practice of Critical Discourse Analysis: An Introduction*.
London: Hodder, 2007.
Botha, Eugene J. *Jesus and the Samaritan Woman: A Speech Act Reading of John 4:1-42*. The Netherlands: E.J Brill.1991.
Brown, Penelope and Stephen C. Levinson.*Politeness: Some Universals in Language Usage*.
Cambridge: Cambridge UP, 1987.
Bruce, Fraser.' Pragmatic Competence: The Case of Hedging' *in New Approaches to Hedging*.
Gunther Kaltenbock, WiltrudMihatsch and Stefan Schneider(eds) Emareld Group Publishing Limited.
Cruise, D. Alan .*Meaning in Language: An Introduction to Semantics and Pragmatics*. Oxford: Oxford UP, 2000. Print.
Crystal, David. *The Cambridge Encyclopedia of Language*.2nd Ed. Cambridge: Cambridge UP, 2003.
Emeka, Acheoah John. Saying X: The Pragmatics of a Nigerian Context. *In CS Canada. Studies in Literarture and Language*.Vol. 6 No. 3. 2013. www.cscanada. Accessed 18/3/2013.
Fairclough, Norman. *Media Discourse*. London: Edward Arnold, 1995.
Finegan, Edward. *Language, its Use and Structure*. Boston: Thomson Wadsworth, 2008.
Jerry L. Morgan *Linguistics: The Relationship of Pragmatics to Semantics*. http//www.annualreview.org/doi/pdf/10…/annorev.an.06.100177.000421
Karttunen, Lauri. *Theoretical Linguistics*. Oxford: Oxford UP, 1974.
Kempson, E. G. H. *Presupposition and the Delimitation of Semantics*. Oxford: Alden, 1975.
Thomas, Jenny. *Meaning in Interaction*. London: Longman,1995.

Lawal, Ade Bayo. 'Pragmatics in Stylistics: A Speech Act Analysis of Soyinka's Telephone Conversation' in Adebayo Lawal (ed). *Stylistics in Theory and Practice.* Ilorin: Paragon, 1997. 150-173.

Levinson, Stephen.C. *Pragmatics.* Cambridge: Cambridge UP, 1983.

Leech, Geoffrey.N. *Explorations in Semantics and Pragmatics.* Amsterdam: John Benjamin, 1980.

Melchenko, Liana. *Inferences in Advertising: A Case Study of Swedish and Russian TV Commercials.* M. A Thesis in General Linguistics. Lind University: Department of Linguistics. http//www.ling.w.se/education/essay/lianamelchenkod.pdf. Accessed 23/03/2015.

Mey, Jacob. *Pragmatics: An Introduction.* Oxford: Blackwell, 2003.

Helen Spencer-Oatey and VladimirZegarac 'Pragmatics' in Norbert, Schmitt (ed) *An Introduction to Applied Linguistics.* London: Hodder Arnold.

Odebunmi, A.' Explicatures and Implicatures in Magazine Editorials.: The Case of the Nigerian Tell' inTaiwo, R. Odebunmi, A. (eds) *Perspectives on Media Discourse.*.Mvenchen: LINCOM, 2007.

Osisanwa, Wale. *Discourse Analysis and Pragmatics.* Ebute-Meta: Femolous-Fetop, 2008.

Rami, Arav.*Similarities and Differences between Semantics and Pragmatics.* http://ramialghamdi.wordpress.com/.../similarities-and-diferences-betwe...(2013).

Saeed, John.I. *Semantics.* Oxford: Blackwell, 1997.

Searle, J.R..*A Classification of Illocutionary Acts in Society,* 5, 1-23.(1976)

Stalnaker, Robert. "Assertions" in Syntax and Semantics,.Vol.19. Pragmatics...... 1978.

Verschveren, Jef. *Understanding Pragmatics.*Yew York: Oxford UP,1999.

Watson, James Arnold and Hill, Anne."Dictionary of Media and Communication Studies."7th Ed.London: Hodder Arnold.

Yule, George. *Pragmatics.* Oxford: Oxford UP, 1996.

---. *The Study of Language.*Cambridg: Cambridge UP, 1996.

YemiOgunsiji&Farinde, R.O. Analytical L;inguistics. Ago-Iwoye.OlabisiOnabanjo UP.

The English Language and Literature in English: An Introductory Handbook. Eforos, Bune Adegbiya. Ilorin:

Huang, Y. Pragmatics. Newyork: Oxford University press,2007

Odebunmi, Akin. *Meaning in English: an introduction.* Ogbomosho.Critical sphere, 2006

Allot, N. *Key terms in pragmatics.* New York: Continuum,2010

Ariel, M.. *Defining pragmatics.* New York:Cambridge University press,2010

Grundy, Peter. Doing pragmatics. London. Arnold,2000

Kempson, R. *Semantic theory.* London: Cambridge university press, 1989

Levinson,S.C. Pragmatics. New York; Cambridge university press,1983

Thomas, Jenny. *Meaning in interaction; an introduction to pragmatics.* London and New York: Longman press,1995

Lawal, A., Ajayi, B.,& Raji, W.. 'A pragmatic study of selected pairs of Yoruba proverbs'. *Journal of Pragmatics.* 27: 635-652.1997

Osisanwo, Wale *Introduction to discourse analysis and pragmatics.* Lagos: Femous Fetop Publishers, 2008

Verscheuren, J. *Understanding Pragmatics.* London: Arnold, 1999

Odebunmi, Akin. A pragmatic reading of of Ahmed Yerima's Proverbs in Yemoja, Attahiru, and Dry Leaves on Ukan Trees. *Intercultural Pragmatics* 3. (2), 153-169. 2006

Kasher, A. Pragmatics and the modularity of mind. *Pragmatics: a reader* in S. Davis ed. (Pp.567-582). Oxford University press, 1991

Chapter 5

Speech Acts as States-of-affairs: A Pragmatic Overview of a Mobile-Phone Message of August 31ˢᵗ 2012

- John Emike Acheoah

1. Introduction

Pragmatics emerged as a reaction against the hitherto-purely formalist approach to language study; an approach which had deprived man of the most outstanding of his ability – the ability to negotiate a meaning to the world instead of extracting a meaning that was already there. In this paper, I contend that when speech acts are performed to decoders who have embraced the environmental, socio-cultural, psychological, historical or diachronic contexts of such acts, then language meaningfully picks out societal phenomena, rather than existing in a vacuum. Hinging on Acheoah's (2015) Pragma-crafting Theory, micro-structures from a mobile-phone message are subjected to pragmatic analysis. However, the paper relies on Bach and Harnish's (1979) speech act taxonomy to categorize speech acts performed as language is used to address states-of-affairs. The Keywords are Pragmatics, Pragma-crafting Theory, speech acts, mobile-phone message

The emergence of pragmatics replaced "linguistic competence" with "communicative competence". Linguists who champion the cause of a context-dependent layer of linguistic study include: Austin (1962), Lyons (1977), Searle (1969), Leech (1983) and Halliday (1970).
The mobile-phone message being analyzed in this paper was received on 31ˢᵗ August 2012 from an anonymous source. The message is titled: "8 Best Selling Books in Town" and ends thus: "*Available in all bookshops nationwide. GRAB UR COPIES NOW!!"

2. Speech Acts

A major feat of Austin's theory is that it generated a widespread interest on "doing things with words." He makes a distinction between Performatives and Constatives. Constatives are statements which have been traditionally treated as having the property of truth or falsity. But performatives may not meet this criterion. They index the fact that an utterance uttered, is the performance of an action; they transcend, mere stating. Rather than being true or false, performatives are either "felicitous" or "infelicitous". In Austin's view, performatives and constatives differ in the areas of "doing" and "saying" (p.47). The felicity condition for performatives is that certain conventional procedures be fulfilled; certain words have to be uttered in certain circumstances, all participants of the discourse must execute such procedures correctly and completely, the particular persons and circumstances in a given situation must be appropriate for the particular procedure, and their thoughts and feelings should also be germane to the situation (pp.14-15). The violation of these procedures, makes performatives infelicitous. Austin goes further to define "perlocutionary acts" which are the effects on, or thoughts or feelings of the audience or the speaker produced by the act of saying something. Unlike illocutionary acts, perlocutionary acts are unconventional. They involve either the achievement of a "perlocutionary object" (e.g. warning, informing) or the production of a "perlocutionary sequel".

There is "uptake" in the performance of illocutionary acts, and this implies bringing about an understanding of the meaning and the force of the locution. By convention, many illocutionary acts bring about a response or a sequel e.g. an order brings obedience as a response, and a promise brings about fulfillment (pp. 117-118). Thus, "uptake" is the force of illocutionary acts, whereas perlocutionary sequel is the response which such an "uptake" (understanding) brings about.

Searle's seminal book, *Speech Acts: An Essay in the Philosophy of Language* which was developed in subsequent works such as Searle (1969), was a speech act proposal. His work mainly explains that communication is rule- governed, and that speech act is the core of communication. Like Austin, Searle distinguishes "illocutionary acts" which he regards as the "complete" speech acts, from "perlocutionary acts" which concern the consequences or effects of illocutionary acts on hearers. He further distinguishes "utterance acts" (the act of uttering words, which Austin calls "Phatic Acts"), from "propositional acts", which are used to refer and predicate. Searle's speech act taxonomy is one of the attempts to refine Austin's and this taxonomy is based on "illocutionary point", "direction of fit" and "sincerity conditions" (as well as other features including the role of authority, discourse relations, etc.). By "illocutionary point", Searle means the "purpose" of speech act in question. The second criterion, "direction of fit", concerns the match between our words and the world. While some speech acts try to get the words (or, more specifically, their propositional content) to match the world, others try to get the world to match the words. A third major criterion concerns differences in the psychological states expressed. Thus, a person who "states, explains, asserts, or claims that P <u>expresses the belief that P;</u> a man who promises, vows, threatens, or pledges to do A <u>expresses a desire (want, wish) that H do A;</u> a man who apologizes for doing A <u>expresses regret at having done A;</u> etc." (1979:4). The psychological state expressed in the performance of a speech act is therefore the "sincerity condition" of the act.

Apart from these three major criteria, which Searle considers the most important, he also examines other important aspects of a speech act in his taxonomy. These include the role of authority, discourse relations, the force or strength with which the illocutionary force is presented, differences in the status of speaker and hearer, differences in the way the utterance relates to the interests of the speaker and hearer, differences between acts that are always speech acts and those that can be but need not be performed as speech acts, differences between acts that require extra-linguistic institutions for their performance and those that do not (pp. 2-8). According to Bloomfeild (1933), "the meaning of a linguistic form is the situation in which the speaker utters it, and the response which it calls forth in the hearer". Austin himself acknowledges that "the meaning of one's linguistic vehicle cannot be relied on to determine the illocutionary force of one's utterance." He took this position to demonstrate that illocutionary force transcends meaning when meaning is viewed as "sense and reference".

3. Theoretical Underpinnings

This chapter mainly explores Acheoah's (2015) Pragma-crafting Theory to investigate the referential potency of speech acts. However, Bach and Harnish's (ibid.) speech act taxonomy facilitates the categorization of speech acts in the analysis done in this study.

3.1 Acheoah (2015)

To underscore the systematic, comprehensible and dynamic nature of human communication, Acheoah (2015) evolves the Pragma-crafting Theory. Contending that effective use and interpretation of language is essentially a "pragmatic" process of "crafting" (skillful selection and arrangement and interpretation of verbal and non-verbal elements of communication from smaller structures to larger ones), Acheoah presents a scholarly overview of hitherto-neglected issues in the literature of pragmatics. "Every Pragma-crafting (P-crafting) involves "illocrafting", "uptake" and "sequel". Therefore, P-crafting is a super-ordinate pragmatic act which produces linguistic and extra-linguistic elements of communication. At different stages of a communicative event, there is a candidate for inference. At every such stage, the interactive and non-interactive participants explore P-crafting Features (inference features): indexicals (INDXLs), Shared Macro-knowledge (SMK), Shared Contextual Knowledge (SCK), Shared Knowledge of Emergent Context (SKEC), Geoimplicatures (GIs), Linguistic Implicatures (LIs), Behavioural Implicatures (BIs), Contextual Presuppositions (CPs), Pragmadeviants (PDs), Object Referred (OR) and Operative Language (OL) – to ascertain messages and sequels (ibid. p.21-32)." Notions in the theory include:

(i) P-crafting: This is a super-ordinate notion which has dual components: Event and Text; these two components unfold as discrete multiple categories in the explanation of how communication is interpreted from speaker-hearer or writer-reader ends.

(ii) Event: It concerns participants of discourse who are either interactive or non-interactive. The interactive participants perform any or all of these acts to the discourse: linguistic, extra-linguistic and psychological acts. On the other hand, the Non-interactive Participants are those who are present in the setting, but do not perform any act in the discourse. This kind of participants is typical of certain discourse settings. Even when they perform linguistic, extra-linguistic or psychological acts, such acts are not connected to the discourse in progress, so they are labeled as "Non-interactive Participants". Acheoah (2015) exemplifies the notion thus: Billy, Gerald and Jane may begin a conversation from school and sustain it until they get to Hardy's shop, only to meet Hardy and his customer bargaining over the price of certain commodities. In this situation, all acts performed are only meaningful in terms of how they affect an on-going discourse. In another vein, the students in a classroom lecture are fragmented: some are discussing issues unrelated to the lecture; some are making linguistic, extra-linguistic and psychological contributions related to the lecture and others are just physically present in the setting. However, in certain discourse situations, an interactive participant may perform linguistic, extra-linguistic or psychological acts as an indirect communicative strategy targeted at a non-interactive participant towards achieving certain goal(s). Indeed, Non-interactive Participants affect communicative events. For example, the sociolinguistic particulars (age, status, ethnic background) of the Non-Interactive Participants determine how and what Billy, Gerald and Jane say in Hardy's shop. Acheoah (2014a) uses the label "H_2" to refer to participants who are present in discourse, but are not speakers' interlocutors.

(iii) Text: Components of Text are Setting, Theme and P-crafting Features. The trio constitutes the communicative features in Text. However, the dynamics of communication are captured by P-crafting Features which have discrete theoretical notions demonstrated by the Interactive Participants in three different frames: linguistic acts, extra-linguistic acts and psychological acts.

(iv) Interactive participant: This is an interlocutory participant. He makes linguistic, extra-linguistic and psychological contributions that do not only impinge on the interpretive process in discourse, but also determine or generate sequel. An Interactive Participant demonstrates pragmatic awareness in the encoding and decoding of utterances.

(v) Non-interactive Participant: A participant is categorized as non-interactive when he does not function in an on-going communicative event, although he is intentionally or accidentally present in the physical context.

(vi) Setting: This is the physical context of the communicative event (Text) in both remote and immediate sense.

(vii) Theme: This category is the message conveyed in/by Text. Text may convey one or more themes that can only be identified when communicative acts (acts performed by Interactive Participants) interact with communicative features (P-crafting Features).

(viii) P-crafting Features: These elements are instrumental to understanding the interlocutory roles of the Interactive Participants. The elements include: Inference, Indexical Shared Macro-knowledge, Shared Contextual Knowledge, Shared Knowledge of Emergent Context, Geoimplicatures, etc.

Inference has to do with making logical deductions from available linguistic and extra-linguistic data. Indexicals are grammatical categories that have the potential to establish the relationship between language and context. Shared Contextual Knowledge is the available pieces of information which only participants of the on-going discourse have for the communication to thrive. When discourse has an Emergent Context, perlocutionary effects may not occur (effects intended by speakers), despite the appropriateness of participants and circumstances. Any situation that suddenly emerges in an on-going discourse is emergent. An Emergent Context becomes Shared Knowledge of Emergent Context when it translates to common knowledge to the participants of discourse. It is vital in terms of its potential to determine illocutionary forces and relocate sequel. It is a candidate for inferences. The term "Geoimplicature" is coined from "geographical" and "implicature" to refer to practices that have geographical restriction in terms of people, and not just in terms of physical boundaries (cf. Acheoah, 2011). Such practices are not universal, and they are both verbal and non-verbal. Linguistic implicatures are meanings implied through language while Behavioural implicatures are meanings implied through extra-linguistic and psychological acts. Contextual Presuppositions are products of Shared Contextual Knowledge; in a specific discourse, participants deduce meanings from verbal and non-verbal data limited to them. The meanings deduced are treated as Background Assumptions (BAs) which direct interlocutory roles. DCs (Decoders) imply that ENCs (Encoders) know that certain VEs (Verbal Elements) and NVEs (Non-verbal Elements) are deduced as OR (Object Referred) in OL (Operative Language).

(ix) Linguistic Acts: There are five components in this category:
1. Speech acts (direct, indirect and pragmadeviant);
Pragmadeviants are deviant forms of expressions which participants use as part of illocutionary strategy or creative indulgence.
Acheoah (2011) coins the term "Pragmavediant" (PD) from "pragmatics" and "deviant". It is not a duplication of the notion of indirect speech act as it is any expression used as a literal but deviant communicative strategy. For example, in the conversational exchange below, Sam deviates from the conventional use of the verb "stole" since he owns the book:
Sam: I stole my book from the teacher's bag.

Mary: But it's yours.

There is always a pragmatic justification for pragmadeviating; Sam's book was no longer his, because his teacher who seized it did not promise to return it.

Object referred (OR) is the referent of an utterance. This referent is either in the remote world or immediate context of speech. One of the strengths of "meaning as object" (an approach to the study of meaning in semantics) is that words have or pick referents (objects) in the world.

Every natural communication is conveyed through a particular language, whether indigenous or alien to the participants. This is what Acheoah (2015) refers to as Operative Language.

2. Supra-segmental Features (stress, intonation, rhythm, pitch);

Stress is the degree of emphasis with which a syllable is uttered. Intonation is the rising and falling of the voice during speech production. The noticeable pattern of sound produced as a result of stressed and unstressed syllables produces rhythm. Therefore, speakers' intentional violation of the stress patterns of words or stretches can convey varied messages in discourse. During a class lesson, the pupils who have become too tied to continue the lesson may choose repeated pitch rhythm (and this can generate the perlocutionary effect of annoying the teacher) to respond to the teacher when they are asked: "Pupils, do you understand?" Indeed, stress, intonation and rhythm are mostly inseparable. These prosodic features convey messages in communicative events.

3. Phones (Ssss, Shhh, Mmmm, Ehmnn);

The term 'phones' refers to speech features between the phoneme and the word. They are common components in both written and spoken discourse. Small as they are, they express emotions of various kinds besides having speech acts illocutionary potential in context.

4. Exclamations (Wao!, Oh!, Ah!, Abah!, other categories);

Psychological acts are sometimes performed through exclamations. A speaker may utter "Oh!" in a particular context of situation to perform the act of approving whereas the same speaker may utter "Abah!" to agitate in the same context of situation.

5. Music (lyrical).

Participants can sing without using words (lyrics). However, it is when words are used that it can be said that a linguistic act has been performed. Lyrics convey diverse messages in discourse. Sometimes, the context in which a participant of discourse sings, and how it is sung, determines the implicature.

(x) Extra-linguistic Acts: Extra-linguistic acts in the Pragma-crafting Theory include:
1. Sociolinguistic Variables: These include: age, cultural background, social status/class, gender and relationships).
2. Music (non-lyrical): Non-lyrical music operates as non-verbal communication. It can be rhythmic, but its importance in the Pragma-crafting Theory is its communicative value in discourse. Sounds produced in rhythmic pattern in certain contexts may negate world knowledge, and so become an implicature or an illocutionary strategy.
3. Drumming: Where a group of students are writing an examination, drumming generates a Behavioural implicature (BI), which is produced when extra-linguistic acts negate the context of discourse.

   Semiotic particulars (weather, time, contextual object (CO), colour, clothing, posture, perfume, location/position, size, body mark and silence);
4. Laughter: Laughter is capable of conveying expected emotions of solidarity, peace, approval, admiration, etc.
5. Body Movement: Not all body movements are gestures. Like gestures, body movement can reveal psychological states of participants, besides being able to achieve communicative goals.

(xi) Psychological Acts: These are the different emotions expressed through linguistic and extra-linguistic acts.

Figure 1 shows theoretical concepts in the Pragma-crafting Theory (cf. Acheoah 2015:23):

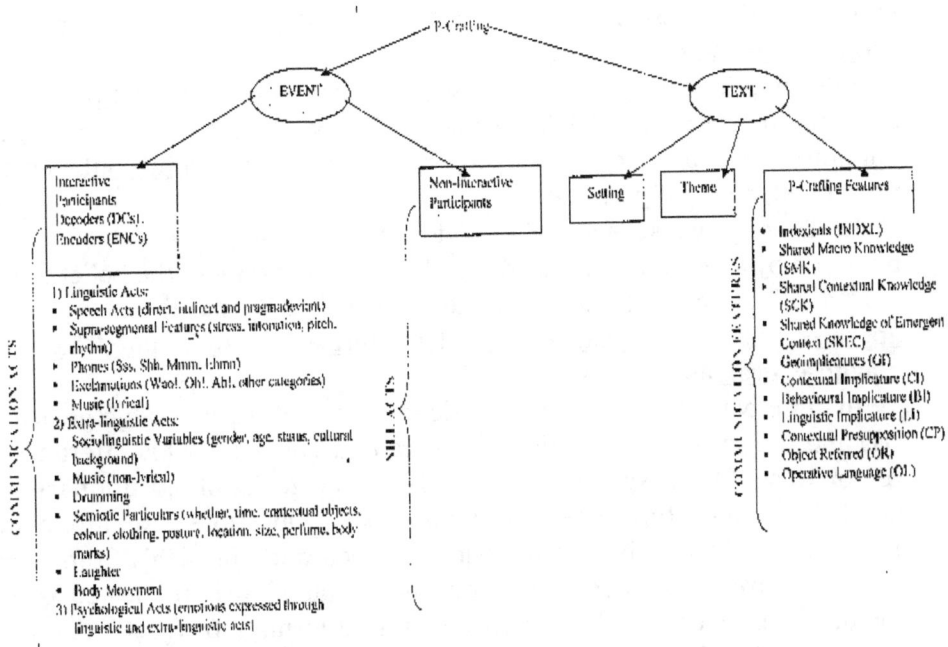

Figure 1: Theoretical Concepts in the Pragma-crafting Theory

3.2 Bach and Harnish (1979)

The approach of Kent Bach and Robert M. Harnish to Speech Acts is intention and inference-based. They contend that for speakers to perform illocutionary acts, it is intended that listeners have the understanding of the acts. It is their claim that the act of conversation or interactional talk has to involve an inferential process. Their terminology Speech Act Schemata (SAS) refers to an inevitable part of the inferential process in a communicative event. To them, mutual contextual beliefs (MCBs) between a speaker and his hearer facilitate the inferential process, as the inference made or is expected to be made by the hearer does not depend on what the speaker says but on the contextual knowledge shared commonly by the speaker and hearer in discourse. For proper understanding of their theory, see Bach and Harnish (ibid.).

Speech act categories in Bach and Harnish (ibid.) taxonomy include: Assertives, Informatives, Confirmatives, Concessives, Acriptives, Retractives, Assentives, Dissentives, Disputatives, Responsives, Suggestives, Suppositives, Descripives, Directives and Advisories (Ibid. pp42-46). According to them, Assertives are characterized by S's expression of belief that the hearer (H) also believes that P. "Examples of verbs denoting Assertives speech acts are affirm, allege, assert, aver, avow, declare, and deny (p.42).

Informatives are speech acts in which S expresses the belief that P and also "the intention that H form the belief that P." Examples are advise, announce, appraise, disclose, inform, insist, notify, point out, report, reveal, tell, and testify (p.42).

In Descriptive speech acts, S declares that a particular quality is possesed by a person, place or thing. That is, S expresses "the belief that O is F" and "the intention that H believes that O is F" (p.42). Examples are appraise, asses, call, categorize, characterize, classify, date, describe, diagnose, evaluate, etc. (p.42).

In directives, the speaker's attitude toward a future action by the hearer (H) and the speaker's intention or desire that H consider his utterance as reason to act (A) is expressed (p.47). Six subcategories of illocutionary acts are listed under this category: Requestives, Questions, Requirements, Prohibitives, Permissives, Advisories. In Bach and Harnish's framework, Questions are "special cases of requests in that what is requested is that the hearer provide the speaker with certain information" (p.48). A speech act is considered a question if S expresses "the desire that H tell S whether or not P" and "intention that H tell S whether or not P because of S's desire" (p.47). Examples of verb denoting Questions are ask, interrogate, query, questions, quiz, etc. Advisories, they explain, is a speech act in which the speaker expresses the belief that "there is (sufficient) reason for H to A," and "The intention that H takes S's belief as (sufficient) reason for him to A" (p.48). Examples are advise, caution, counsel, propose, recommend, suggest, urge, warn, etc.

The third major category of speech acts established by Bach and Harnish, Commissives, are acts involving the undertaking of an obligation or proposal to undertake an obligation. Two main types of this category are distinguished: Promises and Offers. S promises H to A if S expresses "the belief that his utterance obligates him to A", "the intention to A", and "the intention that H believes that S's utterance obligates S to A and that S intends to A" (p.50). Contracting, Guaranteeing, etc. are examples of this category. Promise include swear, vow, surrender and guarantee. A speech act is said to be an Offer if S expresses "the belief that S's utterance obligates him to A on condition that H indicates he wants S to A" and "the intention that H believes that S's utterance obligates S to A and that S intends to A on condition that H indicates he wants S to A" (p.50). Examples of verbs denoting speech acts in this category are volunteer, offer, and propose. Acknowledgements, the final category of Bach and Harnish's communicative illocutionary acts, are very common in our day to day interaction. They express perfunctorily, if not genuinely, certain feelings toward the hearer" (p.51). Examples of verbs denoting members of this category include greet, thank, condole, apologize, congratulate, etc.

Bach and Harnish's non-communicative (or conventional) illocutionary acts are divided into two classes: Effectives and Verdictives.

4. Presentation and Analysis of Data

I present and analyse the entire message as Best Selling Book 1 – 8 (henceforth BSB 1 – 8): I do not attempt a refined, extensive analysis; my aim in this paper is just to locate the states-of-affairs that speech acts address in the corpora. I strongly believe that the brief but integrative analyses (simply pragmatic comments) done in this paper suffice as far as the goal of the study is concerned.

BSB 1.
Beauty Tips by Olusegun Obasanjo

Speech Act Categories: Informative, Ascriptive, Descriptive, Assertive, Dissentive, Disputative
Illocutionary Forces: Informing, Describing, Declaring, Amusing, agitating.
Perlocutionary Acts: The audience is informed and amused.
Pragmatic Implications: To amuse the readers, the writer explores the background assumption (BA) that the former Nigerian Head-of-State and President, Olusegun Obasanjo, is so ugly. The text therefore explores Geoimplicature (GI) since the target audience understands the Object Referred (OR). Since the meaning of the word "beauty" in the Operative Language (OL) which is English is known to the readers, there is uptake. When speech acts (locutionary) are used to refer to states-of-affairs, the interaction between pragmatics and semantics becomes evident. According to Leech (1983), there is a clear relationship between semantics and pragmatics. He posits: "Semantics is primarily rule-governed (grammatical) while pragmatics is believed to be principle-controlled (rhetorical)". The above text reveals the writer's idiosyncratic, indirect and thought-provoking way of addressing the state-of-affair. Fowler (1981:28) posits: "Linguistic structure is not arbitrary but is determined or motivated by the functions it performs."

BSB 2.
Value of Family Planning by 2face Idibia

Speech Act Categories: Informative, Descriptive, Disputative, Assertive, Declarative, Ascriptive, Dissentive
Illocutionary Forces: Informing, Condemning, Dissenting, Mocking
Perlocutinary Acts: The readers are informed and amused.
Pragmatic Implications: The decoders are aware that the famous Nigerian musician, 2face Idibia, has impregnated several ladies. He carries this stigma in the country, despite his feat in the musical industry. His name, as the text suggests, has become a usual collocate of "polygamy" or "womanizing". Against this background, the writer detaches from the readers' expectation; the readers' mind set and puzzle is: Why should a polygamist be the author of a book which teaches the value of family planning? BSB 2 shows the writer's consistency in using indirect illocutionary strategies to mean or refer to states-of-affairs. Within the context of family planning, the Object Referred (2face Idibia) is a deviant reference, therefore the readers presuppose (Contextual Presupposition) that the encoder is being indirect in the selection of Verbal Elements (VEs) of communication[1]. There are three Contextual Objects that have been used as P-crafting Features (inference features) in BSB 2: "value", "family-planning" and "2face Idibia". The decoders' uptake is that "the encoder is amusing the readers as well as mocking 2face Idibia". In addressing states-of-affairs, BSB 1 and BSB 2 parade different domains. Unlike BSB 1 which takes on a political subject/personality, BSB 2 takes on a subject/personality from entertainment industry. Adegbija (1982) rightly notes that different contextual structures produce speech acts, and by this, he means that speech acts address issues in different domains of society. In establishing the relationship between the Master Speech Act and other speech acts in a given discourse, Adegbija (ibid.) contends that the pragmatic analyst should be able to: locate the contextual structure that produces the speech acts; investigate the thematic relevance of their selection and sequencing.

Figure 2 represents the contextual domains of speech acts:[2]

Contextual Structures of Speech Acts:

a) Political/Government Context;

b) Religious Context;

c) Socio-cultural/Philosophical Context;

d) Educational Context;

e) Domestic Context;

f) Administrative Context;

g) Occupational Context;

h) Scientific Context;

i) Business/Commercial Context.

BSB 3.
Peaceful Co-existence by Boko Haram Sect

Speech Act Categories: Informative, Ascriptive, Dissentive, Descriptive, Assertive, Disputative
Illocutionary Acts: Informing, Describing, Rejecting
Perlocutionary Acts: The decoders are informed, amused and refreshed.
Pragmatic Implications: The objects: "peace" and "Boko Haram" are contradictory. The decoders are part of the social realism of Boko Haram's anti-peace posture and activities (Shared Macro-knowledge), so BSB 3 is decoded as thematic humour: any desire for peaceful co-existence cannot emanate from those who traditionally fight peace with unending passion. It is obvious that the encoder is a Nigerian where the Boko Haram Sect operates. First-hand knowledge of the linguistic conventions of OL facilitates the use of indirect speech acts to make reference to states-of-affairs. Speech act theory "provides a way of talking about utterances not only in terms of their surface grammatical properties but also in terms of the context in which they are made, the intentions, attitudes, and expectations of the participants, the relationships existing between participants…rules and conventions that are understood to be in play when an utterance is made and received" – (Pratt 1977).
Bach and Harnish opine that communicative intentions are the mental causes of communicative acts, and those that the hearer has to understand for the communicative act to be successful.

Communicative intentions have the following features:
- They are always oriented towards some other goals (the addressee);

- They are overt, that is, they are intended to be recognized by the addressee;
- Their satisfaction consists precisely in being recognized by the addressee.

Acheoah (2014b) contends that extra-linguistic factors (the socio-pragmatic motivations of language use in regional communication, which invariably presupposes the social, environmental, situational, cultural and diachronic contexts of linguistic elements used "beyond the sentence) are the core of pragmatic use of elements of communication. Halliday (1970) has a similar view: "The particular form taken by the grammatical system of language is closely related to the social and personal needs that language is required to serve."

BSB 4.
Tactics to Win Trophies by Nigeria Olympic Committee

Speech Act Categories: Informative, Assertive, Ascriptive, Dissentive, Descriptive, Disputative
Illocutionary Forces: Informing, Describing, Declaring, Condemning
Perlocutionary Acts: The readers are informed, amused and refreshed.
Pragmatic Implications: The text is addressed to sports domain. It is a product of the most recent (emergent) poor performance of the Nigerian contingents at the Olympics – an Emergent Context which has become Share Knowledge of Emergent Context to the audience. The Background Assumption (BA) of the encoder is that the decoders (DECs) have witnessed or heard about the series of defeats suffered by Nigerian contingents during Olympic Competitions. Thus, BSB 4 is a Disputative (speech act category in Bach and Harnish's taxonomy) which lampoons the Nigerian governing body for the Olympic. Speech acts often have environmental contexts which determine the process of encoding and decoding them. The process of using speech acts to impinge on states-of-affairs inevitably engages dynamic, pragmatic instrumentalities such as implicatures and presuppositions. Linguistic Implicatures (LI) are potent in conveying messages when speech acts are engaged in spoken and written discourses. According to Levinson (1983:226), apart from speech acts, implicature and presupposition are among the central phenomena that any general pragmatic theory must account for. Indeed, linguistic choices and patterning are essentially the process of "crafting" towards achieving illocutionary goals. Adegbija (ibid.) notes that in textual

analysis, while a synchronic perspective would be primarily concerned with the text *per se*, its present life, context and contemporary meaning, a diachronic perspective would introduce dimensions of meaning relating to the historical and global context enclosing a text. Such access to diachronic context is particularly relevant for a full elucidation of indirect speech acts. Diachronic context typically forms central aspects of the mutually shared beliefs that are important for the understanding of linguistic, extra-linguistic and psychological acts performed when speech acts refer to states-of-affairs.

BSB 5.
How 2 make ur Marriage Work by Rev Chris Okotie

Speech Act Categories: Informative, Disputative, Assertive, Dissentive, Desrciptive, Ascriptive
Illocutionary Forces: Informing, Declaring, Describing, Condemning
Perlocutionary Acts: The audience is informed, amused and refreshed.
Pragmatic Implications: Rev Chris Okotie is widely known by Nigerians for pluralistic divorce; his present wife is not the first, irrespective of his position as a Pastor. The Pragma-crafting Theory contends that sociolinguistic variables determine implicatures and presuppositions in discourse. In the case of the OR (Rev Okotie) the sociolinguistic variable that impinges on meaning is "status". BSB 5 engages religious domain, where morality is expected (SMK). If Rev Okotie epitomizes "failed marriage" in the mindset of Nigerians as a result of the recurring divorce he is known with (Behavioural Implicature), then the Encoder (ENC) indirectly uses Verbal Elements (VEs) to target the state-of-affair in question. BSB 5 conveys different speech acts: Ascriptive (ascribing negative quality to OR/Rev Okotie), Informative (the secondary illocutionary act of "informing" the readers as if, or in case they do not know about Rev Okotie's antecedents) and Dissentive (condemning broken marriages or even polygamy). In making reference to societal phenomena, the indirect speech act potentials of speech act verbs are evident when such speech acts are used alongside other speech act categories in an utterance. To convey messages effectively, writers/speakers ensure that their selection and sequencing of speech acts are not incidental.

BSB 6.
Say No 2 Corruption by James Ibori

Speech Act Categories: Informative, Ascriptive, Disputative, Descriptive, Dissentive

Illocutionary Forces: Informing, stating, describing, condemning, rejecting

Perlocutionary Acts: The audience is informed, amused and entertained.

Pragmatic Implications: Many Nigerians are well informed about the ordeal of the former Delta State Governor, James Ibori, who was arrested and detained for stealing government funds. A Nigerian as well, the encoder of this text amuses his readers who do not expect a thief to protect money. BSB 6 captures politics, a domain where money laundering is a recurring decimal. Indeed, speech acts have their thematic concerns tied to the psychological states they express; although comic, BSB 2 expresses the degree of disgust ("psychological act" as explained in the Pragma-crafting Theory) which Nigerians feel concerning politicians or political leaders. It is logical to state that indirect illocutionary strategies are persuasive. Leech's view of style as "the dress of thought" makes it clear that the concern of persuasive speech (rhetoric) is the relationship between "what" is said and "how" it is said.

BSB 7.
My Love 4 America by Osama Bin Laden

Speech Act Categories: Informative, Ascriptive, Disputative, Descriptive, Dissentive

Illocutionary Forces: Informing, Describing, Disputing, Stating

Perlocutionary Acts: The audience is informed, amused and refreshed.

Pragmatic Implications: The writer expects many Nigerians to know the man who masterminded the September 11th terrorist attack in the United States of America. The devastating effects of the tragic incidence are common knowledge across the world. As an indirect speech act, the writer patterns unexpected lexical items in the linguistic stretch to create humour; Osama Bin Laden who hates America to the extreme cannot be the one who have written a book about his love for America. The writer of BSB 1 – 8 may be one of the contemporary Nigerian comedians who extract their themes from the existential experiences of different societies. There is the issue of felicity or appropriateness conditions for the performing of speech acts, which many speech act theoreticians emphasize. The speech acts in BSB 1 – 8 can only be fully understood within the felicity conditions involving the audience's awareness of the different states-of-affairs addressed.

BSB 8.
How 2 Speak Good English by Dr. Mrs. Patience Jonathan

Speech Act Categories: Informative, Ascriptive, Descriptive, Assertive, Dissentive, Disputative
Illocutionary Forces: Informing, Describing, Mocking
Perlocutionary Acts: The audience is informed and amused.
Many Nigerians are familiar with the linguistic incompetence (in OL) of Nigeria's former First Lady. I am not aware that she holds a PhD. If she does not, then the title in BSB 8 is sarcastic. Indeed, certain Verbal Elements have been attributed to her by Nigerians (SKEC) due to her response to a particular incidence – when Nigerians say: "There is God ohhhh!" the name "Patience Jonathan" immediately comes to memory as Object Referred". The social context is that of power relations; the aristocrats in different human societies are expected to be above certain human weaknesses. A public personality, Patience Jonathan is expected to have acquired good, extensive Western education – the type that will enable her speak correctly at all levels of effective speech-delivery whether in private or in public. For this reason, the writer of BSB 8 takes up the antecedents of this former Nigeria's First Lady as subjects of ridicule. I posit at this juncture, that the comic and refreshing potentials of this datum is predicated upon by the sociolinguistic variable (mentioned in the Pragma-crafting) therein – the high status of the Object Referred (Patience Jonathan).

5. Discussions and Conclusion

Language use is a thing of credit. Selecting and sequencing speech acts is not just an act (mechanical process), but it is also an art (social competence is infused with the mechanical process of selecting and sequencing speech acts). Every good writer is influenced by situational or contextual variables, and these variables give his/her writing direction. The writer of the mobile-phone message analyzed in this study uses language with principles that corroborate Aristotle's three steps of rhetoric: invention, arrangement and style. In pragmatics, it is from the angle of a writer's (or speaker's) intention that meaning is defined. This explains why perlocutionary acts mostly show consequences that are in line with what the encoder intends. It is therefore often the case that the encoder of an utterance presumes that his decoder has the cognitive maturity to make logical presumptions about utterances being that this decoder is part of what Allan (ibid.) calls the "world-spoken-of". Apart from making utterances worthy of inferences, encoders try to make such utterances easy to mean. This process necessitates the use of world knowledge, implicatures and presuppositions. This is a way of ensuring that the fundamentals of communication theories are met. A speaker, despite his right to idiosyncratic use of utterances in discourse, should not make the inferential process of his utterances personal. A speaker's utterance is impersonal and meets the fundamentals of human communication if "in saying x in a particular same context to any member of that speech community, this speaker has meant p to all members of that speech community[3]."

Bronislaw and Archibald (2004) opine that there are usually constraints which inform the different components of speech. A speaker or writer does not merely use language to convey "social system", but also to influence it. In a similar vein, Jawoski and Coupland (1999) cited in Ayoola 2006:3 (Paper presented at the 23rd Annual Conference of Nigerian English Studies, Ilorin, Nigeria) notes "that discourse analysis is not only language reflecting social order, but language shaping social order." David Harrah, cited in Savas (1994:375) posits: "Most speech acts seem to be focused and directed. They are intended as coming from the agent and going to the receivers or audience. They are intended to have a certain point, and they are intended to be construed as having a certain point." It is natural for participants of discourse to make utterances that have in-built contexts. On the whole, the mobile-phone message analyzed in this study is a Constative (thought-provoking statement) which declares that deceit and hypocrisy characterize the Nigerian society and by extension, human society at large. This Constative is generated with the in-built ironical humour in BSB 1 – 8 as conveyed by varied, versatile speech acts which include: Descriptives, Assertives, Ascriptives, Disputatives, Dissentives and Informatives. Figure 3: shows the versatility (fusing) of speech act categories as well as their illocutionary forces:[4]

Speech Act Category	Illocutionary Force
Informative	• to inform the readers
Ascriptive/Descriptive	• to ascribe qualities to Object Referred (something or phenomenon); • to condemn Object Referred (something or phenomenon)
Disputative/Dissentive	• to dislodge, reject or condemn Object Referred (something or phenomenon)
Assertive	• to state that Object Referred (something or phenomenon) possesses the quality or qualities ascribed to it

Notes

1. The Pragma-crafting Theory views each Object Referred as a person, animal, place, thing or idea (concept) that is a candidate for infinite pragmasociolinguistic phenomena (attitudes, norms, values, practices, beliefs, etc.) that can be subjected to logical interpretation.
2. Although each domain can be viewed as a state-of-affair, there are usually several states-of-affairs that can be addressed within each of the domains according to thematic preoccupations of writers or speakers.
3. This view aligns with Searle's (ibid.) "word-to-world direction of fit".
4. The literature acknowledges the versatility of speech act verbs and posits that the classification of speech acts is intractable. I therefore contend that: "to advise h" is "to suggest to h"; and "to ascribe certain qualities to x" is to "describe x" as having such qualities. Speech act categories in BSB 1 – 8 are same. There are other speech act categories in BSB 1 – 8 which I have ignored because of their homogeneity; I seek refuge in the Projection Principle (cf. Jolayemi, 2000) to conclude that BSB 1 – 8 (or the mobile-phone message) produced same speech act categories even when all the categories are not mentioned in the analysis. According to the Projection Principle, a textual analyst can procure the entire messages in a text (macro text) via selected linguistic structures (micro text). If the data analysed in this study were to be from a play or the novel genre, variegated speech acts could have been easily produced.

References

Acheoah, John. (2011). "A Pragmatic Analysis of Ayi Kwei Armah's *The Beautyful Ones Are Not Yet Born* and *Ola Rotimi's Hopes of the Living Dead.*" PhD Dissertation. Zaria, Ahmadu Bello University.

_____. (2014a). "The Illocutionary Frames Principle (IFP) and the Austinian Postulations: A Clause-structure Investigative Discourse." *Global Journal of Human and Social Sciences*, Volume 13, Issue 13, Version 1.0, pp. 21 29.

_____. (2014b). Saying x: The Pragmatics of a Nigerian Context." *Studies in Literature and Language Vol.* 6, No 3: 39 44.

_____. (2015). "The Pragma-crafting Theory: A Proposed Theoretical Framework for Pragmatic Analysis." *American Research Journal of English and Literature*, Volume 1, Issue 2:21-32.

Adegbija, E. F. (1982). "A Speech Act Analysis of Consumer Advertisements". USA: Indiana University. Ph.D Dissertation.

Austin, John. (1962). *How To Do Things With Words.* Cambridge: Harvard University Press.

Ayoola, K. A. (2006). "Ken Saro-Wiwa's Discourse Strategy in the Niger Delta Struggle". Paper presented at the 23rd Annual Conference of Nigerian English Studies, Ilorin.

Bach, Kent and Harnish, Robert. (1979). Linguistic Communication and Speech Acts. Cambridge: Massachusetts. The MIT Press.

Bloomfeild, L. (1933). Language. New York: Reinehart and Winston.

Bronislaw M. (2004). "Language in Social Context" in O' Grady, William and Archibald John. eds. *Contemporary Linguistic Analysis: An Introduction.* Canada. Pearson Education.

Fowler, Roger. (1981). *Literature as Social Discourse: The Practice of Linguistic Criticism.* Bloomington: Indiana UP.

Halliday, M. A. K. (1970). "Language Structure and Language Functions" in *New Horizons in Linguistics.* (Ed.) J. Lyons. Harmondsworth. Penguin. pp.140-165.

Jolayemi, D. (2000). "Language and Style: A Systematic Textlinguistic Study of Olu Obafemi's Plays" in Oni D, Ododo S. eds. *Larger than His Frames: Critical Studies and Reflections on Olu Obafemi.* Lagos. Centre for Black and African Arts and Civilization, National Theatre. 2000. p.118.

Leech, G. (1983). *Principles of Pragmatics.* London: Longman.

Levinson, Stephen. (1983). *Pragmatics.* Cambridge: Cambridge University Press.

Lyons, J. (1977). *Semantics.* Cambridge. Cambridge University Press.

Pratt, Mary. (1977). Towards a Speech Act Theory of Literary Discourse. Bloomington: Indiana University Press.

Savas, T. (1994). (Ed.). *Foundations of Speech Act Theory.* London: Routledge.

Searle, John. (1969). Speech Acts: *An Essay in the Philosophy of Language.* New York: Cambridge University Press.

Chapter 6

Deixis

– Christiana Rakiya Ogidi-Andrew

1.0 Introduction

Deixis expresses the relationship between words, signs, and what the signs represent. It concerns the function of the meaning of gesture (the so called stroke) and specifies these gestures from the perspective of the participants in a speech event. The interpretation of deixis is based on background knowledge, context of speech and the interplay of activities in which communication occurs (Jespersen, 1951:7). The function of deixis in language is to point the utterance of a speaker at the moment of speaking to objects and issues of discourse (Gillian, 1995). More so, deixis encodes features of the context of utterance. As a result, its interpretation depends on the listener who interprets the relevant context.

Deixis expresses the function of pointing and specifying. Adrian, Richard, Farmer and Robert (2001) assert that, "indexical expressions are the ones that have indexical uses and refer to something in rectitude of its relation to the actual physical utterance." For instance, the word 'I' is applicable to any referent which could be another person within the context of speech or to whoever utters it. Deixis is that aspect of pragmatics which entails understanding the meaning of definite words/gestures, expressions and strokes used in an utterance based on contextual information. It includes lexemes that have fixed semantic explanation. For example, units such as; Go/Goes, Do/Does and so on have fixed semantic interpretation but connotative meanings that constantly change depending on the time, place and context of utterance (Saeed, 2006).

Deixis include types of expressions that are especially handy for referring to objects, persons, things and events whose interpretations are relative to the extra - linguistic context of an utterance which concerns speaker, time and place of speaking, gestures of speaker and or, the current location in the discourse (Crystal, 1980:103). They are inexhaustible because, in some instance, the deictic *origo* changes as roles shift from one speaker to the other in the context of 'talk', especially with regards to the first person pronouns 'I/you/we' (these and some other examples are illustrated also in Igala, Yoruba, Hausa and Ibo accordingly),*ọ̀mí/ùwẹ/àwa,emi/eyin/awa, ni/kei/mu*, ...and the adverbs 'here/now/there' *émí/ábajóí/ọ̀mọ́, ibiyi/nsi/ibeyen, nan/yenzu/chan*...which is continuously redefined as the deictic centre changes.

Deictic terms and expressions are very crucial to language studies and cannot be ignored in the study of meaning because such items aid immensely in disambiguating utterances (Palmer, 1981). However, they are subjective in the sense that they differ from language to language and from speaker to speaker hence, they can be interpreted with reference to a speaker's understanding; but language propositions are often objective and independent of speaker (Inyang, 1998).

Deixis is the study of deictic or indexical expressions in any given language. Words such as, 'you', 'now', 'here' 'there' 'that' and so on are deictic. They are described as a special kind of grammatical form which is expressed in the more common grammatical categories of person, place, tense, time and so on. Deictic expressions make use of gestures which involve indexing acts with our index finger, lifted chin and poked lips, outstretched arm, stretched feet, folded arms and so on. Gestures define spatial reference in the physical world through projected hands/arms specifying a region that is proximal or distal from interlocutors or deictic centre. Through deixis, people anchor their speech signals to the context of the communicative event thereby making the content of their propositions a function that maps a world in its contextually-specific time and space to truth values. Gesture is an aspect of kinetics which involves movement that conveys meaning as derived from the movement of the body parts as accompanied by speech.

Deixis can be gestural and symbolic. Gestural deixis, in a broad sense, refers to deictic expressions whose understanding requires some kind of audio - visual information accompanied by pointing to objects using words such as (as expressed above), 'this/that/there' *ei/èéle/omo, iyi/iyen/owun, wonan/wochan/* (Lyons, 1996). Sometimes, these categories, other than pointing, combine the directions of gaze, tilting of the head, tapping of the fingers, twitching of the eye lashes and change in tone of voice and so on. The symbolic usage usually necessitates basic spatio-temporal knowledge of an utterance and requires being able to see the object of discussion. Therefore, to utter a statement such; 'this hand is bigger than this' (said while lifting up the hand in question is symbolic).

Specifically, non-verbal communication involves sending and receiving messages in different ways. It includes the intentional/unintentional non-use of verbal codes and a variety of behaviours touch, glance, eye contact, facial expression, posture, dress, gesture, intonation, and so on. Non-verbal communication concerns the generating of non-verbal stimuli in a communication by interlocutors. Such forms of communication basically comprise non - verbal messages produced by the body and that produced by the broad setting of time, silence, space and so on. Ruesch (1955) categorises non-verbal signs into sign language, action language and object. Sign language involves the use of non-verbal symbols in place of actual articulation. Such form of non-verbal symbols varies from culture to culture.

Nonetheless, some cultures share certain similarities that are noticeable in general appearance and dress (all cultures are concerned about looks and dressing), body movement which entail tapping of the fingers, moving towards or away from speaker or listener, twitching of lips, nodding of head and posture which involve genuflecting, looking straight into an elder's eyes, touching or leaving hands in pocket when an elder is talking with a younger person (which is considered rude in most African cultures) and so on.

2.0 Deixis

Deixis is concerned with the way languages encode features of the context of utterance and the interpretation thereof. It is a crucial aspect of language study which aids second language (L2) learners and by enhancing their understanding in discourse. It is best described as verbal pointing because it is sometimes accompanied by speech. It is important to know that deixis is not exhaustible by the study of inherently indexical expressions. Any referring expression can be used indexically (Frege1952). See some examples below:

3. I love her (said of a lady who just walked away).
4. The building is fine (said eyes focused on a just completed duplex).
5. What a wonderful performance! (said looking at an artist).
6. How beautiful (Said chin pointing to a kitchen)! These examples express some kind of gesture or pointed gaze (deictic but are sometimes mistaken for demonstratives).

7. She is truly crazy (Pointing index finger to own head).
8. The principal's order (indicating a written document).
9. The marriage is hereby dissolved (said by a court judge).
She owns the three large estates (said walking down the street). The question is how to identify 'here' and 'now' on particular occasion of utterance. There is no other way of defining this phenomenon in natural languages except by relating them to;
 i. Place and time of utterance.
 ii. Time and place of mental act of more or less conscious awareness.

If defined in terms of illocutionary Deixis, the words '*here*' and '*now*' in English and some natural languages (the Ígálâ adverb '*émí/ábajóí*', the Yoruba '*ibiyi/bayi*', *the* Hausa '*nan/yenzu* and the Ibo '*ebea/ugbua*)) refer to where the speaker is at the specific time of utterance and period of time that contains the utterance. For example, the demonstrative adverbs '*there* and then'(the Ígálâ '*Òmó/Ùgbálé*, the Yoruba **Ibeyen/asikoyen** *the* Hausa '*Chan/lokachin*' and the Ibo '**Ebeni/ugbua**))is contrary and negatively defined in comparison to the pronoun '*here*' and '*now*'

The deictic context is centred on the person or speakers 'here - and - now'. As the role of the actual speaker shifts (the roles of the illocutionary agent shifts), passing from one person to another in a given conversation. So, the centre or zero point shifts back and forth together with the reference of 'here and there'. The reference of 'now', unlike 'here and there', does not shift back and forth. Speaker and hearer normally operate with the same temporal frame of reference and common assumptions about passage of time. 'Now' is continuously re-defined by utterance within the shared temporal frame. In the same vein, the past, present and future are explicitly defined in relation to the 'now' of utterance. Primarily, deixis involves acts of utterances by interlocutors and listeners, place and time of utterance. The following are some examples of deixis in English and some Nigerian languages (Ígálâ, Yoruba, Hausa and Ibo):

a, person/possessive pronoun – 'I' (*òmí/emi/ni/mua*),'you' (*ùwẹ(wẹ)/eyin/kei/mmgi*),'yours' (*èwé/tiyin/nkegi*), 'ours'(*èwá/tiwa/namu/nke'ayi*),

b spatial – 'here' (*èmí/ibiyi*/nan/ebea), 'there'(***omo/ibe/chan/ebani***), 'over-there' (***ànumo/ibeyen/chan-chan/eba'hu***), 'now' (***fài/isin/yenzu/ugbua***),

c   possessive adjective – 'my' (***emí/temi/na (nawa)/***)/ 'your' (***ewe/tiyin/naki/***)
d   demonstrative adjective – 'this' (***eì/iyi/wonan/nka***)/ 'that' (***èléè/iyen/woshan/nkani***).

Through the physical co-location of people known as co-presence (Goffman, 1963), individuals convey information using various meaningful and visible accessible channels such as the arrangement of the body parts in shared space that is, body movement includes pointing signals with the use of the hands, heads, lips and even legs and so on. Deixis includes all of the following:

i.   Non-obligatory preparation which entails the lifting of the hands from a rest position to the indicated space thereby performing the semantic intension;
ii   A non-obligatory pre-stroke hold which involves sustaining the hand in a position in a given speech event;
iii An obligatory stroke and a non-obligatory stroke. Post stroke holds where interlocutors sustain their expressing position alongside an obligatory resting of the body part used in its normal rest position. The deictic stroke expressed may be static or dynamic (Lascardes and Stone 2009).

Deictic gestures define spatial reference in parallel/definite terms by projecting the hand to a region that is distal/ proximal in relation to speaker's position. Often, people anchor their speech signals to the context of communicative event through deixis. However described, the term refers to the expressions we use in which meaning is directly traceable to eminent features in a conversation (Rodney and Geoffrey, 2006). Deixis involves the context surrounding an utterance. Deixis broadly falls into the following categories:

2.1 Traditional Category

Deixis 'signifies', 'display', 'demonstration' and points interlocutors to referents. It denotes an occurrence by which the understanding of definite words, phrases and utterances are made possible with regards to contextual information. Also, it includes words that have fixed semantic and denotative meaning which changes frequently depending on a number of factors, i.e., time and or place of utterance. These are discussed under two broad categories; traditional and other categories.

2.1.1 Person Deixis

Person deixis is the most common category of contextual information – person, place and time. Fillimore (1982) calls them 'the major grammaticalized types.' The person category directly shows the roles individuals play in a speech event. The roles include the activities of the speaker, addressee and others. When roles shift in the course of conversation, the deictic *origo* also shifts.

Person deixis concerns the encoding of the role of participants in a speech event in which an utterance is delivered. The category 'first person' is the grammaticalization of the speaker's reference to his/herself. The 'second person' is the encoding of speaker's reference to one or more addressees, while the 'third person' is the encoding of reference to persons or entities which are neither speakers nor addressees of the utterance in question (Levinson 1985).

Following the description of (Levinson 1985), Lyons, (1995) and Saeed, (2006)), person deixis constitutes the following:

1st PERSON SINGULAR: 'I' (mine possessive) (*Òmi, Ù, Èmi, Na, Mi,*
   (*Èémi/temi/nawa/* nmua/possessive)
1ST PERSON PLURAL: 'We' (ours possessive) (*Àwa, Wa,*
   (*Èéwa/tiwa/namu/anyi*/possessive)
2ND PERSON SINGULAR: 'You' (*Ùwe, E, Wẹ'*
   (*Èéwẹ/tiyin/naki/nguwa*/possessive)
2ND PERSON PLURAL: 'You' (*Àme, Mẹ,*
   (*Èéme/tiyin/naku/unuwa/possessive*)
3rd PERSON SINGULAR: 'He/She/It' (*Òun,Un,*
   (*Èéun/tire/nata/nashi/nya*/possessive)
3RD PERSON PLURAL: *Àma, Mà*
   (*Èéma/tiwon/nasu/nyawa/possessive*)

Etu (2000), further categorized the Igala pronouns into the following constituents:

1st PERSON SINGULAR - *Òmi, ,Ù, Èmi, Na, Mi* and
   Èémi,nmua(possessive)
1ST PERSON PLURAL – *Àwa, Àwa, Wa* and *Èéwa,nmua*(possessive)
2ND PERSON SINGULAR - *Ùwe, E, Wẹ* and *Èéwẹ,nguwa* (possesive)
2ND PERSON PLURAL – *Àmẹ, Àmẹ, Mẹ, ẹ* and *Èéme,unuwa* **(possessive).**
3rd PERSON SINGULAR - *Òun, Òun, Un* and *Èéun,nyawa* (possessive).

3ʳᴰ PERSON PLURAL - *Àma, Àm, Mà,* and *Èéma,nyawa* (possessive).

Person Deixis directly shows the diverse roles individuals play in a speech event. The roles include the activities of the speaker, addressee, other persons involved in an utterance. That is, those directly involved and those mentioned in the utterance – the speaker and addressee shift roles in the course of turn taking. Consider the following illustrations in Ígálâ and English:

10. Ígálâ: *Ú nalótáájá.*
    Transliteration: I will go to the market.
    Meaning: 'I am going to the market.'
11. Ígálâ: *Mácheki ma chemíagbe, Àmáa ì mu mìgbatuànè*
    Transliteration: They do that they do me hurt, But he catch me collect/take to ground.
    Meaning: 'They tried to hurt me, but he rescued me.'

These (as exemplified above), are the deictic reference to the participant role of a referent which directly reflects the different roles individuals play in any given speech event. According to some schools of thought (Hartman and Stock (1972: 168), Crystal (1980:263), Levinson (1985: 62), Lyons (1996:302)), deixis is commonly expressed by constituents like possessive affixes of nouns and agreement affixes of verbs and it includes first, second and third person pronoun. A further interesting aspect of person deixis that cannot be overlooked is the special role the speaker and addressee play in grammatical hierarchy/the role reflexives play in some natural languages especially with regards to how reflexives occur in some Nigerian languages. See illustrations of some Ígálâ and English reflexives in the following examples:

12. Ígálâ: *Ì làkpàìójikaọ́laun.*
    Transliteration: He/she bought with shoulder body his/her.
    Meaning: 'He bought it himself.'
13. Ígálâ: *Òmiọ̀tọ́tọ́ ọ́la mi.*
    Transliteration: I myself body me.
    Meaning: 'I myself.'
14. Ígálâ: *Ùwẹ ọ̀tọ́tọ́ ọ́lawè.*
    Transliteration: You your your body you.
    Meaning: 'You yourself.'
15. Ígálâ: *kpàiẹ̀dọ̀ mì.*
    Transliteration: With heart my.

Meaning: 'Myself'.
16. **Ígálâ:** *Ọma ì fuọ́launkpabìe.*
    Transliteration: Child this has body self spoilt.
    Meaning: This child has spoilt himself.
17. **Ígálâ:** *Ma nékè hi óje un ólama n.*
    Transliteration: They not could cook food for body them not.
    Meaning: They could not cook food for themselves (culled from Atadoga in Omachonu)

2.1.2 Temporal /Time Deixis

Time deixis refers to the various times involved and referred to in an utterance. It includes time adverbs such as: 'yesterday', (**onale/ano/gia/**), 'now' **(àbajóí/baiyi/yanzu/ugbua)**, 'tomorrow', (***ona/ola/gobe/echi***), 'then', (***ugbalẹ/igbayen/lokachin/oge***) 'right now' (***fàí-fai/nsi-nsi/yanzu-/ugbua***), 'This night', (***òduí/oruni/wonandere/abani***), 'today' **(*engíni/ani/yo/taa'*)** and different tenses'. These adverbs can be relative to the time an utterance is made – encoding time (ET) and decoding time (DT) (Fillimore 1982). Temporal deixis locate points and intervals on the time axis particularly with regards to the moment of utterance as a reference point. Cruze, (2000: 321) classified time axis into three:
 i. Before the moment of utterance;
(ii) At the time of utterance; and
(iii) After the time of utterance.

In Levinson's, (1985) opinion, "most language systems of recoding and measuring time seem to be the natural and prominent circles of day, night, lunar months, seasons and years which can either be used as measures comparative to some fixed point of interest and even calendrically (Levinson *ibid.*).

Temporal deixis describes the moment at which the utterance is made. In Fillmore's (1997) terminology, it is referred to as 'coding time'. Therefore the deixis 'now', (***ábajóí/nsi/yenzu/ugbua***) becomes the span of time including the moment of utterance and the basis for the systems of estimating and measuring time in most languages. Sometimes, we treat the near and immediate future as being close to utterance by using the proximal deictic expressions such as 'this night', *òdui/oruni/wonandere/na'bania* 'Sunday', (*àládi/ladi/uboshi-*

uka) 'month', *(òchú/ osu/ wata/ owa),* 'year', *(ọ́dọ́/ odun/ shekara/aro)* and so on.

Therefore, counting back from the present, tenses distinguish happenings according to events that happened earlier today from yesterday and the tense particles of tomorrow incorporate those of yesterday and, the word for the day before yesterday incorporates that for the day after tomorrow). This phenomenon signifies a partial cyclical property around encoding-time which Jespersen (in Brown 1995) refers to as "among expressions for the simple past. We must here also mention 'the so – called historic present'

Examples of time deixis are words like 'tomorrow', *(ọna/ ola/ gobe/ echi)* which means 'the successive next day after every other day, or the day after the day of an utterance or the tomorrow of a day last year **(èchí/odun to koja/wochanshakara da yawuche/aro-garaga)** is distinct from the tomorrow of a day next week. Time adverbs are usually relative to when utterance is made or heard. - 'encoding time' (ET) and 'decoding time' (DT). While these are on many occasions the same time, they may differ especially with regards to pre - recorded broadcasts or texts.

The most prevalent aspect of temporal deixis is the 'tense' which is a grammatical category that generally encodes a combination of deictic time and aspectual distinctions which are often difficult to distinguish. Sometimes we set up series of pure temporal distinctions that roughly corresponds to the temporal aspects of natural language tenses. For instance in most natural languages, the present tense specifies that the state or event hold or occurs during a temporal span including the encoding - time; the past tense as indicating the relevant span held before encoding time, the future as indicating the relevant span that succeeds encoding time and the pluperfect as specifying that the event happened at a time before an event described in the past. These clearly show that there are temporal deictic components in most of the grammatical distinctions with regards to tenses.

Temporal deixis describes the moment at which the utterance is issued and it denotes the position of actions and events in time. Some **Ígálâ** lexemes that mark temporal deixis include terms such as ***ábajóí*** (now), **ikole** (then), **ọ̀rọ́ka** (afternoon), **ọ̀nale** (yesterday), ***engini*** (today), ***ọ̀na*** (tomorrow), ***òchú*** (month) ***ọ́dọ́*** (year), and ***aneí*** (this evening).Also, temporal deixis can be marked through tense, which is encoded in the form of the verb with affixes and or sometimes expressed in an independent morpheme. Therefore, 'now' (***ábajóí***) becomes the span of time including the moment of utterance and the bases for the systems of estimating and measuring time. Obviously, some deictic expressions in the temporal domain are borrowed from the spatial domain.

2.1.3 Spatial/Place Deixis

Spatial deixis refers to a speaker's ability to project him/her into a location from which he/she is actually not present. Spatial deixis is also referred to as place deixis and it concerns the spatial locations relevant to an utterance Gillian, (1995). This includes speaker cum addressee's location and persons and objects referred to. Cruse (2000) sees spatial deixis as belonging to the class of locative adverbs such as 'here', (***èmí/ibiyi/nan/ebea***) and 'there', (***òmó/ibe/shan/ebahu***); demonstrative adjectives such as 'this' (***éí/iyi/wonan*/nka**) and 'that', èléè/***iyen/woshan/nkani***). The adverb '*here* can be very ambiguous and evasive especially during electronic communication – telephone conversation, leaving a message on the answering machine, responding to a text on phone or e-mail. The question is, where exactly is 'here'?[1] Natural languages carry an implicit division of space around the current speaker - a division of time relative to the act of speech event.

The adverbs 'here and 'there' pick out places according to their proximity to speakers location while speakers project themselves to locations where they are not yet present at the time of speaking. Spatial deixis include the demonstratives and locative adverbs which focus the attention of the hearer or addressee by picking out an object or entity from the real world and identifying it by referring or pointing. The spatial system of some natural languages distinguishes more than two or three points in the distance scale; English distinguish two 'here and there', **Ígálâ** distinguishes four points and an extra category; *here*/**èmí**, *there*/**òmó**, *over there*/***anumo****, away from interlocutors/* **ànúmó – ànúmó** *and distal from interlocutors/****ànúmó – ànúmó – ànúmó – ànúmó****.* This phenomenon occurs in languages that are distance-oriented system; otherwise, there are two points – proximal and distal, and or three points, which are proximal, medial, and distal from the speaker centre.

---

[1] See: Ibileye, Gbenga (2008) 'Adjusting the Indexical Zero Point in Mobile Telephone Conversations' in *Zaria Journal of Liberal Arts, ZAJOLA*, Journal of the Faculty of Arts, Ahmadu Bello University, Zaria, Vol.2, No. 2, September, 2008, pp 1-8.

Gillian (*ibid*) identifies three planes within the spatial domain directly relatable to the body parts of the speaker, i.e, symmetrical (cutting through the vertical centre between the eyes which distinguishes left/right, asymmetrical (cutting horizontally through some plane of the body yielding the distinction 'up/down', **ate/*ane*, *oke/ile*, *sama/kasa*,** ...above/below and the third plane as cutting through vertical part of the body through both ears yielding the distinction before/in front/behind etc. This distinction leads to the characterization of the physical space around the speaker as proximal/non-proximal, near/distal from speaker. See some illustrations in **Ígálâ**;

18. Ígálâ: *Ì ténèki ne ǫ́koéfùèwoeí*
    Transliteration: He/she want to marry husband stomach city this
    Meaning: She wants to be married in this city.

19. Ígálâ: *Èmícheúgboki a yankòasipiti*
    Transliteration: Here do where that we will build hospital
    Meaning: We will build the hospital here

20. Ígálâ: *Ì gwánéànúmó*
    Transliteration: She/he sat over there
    Meaning: She sit there.

21. Ígálâ: *Únyi du udabaaji*
    Transliteration: House that available across river
    Meaning: The house is across the river.

22. Ígálâ: *Èmícheúgbo e nyo, ólù í gbèanuǫ̀mǫ́*
    Transliteration: Here do place it good, sun it much over there
    Meaning: Here is a good spot; it is too sunny over there.

23. Ígálâ: *Àbú ùwo de ǫ̀mǫ́?*
    Transliteration: How winta is there?
    Meaning: How is winter there?

24. Ígálâ: *Eíkpàieíanumǫ́*
    Transliteration: This and this over there
    Meaning: This and that.

The analysis of demonstratives is quite complicated because of their multi-functional role in language. They are used to point, track referents in discourse and generally, to contrast with other referring expressions. The exemplification below distinguishes some of the uses (Diesel 1999). However, the relations between these uses are certainly more complicated than the illustration suggests. Again, it is obviously not adequate to distinguish solely between exospheric (deictic) and non-exospheric (non-deictic). See examples below:

25. Ígálâ: *Dúǫtakada le mi.*
   Transliteration: Take book that me.
   Meaning: 'Give me that book'- (This is exophoric because 'book' is available in the physical context).

26. Ígálâ: *Anyiga mi eífuumicheagbe.*
   Transliteration: Finger me this has me do injury.
   Meaning: 'I hurt this finger' - (It is exophoric gestural because statement is uttered with finger pointing out).

27. Ígálâ: *Éwóeínyǫ̀ mi.*
   Transliteration: Town this good me.
   Meaning: 'I like this city' (It is exophoric symbolic because this does not require gesture).

28. Ígálâ: *Ú qwuówóeícheéjódùdukpàièéle*
   Transliteration: I brake hand this break first and that
   Meaning: 'I broke this arm first and then that one' (this is gestural contrastive).

29. Ígálâ: *Ǫmaénekèlęeíkakiniàtáeícheęnęębięnę.*
   Transliteration: Child man this said that father this do person bad.
   Meaning: The boy said that this man is a bad person.' (This is anaphoric).

30. Ígálâ: *Ì lónyakaìdàdá le àwó.*
   Transliteration: She/he went to say foolish that slap.
   Meaning: 'He slapped that stupid person' (This is emphatic).

The grammars of languages almost always describe demonstrative systems in spatial ways. Hence the basic semantic contrasts between sets of exophoric demonstratives are spatial in nature. That is, they encode degrees of distance from speaker or addressee.

31. Ígálâ: *Ì ténèki ne ǫ́koéfùewo í*
   Transliteration: He/she want to marry husband stomach city this
   Meaning: She wants to be married in this city.

32. Ígálâ: *Èmícheúgboki a yankòasipiti*
   Transliteration: Here do where that we will build hospital
   Meaning: We will build the hospital here

33. Ígálâ: *Ì gwánéànúmó*
   Transliteration: She/he sat over there

Meaning: She sat there.
34. **Ígálâ:** *únyi du udabaaji*
    Transliteration: House that available across river
    Meaning: The house is across the river.
35. **Ígálâ:** *Èmícheúgbo e nyo, ólù í gbèanuọ̀mọ́*
    Transliteration: Here do place it good, sun it much over there
    Meaning: Here is a good spot; it is too sunny over there.
36. **Ígálâ:** *Àbú ùwo de ọ̀mọ́?*
    Transliteration: How winter is there?
    Meaning: How is winter there?

The term 'here' *(èmí)* and 'there' *(ọ̀mọ́)* or over - there *(ànúmó) (ànúmó - ànúmó)* usually refers to location proximal, distal and or further distal from speaker or addressee especially if they are not in the same location with the speaker. Sometimes, the deictic item 'there' *(ọ̀mọ́)* may also refer to addressee's location. Nevertheless, place deixis is generally understood to be relative to speaker's location and in another instance, 'there' *(ọ̀mọ́)* can also refer to addressee's location specific to time of utterance.

Here, the speaker-centred medial is the unmarked term which can be used to refer to things just about anywhere, except if the speaker or addressee is actually holding something, the speaker-centred or addressee-centred term pre-empts it. Because of this, the 'medial' interpretation is due only to pragmatic pre-emption from the other more semantically specified forms. Also, the **Ígálâ** '**èélẹ** (that) has dual functions; one of the functions shows that the referent is close to the addressee and the other shifts the addressee's attention to a new referent. 'This and that' are in addressee's attentional focus - specifically, *eí* indicates, objects that are closer to speaker while '*eíànúmó*'(the one over there) is used for referents that are distal from speaker. *Eí*' is a dedicated anaphoric determiner on whose dimension the other plays a cataphoric or other contrastive role.

A final term '**èélẹ**', is a demonstrative which contrasts on other dimensions namely, perceptual accessibility: for example, there is a sudden noise in the night, one could say *èunchelẹ*/*what is that?* Or of a mug that is broken one could say, 'What happened to that? The demonstratives in fact occupy a multi-dimensional space with spatial distance on one dimension, textual reference on another and perceptual accessibility on a third.

2.1.3 Discourse Deixis

Discourse deixis is referred to as text deixis. It refers to the use of expression within an utterance to parts of the discussion that contain the utterance, including the utterance itself. In sentences like: 'This is a big house,' the item 'this' refers to an upcoming portion of the discourse; 'that was a beautiful display,' the item 'that' refers to a prior portion of a discourse.

The use of the thumb distinguishes when an expression refers to another linguistic item or a piece of discourse. This is referred to as discourse deixis. Whether spoken or written, discourse often demonstrates occasion to refer to earlier or forth -coming occurrences. Such frequently used segments in discourse are; 'previously' (*kwúbi/tele/dasu/...*), 'then' (*Íkólẹ/igbayen/lokachin...*). Discourse deictic demonstratives focus the hearers' attention on aspects of meaning expressed by a chunk of words (phrases), sentences, or paragraphs. The proximal demonstrative 'this' can be used anaphorically, that is, to refer to something that has previously occurred, and cataphorically, i.e. to refer to something that is about to happen, while the distal demonstrative is used anaphorically only. In sentences like; 'This is a big house', 'this' refers to an upcoming portion of the discourse and in 'that' was a beautiful display', 'that' refers to a prior portion of the discourse.

When an expression refers to the same item as a prior linguistic expression, it is anaphoric – "He couldn't sit down (*Í nekegwuánè n*), he couldn't eat (*Í nekejẹ́ẹ́un*), he is so sick (*Í á cheòga nana*)". This example is anaphoric because there is repeated reference to the referent. Whether spoken or written, discourse often demonstrates occasion to refer to earlier or forth coming occurrences. Such frequently used segments in discourse, i.e. '*Dabaluku ma kaejuòdùdù*/ 'as previously mentioned'. Obviously references to parts of discourse are typically deictic in character and can only be interpreted by knowing the current coding, reading or recording points.

37. Ígálâ: *Dabu àlu ki à ka ìkólẹ.*
    Transliteration: Like mouth that we say time before.
    Meaning: 'As we mentioned previously.'
38. Ígálâ: *Na ténè nènè I chẹun ke nékè mè imoto wẹ mì.*

Transliteration: I want ask question if you can lend me motor your me.
Meaning: I wanted to ask you if you could possibly lend me your car.

39. **Ìgálâ:** *Ọ́Jọ́nìmicheájọ̀de (kwubi)*
    Transliteration: Ọ́Jọ́nìmido hunter before
    Meaning: Ọ́Jọ́nìmi used to be a hunter' implicates that he no longer hunts, however, this claim is clearly voidable by way of adding, 'and he still hunts'

40. **Ìgálâ:** *Ù cheukolo Abuja àmáa, u d'ódoọ̀mọ́ me*
    Transliteration: I did work in Abuja but, I lived there also.
    Meaning: 'I worked in Abuja and I have lived there.'

41. **Ìgálâ:** *Dabaluku ma kaéjuòdùdù.*
    Transliteration: According that they said eye morning.
    Meaning: 'As earlier stated.'

42. **Ìgálâ:** *Ùma kaki è lí ta n.*
    Transliteration: I know that that you see yet not.
    Meaning: 'I know you haven't seen it.'

43. **Ìgálâ:** *Dabaluku ma kaugbale.*
    Transliteration: According that they said before.
    Meaning: 'As mentioned before.'

44. **Ìgálâ:** *Dabáluku ma gb'áluójọ́ le,*
    Transliteration: According that they confessed day that.
    Meaning: 'Just as they promised the other day.'

3.0 Conclusion

Deictic expressions go beyond the limits of the built-in indexical expressions in any language. Besides, the field of indexical expression is sometimes not clearly demarcated, because most referring expressions are not fully individualized solely by virtue of their semantic content. Rather, they depend on states of mutual knowledge that holds between participants in the discourse. The majority of successful acts of reference depend on indexical conditions (Levinson, 1985).

Works cited

Abdulazeez Mainasara. *Elementary Dictionary and Letters Arabic, Hausa and English*. Zamfara:Maigari and Sons, Printing and Publishing, 2014. Print
Ahmad, Abdullahi. Paralinguistic Phenomena in Igala Communication Patterns. M.A. Thesis Ahmadu Bello University, Zaria. 2004 Print.

Akmajian, A. Ann, K. Farmer, A. Demers, R.A. and Harnish, R.M. Linguistics: *An Introduction to Language and Communication.* Cambridge: MIT Press. 2001 Print.

Alahverdzhiieva, K. and Lascarides, A. *Analyzing Speech and Co-Speech Gestures in Constraint-based Grammars.* In S. Muller. (Eds). The Proceedings of 17th International Conference on *Head-Driven Phrase Structure.* Pp 6-26. Stanford: CSLI Publishers. 2010. Print

Andrew, R. C. "A Comparative Analysis of English and Igala Morphological Processes". Unpublished M.A. Thesis, ABU, Zaria. 2007. Print

Clark, Eve. (1978). From Gesture to Words: on the Natural History of Deixis in Language Acquisition. In J. Bruner and A. Garton (Eds), *Human Growth and Development:* Wolfson College Lectures 1976. Oxford: Clarendon Press.

Cruze, D.A. (1986). *Lexical Semantics.* Cambridge: Cambridge University Press.

Crystal, David. *A First Dictionary of Linguistics and Phonetics.* London: Andre Deutsch. 1980. Print

Diessel, Holger. *Demonstratives: Form, Function and Grammaticalization.* Amsterdam:

Benjamin. 1999. Print

Etu, Yusuf (1999). *Igala Expression and Historical Landmarks.* Lokoja: Enenyo Printers and Publishers.

Fillimore, Charles. Towards A Descriptive Framework for Spatial Deixis. In Robert J. Jarvell and Wolfgang Klein (Eds.) Speech, Place and Action. Studies in Deixis and Related Topics, 31-59. London: Willey. 1982.

(1997). *Lectures on Deixis.* Stanford: Centre for the Study of Language and Information.

Frege, Gottlob. *The Thought: a logical enquiry.* Translated by P. F. Strawson, (Ed).*Philosophical Logic* (Pp. 17-38). Oxford: Oxford University Press. (1952). Print

Hall, E.T. *Handbook for Proxemic Research.* Washington D.C: Society for the Anthropology of Visual Communication. 1974. Print

Laver, J. Language and Nonverbal Communication. In Carterette, E.C. and Friedman, M.P. (Eds) *Handbook of Perception,* Vol V11. New York: Academic Press 1976. Print

Levinson, Stephen. Pragmatics and Social Deixis. Proceeding of the Fifth Annual Meeting of the Berkeley Linguistic Society. 1979. Print

_____ *Pragmatics.* Cambridge: Cambridge University Press. 1983. Print

Lyons, J. (1976). *Semantics* vols. 1 and 11 London: Cambridge Thirsty Press 1996. Print

Mey, J. L. (1993). *Pragmatics: An Introduction*. Oxford U.K and Cambridge: U.S.A. Blackwell Publishers.

Okpanachi, H. *Ukoche Ichi Igala: An Igala Language Lesson*. Ankpa: Cuca Communications Ltd. 2002. Print

Omachonu, G.S. *Igala Language Studies*. Germany: Lambert Academic Publishers. 2011. Print

Salem, O.E. A Grammar of Igala Tones. Department of Linguistics and Communication Studies, University of Port Harcourt:2006. Print

Usman, S.S. *ItaIgala*. Jos: Plateau State House of Assembly Press. 1995. Print

_____ *Olufia Ekeji: Igala Language Dictionary*. Anyigba: Jas Investment Services.

(2014). Print

Chapter 7

The Concept of Presupposition

- Eneojoh Jonah Amodu

Introduction

Using language successfully in a communicative context is a very serious and intricate enterprise. Part of its complexities is the inherent presence of presuppositions in communication. The study of presupposition in linguistics is an issue which was prominent in the early 1980s. Before then, the study of presupposition had been an important topic in the philosophy of language. However, in the middle and later part of the 1970's, a number of attempts were made to deal with the concept within what was called a complementarist framework, both from Linguistics, particularly Semantics and Pragmatics but only more recently has it become a topic investigated with psycholinguistic methods in language learning and pedagogy.

Wilson (1975) and Kempson (1975), reject Semanticist and Pragmaticist's attempt to give a unitary account of presupposition arguing that some aspects of presuppositional phenomena require a semantic explanation and others, a pragmatic one. One thing that remained unclear then was how presupposition was associated with particular grammatical or lexical form. For example, with definite noun phrases and the complements of "factive" verbs such as **know** and **realise**. These have changed as Gazdar's (1979) solution to those problems involves deriving from a sentence's form, its potential presupposition and deducing the actual presuppositions of the sentences in context with the help of pragmatic factors which were beyond Semantics.

Presupposition

In communication, not all that is communicated is said: as there are also several of the said in the unsaid. Speakers or language users usually design their linguistic messages on the basis of assumptions of what their hearer already know for the purpose of economy with words and to boast the excitement in language use. Presupposition simply means that which the speaker assumes to be the case prior to making an utterance. It is an aspect of what is communicated but not necessarily said. The meaning of the word 'presupposes' is to "assume before hand; involves and implies". It simply represents some of the most powerful language patterns in language use. Presuppositions are common in everyday language use but advertisers, lawyers and even law enforcement agents explore this in a special way. Presupposition according to Yule (1995) is a technical term that is borrowed by linguists from the field of logic as echoed in the introduction of this chapter. He further observes that presupposition is one of the most powerful persuasion techniques in language use. That is why it is speakers, not sentences that have presupposition.

This view accounts for its relevance in the study of communication science. In ordinary language use, to presuppose could mean to assume. It could also be seen as one of a number of assumptions that the listener might make on the basis of what the speaker has said. This is why it is referred to as one of the aspects or strategies of organising information for maximum persuasion because presupposition forms part of the knowledge assumed by the speaker in making the utterance.

Stalnarker (1974), argues that presupposition is essentially a pragmatic phenomenon. He opines that it is a part of the set of assumptions made by participants in a conversation which he termed the common ground or mutual knowledge. Common ground here refers to the knowledge a speaker and a listener hold in common, that which is mutually shared. This could be predicated on the physical environment, community, culture, general knowledge and co-text. It is also referred to as mutual knowledge because some utterances require that:

> We know x
>
> Our listener knows x
>
> We know that our listener knows x
>
> Our listener knows that we know x

The above illustration is not something directly derivable from the literal Semantics of the sentence. This is a knowledge that the speaker must assume in advance in order for the utterance to be felicitous. That is why some linguists are of the view that presupposition is a pragmatic phenomenon and not something conventional or semantic.

Mey (1993) further stresses Stalnaker's (1974) view with some emphases. She sees presupposition as essential assumptions underlying a statement, which remain in force even though the statement itself is denied. A pragmatic view of presupposition was also proposed by Sperber and Wilson (1995), who argue that the concept of presupposition is not an independent phenomenon but one of a series of effects produced when the speaker employs syntactic structure and information to show the bearer how the current sentence fits into the previous background. This view is accepted because writers, advertisers and other language users integrate presupposition with other traditional discourse notions like the given and new information and focus in their language use.

Sperber and Wilson (1995), further propose that the same principle of relevance to contextual assumptions cover both presupposition and the choice of the different word orders used in discourse. The logical deduction that can be made from this is that an important aspect of any communication involves the presuppositions that are present. Presupposition indeed is a necessary precondition for the processing of any communication. It typically involves the existence of some objects or ideas.

For example, in the sentence:

John graduated from Ahmadu Bello University.

The above sentence presupposes the following:

>>There is someone called John

>>There is a place called Ahmadu Bello University

>>John is a graduate

In another sentence example:

We can't keep something this juicy a secret.

The above is an advertisement and it presupposes that there is something that is "this juicy" and then makes an assertion about that. One important function of the presupposition here is that it promotes a kind of assumption and sometimes even an ideology with its contents. Presuppositions are also crucial part of every well crafted communication because they can cause the reader/ listener to consider the existence of object, propositions and culturally defined behavioural properties which are the target and desire of peculiar language use like in the examples used in the above advertisement.

The concept of presupposition is unique especially in the context of an advert. It is not out of place to assume that presupposition is basically only an assumption which many people make everyday. This may simply not be the case. To assume is to take to be true without proof or verification but to presuppose is to take for granted or take as given information. For example

... MTN has over a million subscribers.

The above statement is partly a slogan of MTN Company's advert for their products and services. Looking at this slogan, the assumption could be that MTN is successful and has a lot of money but what inherent presupposition is in the slogan? In other words, what would the target audience accept unconsciously as a necessary precondition in order for the slogan to take a meaning? On reading the slogan, especially outside any context, there is a mental adjustment in a split second about the fact that a company is talked about and that the company is MTN. When an advertiser confronts the target audience's current situation or problem, there is an excellent chance that the target audience will agree with what the advertiser will say next. It is a type of strategy of pacing and leading pattern. This could be done through compliments or flattery embedded in the presupposition. Advertisers do this most of the time.

This chapter favours the view that the notion of presupposition is pragmatic since presupposition is defined in terms of "assumptions that the speaker makes about what the bearer is likely to accept without challenge" (Givon 1979). The notion of assumed "common ground" is also involved in such a characterisation of presupposition and can be found in Stalnaker's (1978) definition of presupposition "Presupposition is what is taken by the speaker to be a common ground of the participants in the conversation". Notice that, in both definitions, the indicated source of presupposition is the speaker not the utterances.

Controversial and Uncontroversial Presupposition

Presuppositions may be "fair and uncontroversial" based upon the knowledge which is common to all parties to the communication, or "unfair, counterfeit or controversial"-made upon the basis of covert knowledge by a communicator with a hidden agenda which could be that of persuasion. Consider these sentences:

> Sugar is sweet
>
> Bitter leaf is bitter

These sentences assume the existence of a particular leaf and product commonly known as bitter leaf and sugar and further assume that their attributes are bitter and sweet. By common knowledge and agreement, these facts are 'true' hence the presuppositions made in the sentences are fair, accurate and factual.

Also, consider this advert,

> Peace of mind comes from Entrusting
>
> Your fortunes to Trusted Hands.
>
> Leadway Insurance Managed Funds Trusteeship

In simple terms, the above extract is an advert advertising a company. The advert assumes the existence of some "Trusted Hands" which is Leadway Insurance Company and that the company can be entrusted with the audience's fortune with a guaranteed peace of mind. The assumptions as a matter of widely agreed fact and evidence are unnatural or perhaps in part because there is more to "peace of mind" than Leadway can give. This is all about persuasion rendering the presuppositions unfair and inaccurate just for commercial gain. This is not a shared assumption. It is possible as reflected in the illustration for an advertiser with proper skills and sufficient motivation to subtly and deliberately distort information by means of carefully chosen inferences and implications in the form of presuppositions. The target audience without sufficient insight will inevitably fall prey-to some degree – to such cleverly constructed schemes of counterfeit presuppositions, the ultimate aim of which would be to persuade and get the otherwise questionable point of view accepted uncritically.

The basis of a 'fair' or 'counterfeit' form of presupposition or its underlying assumption(s) or proposition(s) is defined by Mey (1993). He views presupposition as uncontroversial, truthful or factual and the controversial or non-factual. He asserts that true presupposition is based on an unconsidered assumption by the encoder which is shared by the decoder. The assumption is that the decoder will draw the same suppositions from the non-asserted elements of an advert as the advertiser holds hence the notion of a presupposition being uncontroversial. On the other hand, the term counterfeit presupposition describes the kind of supposition that is shared by the advertiser and the target audience but which is forced on the target audience by virtue of the advertiser's choice of words which is not shared innocently by the target audience. This chapter points out that there is a place for factual and counterfeit presuppositions and that what they presuppose in their context of use and the intended effects on the target audience could be based on mutual contextual belief.

Preservation of Presupposition

Presupposition has two crucial properties; first, it is something that is taken for granted by the discourse participants. Second, presupposed contents behave differently from the asserted contents. Since presupposition is something the speaker assumes to be the case prior to making an utterance, it must be mutually known or assumed by the speaker and addressee for the utterance to be considered appropriate in a linguistic context. The presupposition should remain constant whether the utterance is placed in the form of assertion, denial, or question because it has to do with assumed common ground. This way, the presence of presuppositions are tested and preserved in sentences.

Note that presupposition can be tested and preserved under assertion, negation, questioning, embedding under modal and embedding as an antecedent of condition. The following sentences will be used to illustrate the above:

>Joan no longer bakes cake.
>My brother is coming from Lagos.

Assertions are strong statements in discourse and they are most of the time statements of facts and declarative in nature, for example:

>- Joan no longer bakes cake.
>- My brother is coming from Lagos.

These sentences presuppose the following:

>>That someone called Joan exists and she baked cake at a time.
>>That I have a brother.

Negation expresses the opposite or absence of something regarded as actually, positive or affirmative. For example:

Joan does not bake cake.
My brother is not coming from Lagos.

These sentences under negation still presuppose:

>>That someone called Joan exists and she baked cake at a time.
>>That I have a brother.

Questioning even when questions are asked, they presuppose. For example:

Does Joan bake cake?
Is my brother coming from Lagos?

The same sentences under questioning still presuppose that:
>>Joan exists.

>>I have a brother.

Embedding under model verbs e.g. might/it is possible that:

Joan might bake cake.
My brother might come from Lagos.

Still the sentences here presuppose that:
>>Joan exists.
>>I have a brother.

Embedding as an antecedent of conditional (If)

If Joan bakes cake, I will eat.
If my brother comes through Lagos, he will buy a car.

These sentences still presuppose that;
Joan exists.
I have a brother.

From the above, it is obvious that different kinds of utterances are used to make different kinds of presuppositions. This though depends on:

- their form;
- their lexical content; and
- the conventions associated with the use of an utterance of a certain type.

Semantic and Pragmatic Presuppositions

Although the label 'Semantic suggests' a clean split from 'Pragmatic', even semantic presuppositions are pragmatic in the sense that they must be evaluated in the discourse participants' common ground. Most presuppositions hold only in specific contexts, so one always needs to know at least what the background store of knowledge is in order to evaluate them.

On the notion of whether both semantic and pragmatic presuppositions exist, Stalnaker (1974), writes:

> ...I think all of the facts can be stated and explained directly in terms of the underlying notion of speaker presupposition, and without introducing an intermediate notion of presupposition as a relation holding between sentences (or statements) and propositions.

From the views of Stalnaker (1974), pragmatic presuppositions are purely speaker actions, whereas, Semantic presuppositions can be traced to the conventional aspects of the meanings of specific words and constructions. Semantic (conventional or lexical) Presuppositions are referred to as part of the encoded meanings of specific words and constructions called presupposition triggers. Lyons (1977), argues that presupposition can be defined as "proposition to whose truth speaker is committed; it is an utterance to be interpretable and appropriate in the context in which it occurs". He further predicates presupposition on Pragmatics by asserting that presupposition is an assumption the speaker makes about what the hearer is likely to accept without dependence /holding between one utterance and another.

Semantic presupposition is viewed from the point of philosophical tradition that looks at sentences as external objects. The concern here is with the individuality of the speakers or writers and their audience. The relations that hold between two sentences, which may be lexical synonymy or antonym is central. Meaning is seen as a feature of sentence rather than something constructed by the participants (Saeed, 2009). This approach is founded on the principle of truth relations as viewed in logic. The construction below is used to show the semantic presupposition as regards to truth relation:

    A. Joan's son bought a car.
    B. >>Joan has a son.

In the above, a truth relation can be used to identify a semantic relationship between the two sentences: This can further be exemplified by presupposition as a truth based relation.

Step 1 : If P (The presupposing sentence) is true then q (The presupposed sentence) is true.

Step 2 : If P is false, then q is still true.

Step 3 : If q is true, then p could be either true or false.

This can be represented on a truth table

P	q
T	T
F	T
T or F	T

This can be explained as follows;

If it is true that Joan's son bought a car, it must also be true that Joan has a son.

If it is false that Joan's son bought a car, the presupposition that Joan has a son still survives.

Lastly, if it is true that Joan has a son, it does not tell the hearer whether he bought a car or not.

On the other hand, the pragmatic approach to presupposition is from the point of view of the fact that sentences are utterances of individuals engaged in the act of communication. According to Lakaff's (1970), pragmatic presupposition is used to refer to the assumptions and beliefs about the context. Presupposition primarily deals with an assumption that could be drawn from an earlier supposition, which deals with the basic background knowledge of the context of the utterance in any communication setting. Against this background, Stalnaker (1978) opines that "the presuppositions of a speaker are the presupposition whose truth he takes for granted as part of the background of the conversation."

Saeed (2009) posits that while a given sentence always produces the same set of entailment, it seems that this is not true of presupposition. He further cites Levinson (1983) who cites an example of presupposition triggered by adverbial clauses:

> She cried **before** she finished her thesis.
> \>\>She finished her thesis.

On the other hand, if we change the verb 'cried' in the proposition to 'died', the presupposition automatically changes

> She died before she finished her thesis.
> \>\>She did not finish her thesis.

Levinson argues that, in the latter example given, presupposition is blocked by our general knowledge of the world: simply put, dead people do not normally finish their theses. This is what is known as presupposition defeasibility. Presupposition works better in Pragmatics than it does in Semantics. Also, the interpretation of the sentences as far as pragmatic presupposition is concerned, relies on the speakers' assumption about the speech. It deals not only with what people say but also why they say things, and why they say them the way they do. For example, in the statement "Mary's daughter gained admission into university", the pragmatic presupposition will include the reason why the speaker says it, and also why she chooses a particular way of saying it. The reason may be that the speaker narrates this story as a surprise because Mary's daughter had been struggling to get the admission for years; it may be that the speaker tells this to the hearer as a challenge so as to motivate the hearer to read hard in order to get a good result. The message may also be that Mary's daughter needs some financial support for the study which the hearer has already known. The message therefore serves as reminder.

It is worth noting that the notion of the distinction between semantic and pragmatic presupposition is subject to intense criticism. Bach (2010) suggests that the main reason for introducing the semantic-pragmatic distinction is to provide a framework for explaining the variety of ways in which what a speaker conveys can fail to be fully determined by the conventional linguistic meaning of the sentence he utters. He is of the view that the various ways in which the distinction is made has been formulated regardless of the fact that the different versions do not coincide. Bach further asserts that the distinction between context dependence and context independence is inefficient as the ground for distinguishing Semantics from Pragmatics. He argues that what one says cannot be facts about word alone but must also include facts about the circumstance in which one is using them; those facts of course comprise of the "context of utterance".

Patel (2012) suggests a way of identifying the similarities and differences between these two fields of study. He proposes that rather than studying presupposition from different perspectives, it is suitable to see them as possessing a combination of both semantic and pragmatic properties. This to a large extent is so because the extraction of a presupposition from an utterance depends largely on the interaction between the linguistic code (Semantics) and the extra linguistic world (Pragmatics).

Contrary to the broad classification of presupposition as semantic or pragmatic, Yule (1996) classifies presupposition into six levels. This he says is because presupposition has been associated with the use of a large number of words, phrases and structures. These linguistic forms are considered to be indicators of potential presupposition which are: the existential, the factive, the non-factive, the lexical, the structural and the counter- factual.

The Existential Presupposition

This type of presupposition assumes the existence of the entities named by the speaker. It arises whenever a definite NP is used. Reference is something a speaker does: we could consider existence as a presupposition. For example, when a speaker says "John's box is new", it is presupposed that John exists and that he has or owns a box. The existent presupposition is assumed to be present either in possessive constructions such as: "your room" which presupposes you have a room or in any definite noun phrase as in expressions like: The lion, the book etc in which the speaker presupposes the existence of the entities named.

Factive Presupposition

Presupposition is said to be factive when the presupposed part needs to be true (needs to be a fact) for the utterance as a whole to be felicitous. The verbs take sentences as complements. For example;

> I didn't realize that John was married.
> \>\>John was married.
>
> I regret having delayed the editor.
> \>\> I delayed the editor

Non-Factive Presupposition

This is a type of presupposition which is assumed not to be true. Non-factive is an assumption that something is not true. Verbs like; dream, imagine and pretend give an idea of untruth and are used with the presupposition that what follows is not true. For example:

> I dreamed that I am a professor.
> \>\> I am not a professor.
>
> John pretended he was ill.
> \> \>John was not ill.

Lexical Presupposition

With lexical presupposition, the speaker's use of an expression presupposes another concept which is unstated. It presupposes something as a result of using that lexical item. This means that with some lexical items, the utterance makes an assertion for example:

You are late again.
\>\> You were late before.

John stopped running.
\>\> John uses to run.

Structural Presupposition

It is obvious that some kinds of structures seem to trigger presupposition, independently of their lexical content. In this case, certain sentence structures have been analysed as conventional and regular presupposing that part of the structure which is assumed to be true.
For example:

When did you smoke?
\>\> You smoked

Who did you meet?
\>> You met someone

In the above examples, the questions presuppose a statement as a result of its form. The presupposed statement is actually part of the question formation itself. Note that the kind of presupposition conventionally associated with structures like questions can be quite controversial. In legal proceedings, for example, one can be forced to answer questions even though one does not believe in what they presuppose. Similarly, politicians frequently refuse to answer questions if they reject the presupposed content.

Counterfactual Presupposition

Counterfactual presupposition is the assumption that what is presupposed is not only untrue, but is the opposite of what is true or contrary to facts. For instance, some conditional structures, generally called counterfactual conditionals presuppose that the information in the in-clauses, is not true at the time of utterance. A counterfactual conditional is one that posits a reality which is contrary to the actual one. For example in the sentence:

If you were my son, I would not allow you to do this.
\>> You are not my son.

If I had lots of money, I will buy a jet.
\>> I don't have lots of money.

Presupposition Triggers

The following structures have been isolated as sources of presuppositions in sentences. Note that no effort is made in this chapter to claim that presuppositions are limited to these, there could be more but these are common presupposition triggers.

-Definite Descriptions- the X that X..., for example:

Jonah saw the man with four legs.
\>> There is a man with four legs.

-Verbs this could take different forms like;

-Factive Verbs- regret, be aware, realise, and be odd.

Jonah is aware of how proud Godiya is.
>> Godiya is proud.

-Implicative Verbs- manage, forget, happen, avoid etc

Jonah forgot to lock the door.
>> Jonah should have locked the door or intended to do so.

-Change of State verbs- stop, start, continue, finish, come, go, etc

Jonah went to the movies.
>>Jonah was not at the movies.

-Iterative- again, anymore, return, another, time, restore, repeat, etc.

Jonah doesn't like Ruth anymore.
>>Jonah liked Ruth.

-Temporal Clauses- before X, since X, after X, whenever X, as X, during. Etc

During the independence in 1960, Nigeria was buoyant.
>>there was independence in 1960.

-Cleft Sentences – it was x that y (cleft) etc.

What Jonah ate was beef stew.
>> Jonah ate something.

-Contrastives - Contrastive intonation, too, back, in return, comparative as etc.

Jonah hits Mary back.
>> Mary hit Jonah

-Counter-factual- Conditional or modal expressions stating facts contrary to how the world is etc.

If Jonah had competed, he would have won.
>> Jonah didn't compete.

Conclusion

The overall aim of this chapter is to discuss and explore the concept of presupposition, its role and how it works in sentences and utterances. The chapter also examined the concept of presupposition from the semantic and pragmatic perspectives. Presuppositional broad forms were also interrogated and the common presupposition triggers pointed out with examples and illustrations. The chapter sums up therefore that the concept of presupposition is an aspect of the theory of meaning based on the assumption defined by our abstract knowledge of reality. That Presupposition is a child of supposition, which means assumption. Also, while semantic presupposition draws its framework from sentences in abstraction based on logic, pragmatic presupposition is primarily based on assumptions drawn from an utterance in communicative context.

References

Bach, K. (2010). *The Semantics – Pragmatics Distinction*. San Francisco State University. Blackwell Publishers.Cambridge University Press.
Gazdar, G (1979). *Pragmatics*. Academic Press, London.
Kempson, R.M. (1975). *Presupposition and Delimitation of Semantics*. Cambridge
Lakoff, R. (1970). *Linguistics and Natural Language*. In Synthese . 22, 151 – 271
Levinson, S.C. (1983). *Pragmatics*. Cambridge: Cambridge University Press.
Lyons, J. (1977). *New Horizons in Linguistics* Harmondsworth, Middlesex: Penguin Books.
Mey, J.L. (1993). *Pragmatics: An Introduction*. Oxford: Blackwell publishing.
Patel, R. (2012). How is Presupposition Both Semantics and Pragmatics.
Saeed, J.I (2009). *Semantics*. New York, Blackwell Publishers.
Stalnaker, R.C. (1978). "Assertions". In syntax and Semantics, vol 9 pp. 315 – 333. User www.sfsu.Edu/kbach/semprag.htt.
Wilson, D. & Sperber, D. (1975). Relevance: Communication and Cognition. Oxford: www.hmanities. memaster.ca/.../tralques
Yule, G. (1996). *Pragmatics*. Oxford: Oxford University Press.

Chapter 8

A Pragmatic Analysis of Truth Value in Selected Nigerian Newspapers

- Lawal Olarewaju Adesina

Introduction

Newspaper has been held to wield a lot of influence over the mind and imagination the way literature does. The press is seen as a representation of the world in language, because as Fowler (1991:60) observes, language is a semiotic code which imposes structure of values on whatever is represented. And so, news like every discourse, constructively patterns that of which it speaks. As Thompson (1973:25) notices also, serious newspapers exist as a continued tension with government. They seek out and publicize facts that the government may prefer to hide. Therefore, a responsible paper will address itself to responsible readers. A responsible newspaper is rightly so-called because it associates itself with government by seeking to influence the decisions that government takes. However, its readers are responsible in the same way because they too identify with the process of government.

According to Fowler (1991:66), the structure of the news text, under the pressure of the social circumstances of communication, embodies values and beliefs. Perhaps this is why, in his opinion, most people read only one daily newspaper and rely on the news as less biased. In the contemporary papers, a large amount of report is often based on speeches, statements, replies to questions and views. What is more, a number of institutionalized speech situations are regularly sourced by the press e.g debates in the two chambers of the National Assembly, press conferences, court cases, meetings of political parties, trade unions, religious and professional organizations such as the Nigerian Medical Association, Academic Staff Union of Universities etc. These formats provide rich sources of personal utterance from the mouths of people who are perceived as individually important; the way their speech is presented is an integral part of their public personalization. The press is then preoccupied with what such people say.

To this end, a newspaper logically assumes the role of paying particular attention to how what the people say is transformed, because as Rommetveit *et al.* (1979:40) point out, there are clear conventions for rendering speech newsworthy, for bestowing significance on it. This probably goes in line with the views of Thompson (1973:28) as he asserts thus:

> It is taken here for granted that the main business of the press is political and that it carries out its duties by disseminating information about appropriate event, and by sustaining regular debate on their meaning.

Pragmatics, as a branch of Linguistics has continued to dominate attention especially from linguists and philosophers. Writers such as Austin (1962), Searle (1969), Grice (1975) etc. have in fact, reinforced the importance of context in the interpretation of an utterance. Crystal (1985) defines pragmatics as the studies of the factors which govern a language user's choice of utterance. Similarly, Kempson (1988) describes the function of pragmatics as providing an account of how sentences are used in utterance to convey information in context. In fact, the prominent place of the constraints of the society in pragmatics, especially in newspaper representations, as shown in Kempson's submission, confirms Stalnaker's (1970) who defined Pragmatics as the study of linguistic act and the context in which they are performed. The foregoing therefore strongly establishes the link between what people say and how newspapers report such utterances in the society.

Fillmore (1968) gives a description of the deep structure relationships of natural language. He stresses that the system points to the effect that a sentence is made up of a modality constituent which includes tenses and sentence modifiers such as negation and a proposition. This proposition, in his view is a verb or predicator plus one or more noun phrases, each of which is associated with the verb in a case relationship. For instance, in Agent Case, the animate instigator can be used. For example:

'The man wrote the article'

Instrument case could involve the inanimate force or object involved casually, e.g.

'She wrote it with a quill pen'

Palmer (1981) however sees modality as a set of six particles of mood morphemes. In general, according to Palmer, the mood indicates the truth value of the sentence. He gives the six accordingly:

Emphatic: 'indicates that the speaker knows the sentence to be true: if a sentence that ends with the Emphatic mood is false, the speaker is considered a liar.'

Period: 'indicates that the speaker believes the sentence to be true: if it should turn out otherwise, it would mean that he was mistaken, but by no means a liar.'

Quotative: 'indicates that the speaker regards what he has said to be something that everyone knows'.

Report: 'indicates that the speaker was told the information given in the sentence by someone else, but has no evidence of its true value.'

Indefinite/Question: 'both indicate that the speaker does not know whether or not the sentence is true. The indefinite also means that the speaker thinks the listener does know.'

A series of rules specify possible sequences and arrangements of the verb to capture each proposition, either written or spoken. Hence the observation by Palmer that it is not possible to make what one might call an 'unmodalised' statement at all, arguing that the grammar of English language forces the speaker to indicate what is the status of what is being said.

1.1 Literature Review

A proposition is either true or false, and it should be as exact as possible. This is evidently the sort of rationality that is useful in science but when we stop to analyse the meaning of word, propositions tend to be meaningless in the true sense of meaning; that is, they do not really tell us the truth. According to Fowler (1991:30), a speaker or writer must always indicate or imply a commitment to the truth (or otherwise) of any proposition he or she utters. This means that when a certain proposition is uttered, there is always a prediction of the degree of likelihood of an event described taking place or haven taken place.

However, a speaker may utter words which are blatantly untrue or for which he or she lacks adequate evidence. For instance, a speaker who utters the words:

'I always enjoy hardships'

may not appear to deceive the listener in any way but we all know that there is no example in recorded history of people being delighted at hardships. But since the speaker does not show any sign of unseriousness, what the listener needs to do is to work out a possible interpretation of the utterance.

The opinion of Fowler would however be useful for the analysis of this work in the sense that newspaper representations are sometimes or commonly found with truth modality which varies in strength along a scale from absolute confidence to various degrees of lesser certainty.

A straight forward claim for instance does not need any explicit modal verbs in it to be expressed. e.g.

> The cost of the Niger Delta crises <u>has been</u> staggering in all ramifications.
> *Tribune*, Monday, March 6, 2006.

Modality is also found to be indicated by some adverbs such as:

> The underbelly of Nigeria is <u>definitely</u> an apt metaphor. . .
> *Tribune*, Thursday, February 9, 2006.

or by modal adjectves:

> "Without Nelson Mandela's blessing, it is unlikely that any black leader in South Africa can be persuaded to meet the British Foreign Secretary apart from Chief Gatsha Buthelezi."
> *Guardian* February 4, 2005.

From the foregoing, it can be deduced that modality represents a kind of comment or attitude, obviously by definition ascribable to the source of any text, of which editorial writing is an integral part. This comment or attitude can be explicit or implicit in the linguistic stance taken by the writer. Whether these variables are reliable is however left to conjecture.

Allerton (1979:257) seems to take a different view in this context. He opines that *propositional calculus* is somewhat an algebraic system that studies the formation and truth value of complex propositions. He stresses that they may be combined with other propositions in a text of various

relationships such as conjunction, dis-conjunction and implication. To buttress his argument, he gives two sentences:
  i. The weather is pleasant
  ii. John is watching the cricket

Alerton believes that the above propositions may be true (T) or false (F), pointing out that the negation of each sentence will clearly have the opposite truth value. This more or less accords with the natural language, in so far as the truth of "the weather is pleasant" will entail the falsehood of "the weather is not pleasant" and vice versa. This tallies with the view of Thomas (1995:25) who argues that logical positivism is just a philosophical system which points to the fact that the only meaningful statements are those that are analytic or can be tested empirically. He further notes that the logical positivist philosophers of language were only concerned with the properties of sentences which could be evaluated in terms of truth or falsity. For instance, if someone says:

'there are seven words in this sentence',

you can count the words for yourself and judge whether the sentence is true or not.

Kempson (2003) observes that truth condition in propositions is found most difficult in the display of pronouns and other anaphoric expressions. According to her, in order to establish the truth conditional content expressed by a sentence containing a pronoun, some choice as to how the pronoun is to be interpreted has to be assumed, and in her view, these choices are not given as part of the grammar of a language but the language use generally.

Levinson (1983) tallies with Kempson's opinion in relation to context dependency situation in truth conditional propositions. He believes that context-dependency can be traced to specific deictic expressions or indexicals. He argues that sentences which contain such expressions that depend on certain facts about the context of utterance (identity of speakers, indicated objects, places and times, etc.) are not in any way special at all. The reason, according to Levinson, is because every utterance has this context-dependency, due in no small part to tense. He stresses that the following utterance will be true:

'there is a man on Mars'

just in case at the time of speaking, there is a man on Mars, which sharply contrasts 'there was a man on Mars'.

The opinion of Kempson and Levinson are also useful to this study since at times, editorial comments will include meanings that more or less unwittingly get to the press through the complex process of production. At the receptive end, a similarly complex production of meaning through interpretation takes place. When situation reaches this stage, it is context that is the nearest means of detecting the writer's intention since the truth has become somewhat elusive in decoding the proposition.

From the foregoing, it is plausible to deduce that grammar-internal principles do not determine full specifications of truth conditional content but by what is expressed through context. However, Wilson (1974:16) reveals that before one can be certain about the truth condition of any statement, three things must first be ascertained. The first thing according to him, is knowing what the statement means, second, by knowing the right way to verify it and lastly, to have good evidence for believing it.

Based on Wilson's opinion, if one says for instance that the 'earth is round; but insert either 'I don't know what that statement means' or 'I don't know how one could verify that statement' or 'I have no good evidence for that statement' it does mean that any of these conditions makes the original statement absurd.

Wilson's argument sounds convincing in relation to some statements that are used often like 'I sleep all the time, doctor.' In real life situation, it may be possible to evaluate the value of the above mentioned statement to be 'false' or 'meaningless', and make sense of it, in spite of the fact that it is really illogical.

Wilson's view would equally be useful to this work since our successful communication still largely depends on common understanding of the meaning of any statement. Though when understanding is aimed at, it does not really imply that people who use language must come together and consciously agree to use words in certain ways. It means that speakers use words in accordance with a uniform and established set of rules.

In the view of Grice (1975:45), the words 'true' and 'truth' refer to properties of utterances, not states of affairs. On this note then, if I say 'it is true that Tunde is a miser', I am making a comment, not about Tunde but about the assertion, 'Tunde is a miser'. Grice considers that if no such assertion has actually been made, I am implicating that someone might make such an assertion.

Therefore, it can be understood that the assertion about which any claim is made is one with which the reader or hearer is likely to disagree, that is, one is likely to regard as failing to fulfil one or the other of the maxims of Quality. But Watts (1981:50) sees truth value differently. According to him, in the natural narrative situation, the speaker often says things which are either false or for which he lacks adequate evidence, without wishing to implicate anything. The opinion of Watts is probably based on the fact that a narrator, just like an editorial writer, knows that there is no way the reader of any text can immediately check what he or she quotes. This means that propositions of editors are sometimes bedevilled by falsity.

1.2 Theoretical Framework

Linguistic theory exists in several different models, which have widely divergent goals and terminologies. Language, as we are frequently told and as we know, is a human function that pervades and shapes our daily lives. Realistically, the complexity of the English language as any other human language, allows it to be analyzed from different positions over the years. Notable among them are sociolinguistics, syntax, phonology, semantics, just to mention a few.

Besides the aforementioned aspects of linguistic analyses, a language comprises also a pragmatic aspect, to which are reckoned all those mechanisms that relate the language to its context of use, where this context includes the speaker, his audience and the non-linguistic setting.

Two general areas of pragmatic functions are well known. One is the area of speech acts, the other is that of co-operative principles.

The central insight underlying the notion of speech act is that, in addition to saying something, a sentence may also do something – it may assert, question, command, warn or promise.

Thus, as we are saying something, we are also doing something through speaking. This aspect of the interpersonal function of language has been studied particularly by linguistic philosophers and notably by J.L Austin – whose book titled 'How to do things with words' (1955) sums up this perspective – and following him, J. R Searle. To Austin and Searle, we owe the notion of 'illocutionary act' (or a slightly more elegant label) 'speech act'. A speech act is a form of words which, if spoken or written in appropriate conditions and other appropriate conventions, actually constitutes the performance of an action. Austin calls them 'performatives'. Consider the following utterances:

1. The dog is on the mat
2. Dele drinks habitually
3. I declare you man and wife

4. I name this ship Bankole
5. I promise to pay you ₦10

Notice that sentences 1 and 2 above are quite different from 3 – 5 because 1 and 2 only describe states of affairs and sequentially conform to the true/false criterion. Austin therefore names this class of sentences "constatives". The other class of sentences 3 – 5, he labels "performatives". In the view of Austin, in uttering 3 – 5, the speaker does not report a state of affairs but performs an action, bringing into existence a new state of affairs.

Where the utterance literally affects the act referred to: Kola and Dupe are thereby married, the ship is named, the speaker commits himself to pay the addressee N10. Thus, speech acts are integrally enmeshed with the system of conventions that constitute a social and political world, and speech act analysis offers linguistics a direct point of entry into some practices such as newspaper representations.

Basically, the editorial writer, using Searle's sufficient conditions for discourse, makes an assertion in conformity to the felicity conditions of asserting. For instance, the assertion of threat in the following sentence would illustrate further:

Nigeria will know no peace until the Niger Delta question gets its deserved answers

or the following expression:

The Niger Delta region is the underbelly of Nigeria.

The above examples testify to the density of speech act verbs in newspapers which perform action on the reader. They commit the writers to the truth of the propositions contained in their assertions, thereby accounting for the truth value of both statement contained in the texts.

The illocutionary act possesses only one meaning, its illocutionary force; the reader of a text recognizes that the utterance of a particular sentence (such as any of the stated above) in a context counts as a certain action. This means that the presence of many directives, threats and advice expressed in editorial columns only signify that the text stands for attempts by the writer to get his reader to perform future action and the reader will accordingly hold the editor responsible for the felicity conditions of asserting. This therefore qualifies speech act theory as a good framework for the analysis of newspaper editorials.

However, the application of the speech act concept of intentionality to newspaper discourse, especially on the editorials, may not hold enough water because the concept limits itself to those intentions specified by a writer's invocation of felicity conditions established by his linguistic community. The theory cannot handle unconscious intentions or conscious purposes not identifiable by the conventional procedures for making speech acts work.

More so, the notion that only performative verbs could be used to perform actions seems unpersuasive because there is no formal (grammatical) way of distinguishing perfomative verbs from other sorts of verbs in any texts, most especially in editorial columns.

Similarly, the presence of a performative verb does not guarantee that the specified action is performed by the reader.

Based on the above, any attempt to adopt the speech act theory to analyse editorial comment shall be tantamount to pushing it beyond certain limitations.

While Austin makes a distinction between what speakers say and what they mean, Grice (1975:44) formulates a theory to explain how a hearer gets what is said to what is meant, from the level of expressed meaning to the level of implied meaning.

Since Grice conceives of conversation as a purposive, rational behavior, he formulates rules that explain men's conduct in their talk exchanges. First of all, he says, speakers and hearers assume a Co-operative Principle (CP), which he believes should be in force throughout their conversations.

According to Grice (1975:45), the rule states thus: "make your conversational contribution such as is required, at the stage at which it occurs, by the accepted purpose or direction of the talk exchange in which you are engaged." The CP encompasses four principles or maxims:

1. **Maxim of Quantity**
    i. Make your contributions as informative as is required (for the current purposes of the exchange)
    ii. Do not make your contribution more informative than is required.

2. **Maxim of Quality**
    i. Do not say what you believe to be false
    ii. Do not say that for which you lack adequate evidence

3. Maxim of Relation
  i. Be relevant

4. Maxim of Manner
Super-maxim: Be perspicuous
  i. Avoid obscurity of expression
  ii. Avoid ambiguity
  iii. Be brief (avoid unnecessary prolixity)
  iv. Be orderly

  (Adapted by Grice, 1975:45-46)

Just as speech act theory has not provided a fool proof method of detecting authorial intentions in any text, critics also hold that Grice's CP and maxims fail to account for the following:

One, sometimes, an utterance has a range of possible interpretations. How do we know when the speaker is deliberately failing to observe a maxim and hence that an implicature is intended?

Two, how can we distinguish between different types of non-observance (e.g. distinguish a violation from an infringement)? And more in this purpose, Grice argues that there should be a mechanism for calculating implicature, but it is not always clear how this operates. For instance, the same words may convey, in different circumstances, very different implicatures. The implicature so conveyed in one particular context is not random, however.

Yet, Grice's CP and maxims would be more attractive to the attention of this research than Austin's speech act theory in the sense that, two aspects of Grice's maxims are central to the concern of this study. For example, when the maxim of quality is flouted, Grice lists irony, metaphor, meiosis and hyperbole as the outcome whereas the flouting of the maxim of manner results in ambiguity and obscurity. In this light, the theory of conversational implicature is more likely to be of use to this study. CP, which directs the conversational participants to follow the points of the talk exchange, is especially protected in the selection process for editorial writing. Based on this application, any text produced by the writer represents a conversation between the writer and the reader.

Grice's formulation of the CP and the maxims, describes in particular the behaviour of participants in a conversation whose purpose is to communicate efficiently. He does not however, rule out other purposes for other conversations. Taking this hint therefore, this research proposes that the point of the 'interaction' between the writer of an editorial column and his readers is the assertion of untrue propositions as linguistic tools to reach out to the audience (reader). Once this takes place, therefore, such propositions become unreliable. Our attitude to this pragmatic analysis is a single model which is co-operative principles. However, where other useful models could do a particular job better, such would be applied appropriately.

1.3 Analysis of Data

In this section, we have attempted to analyse the extracts of some selected Nigerian newspapers' editorial comments. The pragmatic analysis of truth value is the focus. In doing this, we have made the extracts from the following newspapers – 'The Guardian', 'The Nigerian Tribune', 'The Punch' and 'The New Nigerian'. In the analysis, an attempt has been made to determine the extent to which propositions of the editorials are true. Particularly, we have sought to analyse the texts along the dimension of Grice's Co-operative Principles. According to Grice (1975), the words 'true' and 'truth' refer to properties of utterance, not states of affairs. This illustrates the view that th writer's proposition, based on this study is just to influence, not the belief but the attitudes of his/her readers to the reliability of what is expressed. In addition to these features of true and untrue propositions, we have shown in every text examined, the attitudes of readers towards the verifiability of the editor's comments. Added to this, the pragmatic effects of the proposition on readers are explicated therein.

Text 1
> And what are the issues? Shorn of all peripheral details, there really is only one: who rules Nigeria post 2007. From all evidence, this objective to capture or to retain power literally obsesses the various factions within the ruling People's Democratic Party ton the one hand, and the politicians elected to serve on the other. Every other matter of stat is now consigned to the backburner.
> *The Guardian*, Tuesday, September 13, 2005.

Typographically, the text appears to be narrative prose. The dialogic opening triggered by the rhetorical question, is used to refer back to the shady relationship between the President, Olusegun Obasanjo and his vice, Atiku Abubakar.

The passage however poses problem to the reader. The first issue is now the reader will determine the intentions of the writer towards the questions raised. For instance, is it really the illocutionary act of requesting information, or not?

Another area is ambiguity involved in the questions. The reader is at a loss in pinning down the possible intention of the writer. Note carefully that the expression, "who rules Nigeria post 2007" does not even end with a question mark. And the type of context associated with the expression after the question mark till the end of the sentence is colloquial and does not appear to be relevant to the sub-theme presented here. The writer's violation of the Maxim of Relation must therefore constitute a case of flouting, since the whole lot of the opening sentences is detached from the rest part of the paragraph. There is no thematic cohesion. In flouting the Maxim of Manner also, the writer implicates an attitude of social superiority to unleash his disgust for the PDP controlled regime. This view is supported by the expression "…factions with PDP and politicians elected to serve". He wants readers to believe that PDP members are not out to serve. This is discoursal over-skill since it actually puts the reader at an ambiguous position. What this expression implies is that the writer is sitting on the fence to pound on PDP. The reader is not allowed any chance to evaluate the text objectively since the writer has already situated his opinion.

The last lexeme, 'backburner', ending the metaphorical statement obscures the whole of last sentence. There is therefore a case of violation of the first part of the Maxim of Manner by the writer.

Text 2

> Indeed the trivialization of public office would be so laughable were it not so sad. Pray, where has decorum gone? We ask: must every utterance from any quarter attract a riposte? Whatever happened to golden silence even in the face of provocation? Surely, this is not what leadership is supposed to be about and we can only shudder at what cues, what values our youths pick up from all these. But of course, this is understandable in its proper context. Ensconced in the rarefied environment of Aso Rock, our leaders are far removed from other realities; they hardly grasp the real issues that matter to the people of Nigeria.
> *The Guardian*, Tuesday, September 13, 2005.

The mode of this text appears to be oral, and the style is casual. Abundant markers of an oral model converge here. The syntax is broken up into short information units by frequent punctuation marks. Striking is the employment of question marks which assume a dialogic, an argumentative engagement with the imagined points of view of those referred to by the text. "Pray, where has decorum gone?" We ask: must every utterance from any quarter attract a riposte?" "Whatever happened to golden silence even in the face of provocation?"

Judging from the above cited rhetorical questions, one could deduce that the writer opts out of fulfilling the Maxim of Quality by raising the problems and then dismissing them in the same way as he opts out of telling us how he expects leadership to be handled. The framing of the last question in the text also violates the Maxim of manner in that it is obscure.

The violation constitutes a case of flouting and invites the following implicatures:
    a. that the violation, in some sense, involves the writer's sentiment;
    b. that the writer does not have access to Aso Rock, and that he may have been denied certain opportunity he desired at a particular time in the past.

Text 3

> The reference to the Niger Delta region as 'The underbelly of Nigeria" is definitely an apt metaphor describing both the wealth and the vulnerability of that region vis-à-vis the corporate existence of the country. If Nigeria were to be an immense, docile, reptile the Niger Delta would have been its soft, vulnerable underbelly, at which, for over a month now, darts and poisonous arrows of anger, discontentment, abduction and subterfuge had been hunted by vicious, angry youths of that region.
> *The Nigerian Tribune*, Thursday, February 9, 2006

This text responds to the basic story of the Niger Delta crisis and its attendant consequences.

The writer of this text has violated two Maxims here, that of Manner (the writer should avoid ambiguity) and that of Quality. The violation of the Maxim of Manner is a case of flouting, and the implicature to be deduced is that there is an ambiguous discrepancy between what the writer describes the Niger Delta region to be and what the reader believes, "...the underbelly of Nigeria".

This double violation of the narrative CP throws more light on the way in which the writer wishes us to react to the Niger Delta issue. The reader feels that the writer cannot give substantial evidence for what is reported. Thus, the violation of the second Maxim of Quality is further exemplified. 'If Nigeria were to be an immense, docile reptile, the Niger

Delta region would have been its soft, vulnerable underbelly..." (to the end of the text).

Towards the end of the text, the writer resorts to blatant violation of the Maxim of Relation (the writer should only report such events and evaluations as are thematically relevant to the reported world presented). Lexemes such as "darts and poisonous arrows of anger, discontentment..." only pushes the report so far to the extent of misleading the reader.

However, the non-relevance of the insertion of the lexemes, which makes the maxims of Relation to be violated can only be true if the structure of the text does not allow metaphorical expression. We saw in the text that it actually does. Even the writer, probably unwillingly, introduces metaphors in his first speech. Thus the writer's belief that he has inadvertently violated the Maxim of Relation implicates ambiguity. The lexemes ending the text have been overused for the purpose of portraying his fear. For instance, the relevance of "...poisonous arrows of anger", a metaphor, within the context provided is questionable, since most readers will be unable to relate the two experiences.

Text 4

> We urge law makers to be patriotic and honest, to put the tenure extension saga behind them and do what is right for the country by giving it a body of laws that would usher in peace and propel it towards growth and development. In essence, our advice is that our law makers should revisit the amendment bill and give the country a wholesome, workable constitution.
> *The Nigerian Tribune*, Thursday, February 9, 2006

The editorial enters a dialogic relationship with its readership, starting this paragraph with the pronoun 'we'. There is no doubt that readers are implicated in the ideological position of the 'we' to the extent that they accept the position of the writer.

However, the writer is faced here with a clash between the Maxims of Quantity and Manner. As a writer, he is required by the Maxim of Quality (Make your contribution as informative as is required) to reveal information which would lead to an increased knowledge and understanding of the subject matter. At the same time, the Maxim of Manner (avoid ambiguity) requires that he not knowingly cast his subject in a poor light or leave him open to misunderstanding. For instance, the pronoun 'them' has created problem of co-referentiality because the reader is lost as to whom the writer is referring to by the choice of the lexeme.

Striking is also the use of the colloquial word 'saga' (avoid obscurity) and the use of mundane metaphor 'usher in peace and propel...', which obviously disturb the easy reading of the reader.

The last sentence of this text equally puzzles the reader, when considering how ambiguous it sounds. Though the writer tries to create a familiar, matter of fact relationship with his reader by the use of generic word 'our' in two instances, the whole string is ambiguous. Since no justification is provided for the judgment, it is obvious that CP is put in jeopardy. The reader knows that there is an amendment bill being discussed but does not know which one is right or wrong.

Text 5

> The mounting restiveness indeed holds serious adverse impacts for the nation's mono-cultural economy and corporate existence. An estimated $30 billion was lost to communal unrest and oil theft in the Niger Delta between 1999 and 2003. At a time, up to 300,000 barrels of oil worth $8.5billion (a quarter of the 2.2million barrels exported per day) was stolen daily. It is estimated that the country losses about $6.8million on every violence-induced production determent and another $6.8milion spent annually to replace vandalized equipment in the oil communities.
> *The Punch*, Monday, February 27, 2006.

The writer of this text violates the second part of the Maxim of Quality (The writer should not say that for which he lacks adequate evidence and that of Manner (avoid obscurity). Looking at the text, the reader is bombarded with lots of very high monetary figures and numbers. Such figures may be difficult for some newspaper readers to take in and retain, especially as they refer to counts of different entities (barrels of oil, money in dollars, particularly those lost). And no doubt, the dramatic figures should be an extrapolation from the numbers of reported cases.

Most of these figures are presented in metaphoric context to give the appearance of a great loss to the nation. These ambiguous phrases can testify: 30billion dollars, 6.8million dollars, 8.5billion, 300,000 barrels, etc. The effect is blurring, a diminution in analytic precision; an impressionist style comes over, especially in conjunction with the ubiquitous mentions of large but constantly shifting figures. Thus, the discourse is constantly alarming and hyperbolic but in an obscure way.

Text 6

When the Justice Niki Tobi led National Political Reform Conference was inaugurated last year, many had thought the confab was mainly a vehicle for extending the President's tenure. But Nigerians did not have to speculate for long. A mystery draft constitution, which threatened the credibility of the confab, soon emerged... An attempt to doctor the Electoral Act 2001 also came to the open. The smuggled clause then was section 80(1).
The Punch, Tuesday, February 14, 2006

The language employed by the writer here would be the newspaper's own version of the language of the public to whom it is principally addressed. The metaphoric expression: "...many had thought the confab was mainly a vehicle for the President's tenure extension". The second sentence is opened with another metaphor which complements his implied notions: 'a mystery draft constitution' that underlies a common stock of knowledge which the writer of the paper assumes the audience shares with him. It may not however be certain whether the implied readers would perfectly work out the associations he wants them to draw.

By using the above mentioned metaphor to implicate different meanings concerning the confab's position on the amendment, the first part of the Maxim of Quantity (the writer would not say what he believes to be false) has been violated.

Text 7

The spate of crises in the country's institutions of higher learning is to say the least alarming. This month alone, four universities: Abuja, Bauchi, Ile-Ife and Zaria were closed down to avert a breakdown of law and order. On Wednesday, March 1, the University of Abuja was closed down following a fracas that broke out between students and the police over the alleged killing of a 200level Business Administration student. Exactly two weeks after, Abubakar Tafawa Balewa University, Bauchi was closed down when violent protests erupted in the school over alleged mysterious death of a part 3 student in the Estate Management Department, Abraham Idris who was said to have fallen off a motor cycle outside the campus. He later died at the hospital. The students had earlier agreed to this explanation, but later demanded that the body of their colleague be exhumed for proper post-mortem. This led to the demonstration and the police had to intervene.

New Nigerian, Wednesday, March 22, 2006.

The first sentence of the text is governed by the illocutionary force of fear. Apparently, the writer considers that the fear he mentions is latent to his readers, hence the appropriateness of the illocutionary act.

This text is bedevilled by numerous indexical and demonstrative deictic terms which drive the reader into serious ambiguous position. Examples of these indexicals are 'on Wednesday, March 1,' 'exactly two weeks' and 'he later died at the hospital'. The ambiguity arises from these terms when the reader realizes that the reference on the deictic terms changes every moment, yet none of those words would change their meanings. If they did, it may be impossible for readers to know what they meant and how to work out the interpretation of what is communicated.

The more serious are the demonstrative deictic terms used in the text. They are: 'this month alone', this led to the demonstration'. Demonstratives like these require a supplementary gesture in order to determine reference. Both writer and reader here know that this is impossible. Hence for the reader to simply determine what month, the explanation and the demonstration the writer has in mind respectively is very difficult.

Therefore, to the extent that the deictic formatives cannot fully capture and orientate the spatiotemporal sequence in the story presented, it no doubt presents ambiguity to the reader. And since the writer has put the reader in such ambiguous position, we consider it as a case of violation of the Maxim of Manner (avoid ambiguity).

Text 8

> The New Nigerian is worried at the rate crises are erupting in the universities which are supposed to be not only citadels of learning but also of good behaviour and conduct. Institutions of higher learning such as universities are expected to be the training ground for future leaders...We believe that there are adequate avenues for seeking redress in the schools. The students should endeavor to channel all their grievances to the relevant authorities rather than taking the law into their hands. This would not only ensure a peaceful resolution of problems, but it would also portray the students in a better light. i.e. as civilized members of the society.

New Nigerian, Wednesday, March 22, 2006.

At the heart of the first sentence is a presentation of a clumsy and evaluative expression: "...which are supposed to be not only citadels of learning but also of good behaviour and conduct." The above expression makes the reading of the text to be sluggish. We count this as a brazen violation of the Maxim of Quantity.

In the ensuing paragraph, the writer commits himself by the lexeme, 'avenues' because he only points out one in his explanation instead of more than the reader expects (violation of the Maxim of Quantity). The mundane metaphor – 'taking the law into their hands' in the context confuses the reader because two referents are mentioned – students and authorities. The lexeme 'their' presents ambiguous sense to the reader, he has to decide which of the referents the writer is interested in. What is more, the singular word 'student' is used as deviance here because it is supposed to be in the plural form. It obscures the string altogether. The lexeme 'better light' is superfluous and irrelevant to the sub-theme presented.

1.4 Conclusions

It is fairly obvious that in newspaper presentations, certain attitudes are displayed by writers. Basically, linguistically constructed representation is by no means a deliberate process entirely under the control of the newspaper as a result of their use of journalese.

We found that the editorials display vocabulary that is generally emotive, dramatizing speakers with strong feelings and options. Due to this, evaluative adverbs and adjectives are prominent: 'brutally', 'hideous', 'innocent', 'mercilessly' and so on.

In general terms, when these emotional words are employed by writers, the prepositions do not seem to convey truth or facts. Rather, they just create an influence on the reader. As Stevenson (1944) observes, any proposition that appeals to the emotion through sensational incidents are only ethical judgment which does not indicate facts. Therefore, when strong adjectives and adverbs are made, they just constitute attitudes and not the truth condition of the statement.

It can also be noticed that modality is an important device by editorial writers. This is found in the texts to have the instance of a speaker who has assumed a position of authority. The authority here includes a claim to know what is inevitably going to happen as exemplified in various texts analysed:

> Let the truth be told: Nigeria will know no peace until the Niger Delta questions...get its deserved answers.

> *Tribune,* Monday, 6th March, 2006

However, we must point out that truth modality, in real sense, varies in strength along a scale from absolute to the least confidence because a sentence containing the modal 'will not' cannot be compared with truth content of 'could be'. The same applies to the following sequence of adverbs – 'certainly' and 'unlikely'. All these were found to be instrumental to the conveyance of truth and untruth propositions throughout the texts.

The rhetorical and didactic form of address, though oral in tone, is more like a lecture, presupposing power-difference than a conversation, which gives the appearance of solidarity with the reader.

We however found that most of these claims of institutional authority cannot be fully relied on since readers may not be convinced of their sustainability when it comes to truth-conditionality. For instance, the questions raised by the writers only thicken the doubt of readers towards their reliability to the truth contents, since the illocutionary forces are not specified. They, readers, may not know if the questions should be interpreted as directives or commands.

Generic statements also pervade the texts. These are not affirmative of obligations or necessity, but descriptive propositions which are supposedly true of the instances of the entities to which the editorial refer. *'Niger Delta crisis is the underbelly of Nigeria'*. The function of this to the text is the authoritarian nature, claiming total and definitive knowledge of the topics under discourse; they offer the comfort of the closure as against the openness of enquiry. This often puts the reader in doubt as to the sincerity or truth of such propositions.

On a general note, we found out that the generic sentences offer problem to readers before the meanings are detected. In most cases, the associations used to describe incidents might be far-fetched.

We similarly noticed in the texts that the newspapers used the consensus 'we' and 'us' to achieve some ideological point of view. The important thing to note here is that consensus is posited about a set of beliefs or values, and not facts at all. What we found in the study is that where facts do not seem to square with beliefs, the editorial writers use language which suggests that reality does fit in with belief.

As for value-laden language, the crucial point is that the values are in the language already, independent of the journalist and of the reader. It is therefore, obligatory to select a style of discourse appropriate for each setting in editorial. In selecting the required style, the editor ceases to be an individual subject, and is constituted as something more impersonal, a writer.

It was also found that, newspaper and its readers shared a common discursive competence, know the permissible statements, permissions and prohibitions. For instance, they both know that taking expatriates hostage is inappropriate; strikes are bad, mismanagement of funds is unpatriotic. Newspapers and readers negotiate the significance of the texts around the stipulations of the appropriate discourse. Therefore, any proposition is assessed by readers on the basis of this agreement.

An intriguing feature of these editorials that is worth mentioning again is that much of the texts examined are, among other things, technically speaking, aesthetic. That is to say, they deploy certain structural patterns like metaphors, ambiguities, puns, clichés and sometimes, poetic features to colour their propositions. The effect of these features on readers is defamilairization.

On the whole, it is significant to point out that the relationship which the editorial voice constructs with the reader appears to be dual in nature. One, the source claims the authority to explain an argument and to persuade the reader of its correctness. Second, the editorial claims solidarity by invoking consensus, as earlier stated in this section.

The texts, no doubt, illustrate a discourse of institutional power which emanate from, and in turn helps to construct, the newspapers' claimed authority.

References

Allerton, D. J (1979). *Essentials of Grammatical Theory: A Consensus view of Syntax and Morphology;* London: Routledge & Kegan Paul.
Crystal, D. (1985) What is Linguistics? London: Edward Arnold.
Fowler, R. (1991). *Language in the News; Discourse and Ideology in the Press*; New York: Routledge.
Grice, H.P (1975). *Logic and Conversation*; New York: Academic Press.
Kempson, R. (2003). *Pragmatics: Language and Communication in the Handbook of Linguistics* (ed); London: Blackwell Publishers Ltd.
Levinson, S. C (1983). *Pragmatics*; Great Britain: Cambridge University Press.
Palmer, F. R (1981). Semantics; Cambridge University Press.
Rommtveit, R. et al (1979). *Studies of Language, Thought and Verbal Communication*; London: Academy Press.
Stevenson, C.L (1944). *Ethics and Language*; London: Yale University Press.

Thomas, J. (1995). *Meaning in Interaction: An Introduction to Pragmatics*; London: Longman.

Thompson, D. (1973). *Discrimination and Popular Culture;* London: Heinemann Educational Books Ltd.

Watts, R.J (1981). *The Pragmalinguistic Analysis of Narrative Texts: Narrative Co-operation in Charles Dicken's Hard Times*; Gunter Narr Verlag Tubingen.

Wilson, J. (1974). *Language and the Pursuit of Truth;* Cambridge University Press.

Chapter 9

Speech Act analysis of President Goodluck Jonathan and General Mohammed Buhari's 31st March 2015 Telephone Conversation

- Ayodabo, Joel Olatunde

1.0 Introduction

In the past two years or so, political activities have heightened, in Nigeria, creating tension everywhere, especially in party politics. The two main political parties in contention for power at the federal level were the Peoples Democratic Party (PDP) (a party that had controlled the nation at the federal level since 1999) and the All Progressive Congress (APC) (a party that evolved from an alliance of some progressive political parties).

The political activities climaxed with the general election time table which slated elections for February 14th and 28th 2015. But there was a postponement of the dates of the elections. The presidential election earlier slated for February 14, 2015, eventually took place on March 28th 2015. Out of the 14 political parties that contested for the office of the president, the PDP and APC candidates were the most prominent and celebrated. They were the two parties whose electioneering campaigns were most glamorous and full of 'hate campaign' in terms of linguistic and graphic expression. The tension generated by the campaigns created fears at the local, national and international circles, according to local and foreign media reports. Also, before the elections, issues such as the use of permanent voters' card, card readers and the need for deployment of soldiers during the elections heightened the fears of possible breakout of violence during the elections, and after the release of results.

On March 28 2015, elections took place into the Federal House of Representative and Senate but that of the office of the president was of more concern to most Nigerians. By the midnight of 28th of March, 2015, elections could not hold in some local government areas in some states, and they continued on Sunday 29th of March, 2015. That obviously delayed the release of results. By the evening of Sunday the 29th, the Independent National Electoral Commission (INEC) started a gradual release of results state by state, and by 5pm of Tuesday 31st March, results from about 33 states of the federation had been collated and released to the public. By then, it was obvious that the candidate of the APC was in the lead; thus the sitting President, and the presidential candidate of the PDP, President Goodluck Ebele Jonathan (GEJ), henceforth GEJ, put a call through to General Mohammed Buhari (GMB) henceforth GMB, the Presidential candidate of APC. The text of that telephone conversation forms the data for this study. GEJ and GMB rely greatly on the above as common ground for the progression of the telephone conversation, as no direct mention of the words 'political parties', 'election(s)' or 'result(s)' is made throughout the conversation.

That conversation attracted much attention, and has continued to generate comments and interpretations, locally and globally. The choice of this text as the preferred data is justified by the quality of attention it has attracted; again its content is significant for the political stability of Nigeria, the largest nation in sub-Saharan Africa. The pragmatics of the conversation has continued to shape people's (politicians and the electorate and the international community) views, actions and reactions about the final results declared by the Independent National Electoral Commission (INEC) in the early hours of Wednesday, April 1, 2015.

To properly situate the study, some theories of pragmatics are reviewed, and, in particular, Grice's (1975) Cooperative Principle, which is considered appropriate for analysis of the data. Common Ground is also examined as a veritable tool in conversation analysis. Some typologies of Speech Acts are reviewed, after which George Yule's classification of speech acts is picked for consideration of the speech acts identifiable in this text of the conversation.

2.0 Literature Review

Some comments are provided on Pragmatics, Common Ground, and H.P Grice's Cooperative Principle as literature to generate background for this study. Also some taxonomies of Speech Acts are reviewed.

2.1 Nature and Scope of Pragmatics

Scholars of the field of pragmatics believe that language use is of great importance to mankind. Early philosophers such as Austin (1962), Searle (1969) and later Grice (1975) underline the fact that the occasion of an utterance is important, and that its total context must be understood before the meaning and intention of an utterance can be fully grasped. Crystal (1987:120) explains that Pragmatics studies the factors that govern our choice of language in social interaction, and the effects of our choice on others.

In his own view, Dijk (1992:218) believes that the basic idea of Pragmatics is that when we are speaking in certain contexts, we also accomplish certain social acts. Our intentions for such actions, as well as the interpretations of intentions of actions of other speech participants, he adds, are based on a set of knowledge and belief. Ayodabo (1995) introduces the essence of language function to this discussion on Pragmatics when he observes that Pragmatics focuses on illocutionary acts, an aspect of speech act that specifies what the language is being used for, in a given occasion, whereas Kempson (1996:561) views Pragmatics as the study of interpretation from the perspective of psychology; in other words, the study of the general cognitive principles involved in the retrieval of information from an uttered sequence of words.

Lawal (1997) is of the opinion that Pragmatics evolved as a result of the short-comings of structural semantics to capture satisfactorily the sociological and other non-linguistic dimensions of verbal communication. What can be deduced from the above is that the goal of the pragmatician is to describe, adequately, the components of effective use of language. There is a relationship between how language is used and where it is used. However, Adegbija's (1999) explanation of Pragmatics is rather comprehensive. According to him, 'Pragmatics may be seen as the study of language use in particular communicative contexts or situations.

It is obvious from the few definitions examined above that Pragmatic theory has drawn inspiration from logic. The field draws mainly upon the philosophy of language and 'the theory of speech act', in particular, as well as the analysis of conversations and of cultural differences in verbal interaction. This makes this study a justified one, since telephone talk is in the realm of conversation. Pragmatic theories are basic to the study of human speech. All pragmaticians appear to agree that pragmatic approaches to language study are concerned about language in use in social context, particularly with reference to the functionality of utterances performed in different contexts of interaction. And for the success of any pragmatic analysis, there is usually much shared ground, which has been variously discussed under different concepts and expressions such as mutually shared beliefs, common ground or common knowledge..

2.2 Common ground as a resource for social affiliation

Common ground constitutes the open stockpile of shared presumption that fuels amplicative inference in communication (Grice 1989), driven by intention attribution and other defining components of the interaction engine (Levinson 1995, 2000, 2006). Any occasion of "grounding" (i.e., any increment of common ground) has consequences for future interaction of the individuals involved, thanks to two perpetually active imperatives for individuals in social interaction. According to Enfield (2008:225) an informational imperative compels individuals to cooperate with their interactional partners in maintaining a common referential understanding, mutually calibrated at each step of an interaction's progression. Here, common ground affords economy of expression. The greater our common ground, the less effort we have to expend to satisfy an informational imperative. Also, an affiliational imperativecompels interlocutors to maintain a common degree of interpersonal affiliation (trust, commitment, intimacy), proper to the status of the relationship, and again mutually calibrated at each step of an interaction's progression. In this second dimension, the economy of expression enabled by common ground affords a public display of intimacy, a reliable indicator of how much is personally shared by a given pair of interactants. In these two ways, serving the ends of informational economy and affiliational intimacy, to increment common ground is to invest in a resource that will be drawn on later, with interest. This perhaps accounts for quite a lot of presupposition and implicature that often characterize telephone conversations between and among intimate persons. The case of GEJ versus GMB is not different.

A canonical source of common ground is joint attention, a unique human practice that fuses perception and inferential cognition (Moore and Dunham 1995; Tomasello 1999, 2006). In joint attention, two or more people simultaneously attend to a single external stimulus, together, each conscious that the experience is shared. This time, the presidential election in Nigeria is the external stimulus, which is the main source of common ground.

Let us now look at Grice's Cooperative Principle (CP), as a theoretical model, since our analysis of data will rely mainly on CP's maxims.

2.3 Grice's Model of Verbal Communication

Paul **Grice** proposes that in ordinary conversation, speakers and hearers share a cooperative principle. Speakers shape their utterances to be understood by hearers. The principle can be explained by four underlying rules or maxims. A critical look at the maxims is germane to this study, because we intend to use the CP as a theory for our analysis of the telephone conversation that took place between GEJ and GMB.

Grice's work is for interlocutors to make their conversational contribution such as is required, at the stage at which it occurs, by the accepted purpose or direction of the talk exchange in which interlocutors are engaged. He labels his theory *Cooperative Principle* on the assumption that it is acceptable by the generality of language users. Grice (1975:48) further distinguishes four categories of maxims, each of which has some other more specific maxims and sub-maxims. These are *Quantity, Quality, Relation* and *Manner*.

In summary, the Quantity maxim provides that speakers should be as informative as is required for the conversation to proceed. It should be neither too little, nor too much. Quality maxim expects speakers to be truthful. They should not say what they think is false, or make statements for which they have no evidence. With Relevance maxim, we expect that speakers' contributions should relate clearly to the purpose of the exchange. Lastly, Manner maxim expects that speakers' contributions should be perspicuous: clear, orderly and brief, avoiding obscurity and ambiguity. See Grice 1975: 48 for fuller discussion.

In this approach, utterance interpretation is not a matter of encoding and decoding messages. Rather it involves taking the meaning of the utterance together with contextual information and inference rules, and working out what the speaker meant on the basis of the assumption that the utterance conforms to very general principles of conversation.

Grice's thesis is based on the view that our talk exchanges do not normally consist of a succession of disconnected remarks, and could not be rational if they did. They are characteristically, to some degree, cooperative efforts.

Grice does not of course prescribe the use of such maxims. Nor does he suggest that we use them artificially to construct conversations. But they are useful for analysing and interpreting conversation. However, very often, we communicate particular non-literal meanings by appearing to "violate" or "flout" these maxims.

We find this theory quite useful for the analysis of GEJ and GMB's telephone conversation, because Grice believes that the observance of the Cooperative Principle (CP) and the maxims, in a talk exchange, could be thought of as a quasi-contractual matter, with parallels outside the realm of discourse.

Though Grice did not use the term pragmatics, it seems that he was trying to provide a general framework into which every aspect of utterance interpretation can be accommodated, and that all aspects of the total meaning of an utterance belong either to what is said, or to what is implicated. Justification for the use of this theory, here, rests on the currency of the topic of discussion, the common ground shared by all Nigerians and non-Nigerians on the 2015 general elections in general, and the presidential election in particular, and the fears of possible post-election crises.

All these further constitute common ground for the telephone conversation under study. Having looked at issues in pragmatics, common ground and cooperative principle, there is the need to look at some classifications of speech acts. This is imperative because language is meaningless without its function; the main goal of any pragmatic analysis is the identification of the speech acts that such utterances perform.

2.4 Taxonomy of Direct Speech Acts
Austin (1962) remarks that engaging in a speech act means performing the complementary acts of locution, illocution and perlocution. A locutionary act is a sentence uttered with a determinate sense and reference; an act performed in order to communicate. An illocutionary act is said to be a non-linguistic act performed through a linguistic or locutionary act. Illocutionary acts include commanding, daring, nominating, resigning, etc., and can be effected through performative sentences, whether or not they contain performative verbs (Fromkin and Rodman, 1983). A perlocutionary act results from a language user's utterance, and it is the intended or unintended consequence of, or reaction to what is said. As Lawal (1997) puts it, this act is not part of the conventional meaning of the utterance, but it is derived from the context and situation of the utterance.

Austin (1962) classifies speech acts into five categories of Verdictives, Exercitives, Commissives, Behabitives, and Expositives, while Searle's (1969) categorization of illocutionary acts is based on the argument that

Austin's (1962) classification is deficient; that Austin did not provide a foundation for his classification. Searle also points out that there was too much overlap in Austin's taxonomy. Based on these observations, Seale (1969) comes up with a five-class categorization: Assertives, Directives, Commissives, Expressives and Declarations.

Bach and Harnish (1979) recognize two main categories of illocutionary acts. They are communicative and non-communicative. Communicative acts have four main sub-categories ofConstatives, Directives,Commissives and Acknowledgments Non-communicative class has two sub-categories, which are Effective and Verdictives.

Trauggot and Pratt's (1980) classification of illocutionary acts are: Representatives, Expressives, Verdictives, Directives, Commissives and Declaratives (Trauggot and Pratt 1980:229-230).Leech (1983:105) writing under 'varieties of illocutionary function' classified illocutionary functions into four types (according to how they relate to the social goal of establishing and maintaining comity): these are Competitive, Convivial, Collaborative and Conflictive.

It is instructive to observe that some of the taxonomies, classes and sub-classifications discussed, so far, are products of the efforts by the various scholars to contribute to the dynamic field of utterance analysis. To avoid confusion and verbosity, we have decided to use George Yule's (1996) general classification system, which lists five types of general function performed by speech acts. These are: *declarations, representatives, expressive, directives* and *commissives*. These are simple enough to grasp, particularly when the relationships between worlds and words are considered. Let us elaborate on this classification.

Declarations are those kinds of speech acts that change the *world* via their utterance. The speaker has to have a special institutional role, in a specific context, in order to perform a *declaration* appropriately. In using a *declaration*, the speaker changes *the world* via *words*.

Representatives are those kinds of speech acts that state what the speaker believes to be the case or not. Statements of facts, assertions, conclusions, and descriptions are all examples of how the speaker represents *the world* as he or she believes it is. In using a *representative*, the speaker makes *words* fits *the world* (of belief).

Expressives are those kinds of speech acts that state what the speaker feels. They express psychological states and can be statements of pleasure, pain, likes, dislikes, joy, or sorrow. They can be caused by something the speaker does or the hearer does, but they are about the speaker's *experience*. In using an *expressive,* the speaker makes *words* fit the *world* (of feeling).

Directives are those kinds of speech acts that speakers use to get someone else to do something. They express what the speaker wants. They are *commands, orders, requests, and suggestions.* They can be positive or negative. In using a *directive,* the speaker attempts to make *the world* fit *the words* (via the hearer).

Commissives are those kinds of speech acts that speakers use to commit themselves to some future action. They express what the speaker intends. They are *promises, threats, refusals, pledges,* and they can be performed by the speaker alone, or by the speaker as a member of a group. In using a *commissive,* the speaker undertakes to make *the world* fit *the words* (via the speaker).

3.0 Methodology

This is a survey study, hence the approach is descriptive. The study of discourse is the study of units of language and language use consisting of more than a single sentence connected by some system of related topics. The study of discourse is sometimes more narrowly construed as the study of connected sequences of sentences (or sentence fragments) produced by a single speaker. When more than one person is involved, we talk of a conversation or more generally, a talk-exchange.

Since it was GMB that broke the news of the telephone conversation to the public on Tuesday, April 1, 2015, it was impossible to record the telephone conversation personally. We had to rely on newspaper publications. Data for this study is therefore obtained from *The Punch* newspaper of Friday April 3, 2015 (See the appendix for the full text as published by the newspaper), and presented as such for analysis. Four people participated in the conversation, and these are President Goodluck Ebele Jonathan's Aide (GEJ's Aide), General Mohammed Buhari's Aide (GMB's Aide), President Goodluck Ebele Jonathan (GEJ) and General Mohammed Buhari (GMB). There are twenty-three (23) utterances in all, with each speaker's speech taken as an utterance. Because the entire conversation is not much, we have decided to present and analyse the entire 23 utterances.

To analyse the data, each of the 23 utterances is analysed based on fulfilment or otherwise of the CP maxims of Quantity, Quality, Relation and Manner. The fulfilment is also hinged on the amount of common ground harnessed by the speakers. Then, George Yule's classification of speech acts is visited to identify the speech act(s) that each of the utterances performs. Each of the utterances is labelled U 1– U 23.

4.0 Data Presentation and Analysis

In this analysis, Jonathan's Aide is tagged 'GEJ's Aide', while General Buhari's Aide is tagged 'GMB's Aide'. President Jonathan is tagged GEJ, and General Mohammed Buhari is tagged GMB. The twenty-three (23) utterances (U.1 – U. 23) are presented below for analysis, in pairs. Each pair is established on the basis of initiator/opener and response, that is:

    i)   GEJ's Aide and GMB's Aide;
    ii)   GBM's Aide and GEJ;
    iii) GMB and GEJ.

For analysis, two levels are considered: a) each of the established pairs is analyzed on the extent of fulfilling the four maxims of Grice's CP, given the strength of common ground shared, and b) the speech acts performed by each of the utterances is identified, using George Yule's (1996) taxonomy of speech acts.

4.1
U.1- GEJ's Aide: Your Excellency, Sir
U.2 - GMB's Aide: Good Evening

Fulfilment of CP Maxims
Quantity
U.1 is the opener by GEJ's Aide. It is adequate in terms of Quantity maxim. It is informative enough as a greeting form. U.2 is also informative enough as a response to the opener (Your Excellency, Sir).

Quality
In terms of Quality, the truth value of U.1 lies in the fact that GMB was a former Head of State of the Federal Republic of Nigeria. So, the linguistic expression *'Your Excellency'* is true. U.2 is also of quality because the telephone conversation took place (according to GBM around 5.15pm) in an evening.

Relation
U.1 is relevant as an opening greeting that signals the beginning of the telephone conversation. It is socially acceptable. U.2 is also relevant to the conversation, as it is an appropriate response to U.1.

Manner
In terms of manner, U.1 has substantial courtesy in the sense that the speaker (GEJ's Aide) has aggregated the distance of power relation between himself and GMB. U.1 and U.2 are therefore brief and unambiguous. The utterances are also orderly.

Speech Acts Type
Based on the fulfilment of the maxims against the backdrop of common grounds obtainable from the general background of the text, U.1 and U.2 are Expressive acts.

4.2
U.3 - GEJ's Aide: Hope I'm speaking with General Buhari, Sir
U.4 - GMB's Aide: Yes

Fulfilment of CP Maxims
Quantity
U.3 is informative enough as the aide's utterance is a confirmation request. U.4 also contains enough information to make the telephone conversation progress.

Quality
The speaker in U.3 is making a request because it is true that he or someone else wants to speak with GMB. U.4 is equally true because the speaker is GMB's Aide. Since GMB's Aide is holding GMB's telephone line, his response of 'Yes' is of truth value as he can establish a link with GMB when necessary or required, as we have here.

Relation
U.3 is relevant, since after establishing a relationship through U.1, the speaker needs reassurance about the person he intends to converse with. U.4 is also related to the central content of the telephone conversation. It is also an adequate response to the reassurance being sought in U.3.

Manner
U.3 is clear and unambiguous and orderly. U.4 is very short, brief and straight to the point.

Speech Acts Type
On the basis of the maxims discussed above and the common grounds shared by all, U.3 is a Directive act, while U.4 is a Commissive act.

4.3
U.5 - GEJ's Aide: Ok, President Goodluck Jonathan will like to speak with you, Sir.

U.6 - GMB's Aide: Ok, ok, I'm connecting you, sir.

Fulfilment of CP Maxims
Quantity
U.5 is informative enough as the aide has mentioned the name of his principal (GEJ) who will like to speak with GMB. U.6, in response, is quantitative enough, as U.5 produces enough force which propels the speaker of U.6 to readily agree to act.

Quality
The speaker in U.5 is saying the truth because he is GEJ's aide, and perhaps he has GEJ's mandate to put the telephone call through to GMB. U.6 is also of high quality because what follows validates the promise of the speaker in U.6 to connect the speaker of U.5.

Relation
U.5 is relevant to the subject of the conversation. U.6 is also relevant in content and context to U.5 and the previous utterances. U.6 is a response to U.5.

Manner
U.5 is clear and unambiguous. The request is brief and orderly. U.6 is equally brief and orderly. The use of 'sir' in U.6 is in reciprocity of the manner of language use in U.5.

Speech Acts Type
On the basis of the maxims discussed above and the common grounds shared, U.5 is a Directive act, while U.6 is a Commissive act, in which the speaker commits himself to do something requested in U.5.

4.4
U.7 – GEJ: Your Excellency.
U.8 - GMB's Aide: Hold on.... I'll connect you, Sir.

Fulfilment of CP Maxims
Quantity
U.7 is quite informative. The use of 'Your Excellency' is a fixed address form for any head of a government (past or present), and certain

categories of elected political office holders. GMB who is being addressed as such was a former military head of Nigeria, at a point in the past. U.8 which is a response to U.7 is informative enough too. The mention of the words 'Your Excellency' signals power, since the speaker in U.7 is the sitting President of the Federal Republic of Nigeria.

Quality
GEJ in U.7utters U.7 with the belief that GMB is indeed 'Your Excellency', perhaps based on two premises. One, GMB is seen as being a former Head of State of Nigeria, at a point in the past. And secondly, he is seen as a co-contestant in the presidential election, results of which were still being collated at the time the telephone conversation was taking place.U.8 in terms of quality is also felicitous. The force in U.7 produces U.8, as GMB's aide instantly tells the speaker in U.7 to *'hold on...'*, because GMB's aide believes the speaker in U.7 to be sincere. That belief, perhaps, justifies the inclusion of the word '...*sir*' in U.8.

Relation
U.7 is relevant to the conversation, so far.*'Your Excellency'* has been used before in the opening utterance in U.1. U.8 is also relevant in content and context to U.7.

Manner
U.7 is clear and unambiguous. It is a salutation form to seek the attention of the co-interactant. It is very orderly. Also, the response in U.8 is appropriate and courteous. The use of '... *sir*' is a marker of politeness.

Speech Acts Type
On the basis of the maxims discussed above and the grounds commonly shared, U.7 is a Declaration act, while U.8 is a Commissive (promise) act.

4.5
U.9 – GEJ: Your Excellency.

U.10 - GMB's Aide: Hold on, Sir.

Fulfilment of CP Maxims
Quantity
U.9 is quite informative. The use of *'Your Excellency'* gives adequate information. Situation, here, is similar to what we have in U.7. U.8 which is a response to U.7 contains adequate information too.

Quality
GEJ in U.9 speaks with the belief that GMB is indeed 'Your Excellency'. The premise is the same with U.7. U.10 is also true, as the speaker repeats his promise in U.8. Perhaps he is trying to connect GEJ with GMB, hence the use of the words: *'Hold on, Sir.*

Relation
Utterances 9 and 10 are relevant to the conversation, so far. They are direct repetition of utterances 7 and 8.

Manner
The utterance in U.9 is unambiguous. It is brief and polite. The same is applicable to 10, which is orderly and brief.

Speech Acts Type
U.9 is a Declaration act, while U.10 is a Commissive (promise) act, based on the maxims harnessed and the common grounds shared.

4.6
U.11 – GMB: Your Excellency.
U.12 - GEJ: Your Excellency, how are you?

Fulfilment of CP Maxims
Quantity
U.11 is informative. GMB, a presidential candidate in the general election (whose results were being collated and declared at the time the telephone conversation was going on), recognizes the status and power of his co-conversationist as the sitting President of the Federal Republic of Nigeria. Thus, the uttering of *'Your Excellency'* is understood. U.12 is a response to U.11, and despite the repetition of the exact words used in U.11, there is considerable information in the utterance. The mention of the words *'Your Excellency'* is an acknowledgement of GMB's status as a former Head of State, and perhaps a signal of revealing the overall intention of GEJ in initiating the interview, in the first instance.

Quality
The quality of U.11 is the same as we have in Utterances 1 and 7. A similar quality is produced in U. 12. However, the addition of the clause *'...how are you?'* appears to be a sincere question, given the camaraderie that has characterized the conversation, so far. The tone of the telephone

conversation has not suggested any ill-feeling or insincerity on the part of all the conversationists, so far.

Relation
Utterances 11 and 12 are relevant to the conversation. The two utterances have bearing with U. 1-10. The use of 'Your Excellency' by the two speakers (GBM and GEJ) shows reciprocity and acknowledgement of the status and power ratio of the two main contestants.

Manner
The manner of uttering U.11 and U.12 is clear and unambiguous. The salutation form is to seek the attention of each other.

Speech Acts Type
On the basis of the maxims discussed above and the grounds commonly shared, U.11 likeU.9 is a Declaration act. U.12 is also a Declaration act, with a tinge of Expressive act.

4.7
U.13 – GMB: I'm alright, thank you very much, Your Excellency
U.14 - GEJ: (laughs) Congratulations.

Fulfilment of CP Maxims
Quantity
U.13 is informative. It is an answer to the last part of U.12. U.13 also contains a '...*thank you very much*...', which is an acknowledgement of GEJ's question: 'how are you?' in U.12. He adds the commonly used expression '*Your Excellency*', which has almost become a cliché as used in Utterances 1, 7, 9, 11, 12 and 13 so far. U.14 is just a word, but it is very informative. The non-linguistic element (laughter) adds to the quantity of the utterance, indirectly. Here, it is a measure of expressing conviviality.

Quality
U.13 in terms of quality is true to the extent that GMB couldnot have meant otherwise. His utterance of '... *thank you very much*...' is of high quality because GMB believes in the truth of GEJ's question of '*how are you*' in U.12. '*Your Excellency*' that is added in the utterance is in recognition of the status of GEJ as the sitting President of Nigeria.U.14 is also true in the sense that GEJ's utterance of '*Congratulations*' is sincere and truthful.

Relation
Utterance 13 is a response to the last part of U.12, and it establishes a link with the previous utterances (1-12), hence it is relevant to the theme of the entire conversation. U.14 also establishes relevance with the rest of the conversation in that the speaker is both the sitting President of Nigeria and a presidential candidate in the on-going general election (at the time of the telephone conversation). The uttering of *'Congratulations'* is therefore relevant to the central theme of election result declaration.

Manner
U.13 is not ambiguous; quite brief and orderly. The three parts of the utterance (initial, middle, end) are sequential and logical. U.14 is logical, brief and orderly. The utterance is not ambiguous; it is suggestive of concession of defeat and victory to GMB.

Speech Acts Type
On the basis of the examination of the maxims, and considering the common grounds shared, U.13 is a combination of three acts: Reprsentative (*I'm alright...*), Expressive (*... thank you very much...*) and Declaration (*Your Excellency*) acts. U.14 is a Declaration act on the surface, but a Commissive act at the deeper level.

4.8
U.15 – GMB: Thank you very much, Your Excellency (laughs)
U.16 - GEJ: Yeah, so how are things?
Fulfilment of CP Maxims
Quantity
U.15 is informative in the sense that *'Thank you very much'* is a response to the congratulatory utterance in U.14, and the other part *'Your Excellency'* is in further recognition of the status and power of the speaker in U.14. U.16 is also communicative enough. Though it (*Yeah...*) is a kind of hedging, the question that follows it is an open-ended one, but the import is informative enough to elicit further response from GMB.

Quality
U.15 is true in the sense that it is a response to GEJ in U.14, which is an expression of acknowledgement of success on the part of GMB. U.16 is also true to the extent that the general open-ended question asked is to further convince or prove the genuineness of GEJ's use of the word *'Congratulations'* in U.14.

Relation
U.15 is relevant to the subject of the telephone conversation, as in utterances 1 – 14. It is an expression of gratitude for the utterance of the word *'Congratulation'* by GEJ. U.16 is also relevant to the subject of the conversation. A similar question was asked previously in U.12.

Manner
U.15 is brief and orderly. The use of *'Your Excellency'* also demonstrates decorum and decency.
U.16 is also brief but it demonstrates some kind of superiority. There is absence of 'Sir', or 'Your Excellency', here, which has characterized some of the utterances in the conversation, so far.

Speech Acts Type
On the basis of the examination of the maxims, and considering the common grounds shared, U.15 is an Expressive act that conveys the feeling of GMB. U.16 is a direct Directive act, but it is, given the mood of the nation, an indirect Declaration act.

4.9
U.17 – GMB: Well...
U.18 - GEJ: So, you'd find time to come one of these days so that we can sort out how to plan the transition period.

Fulfilment of CP Maxims
Quantity
U.17 appears empty and hesitant, but given the course of the conversation, it is informative. GMB does not want to say more than necessary, at this point, since he never expects that the conversation would take place, or that such a question would come up. Generally speaking, the question '... *how are things*' can catch any one unawares, and GMB has played safe by using the hedge *'Well...'*. Perhaps, he does not want to flout the quantity maxim, here. U.18 is very informative. GEJ has come out to express in U.18 what matters most. The import of the utterance is that GEJ has conceded victory to GMB in the Presidential election.

Quality
U.17 has quality in the sense that the hedge (*Well...*) coming after the laughter is a way to be economical, and not to communicate what he (GMB) does not have adequate evidence for. It also derives its quality from the fact that it is a response to the general open-ended question (*'how are*

things?). U.18 is true. GEJ who is the sitting President is aware that with the results declared, so far, as at the time he initiated the telephone conversation, GMB is leading, and even if the results of other States being expected are added, GMB will still win. It is on that basis, perhaps, that he has uttered U.18 to concede victory to GMB. The truth value of U.18 lies in the current situation of things at the Independent National Electoral Commission (INEC)'s collation Centre at Abuja, at the time the conversation was taking place.

Relation
U. 17 is relevant to the question asked in U.16, though it does not specifically provide an answer.
U.18 is also relevant as it contains information about invitation to GMB on the transition plan which normally comes after results of elections have been declared. There is also a concrete link between this utterance and the utterance of the expression *'Your Excellency'* and *'Congratulations'* uttered in the course of the conversation.

Manner
U.17 is brief, though hesitant. The use of the hedge *'Well...'* is perhaps a ploy by GMB to deliberately avoid flouting the Quantity and Quality maxims. U.18 is copious, but not ambiguous. The message there is clear.

Speech Acts Type
On the basis of the maxims discussed above and the grounds commonly shared, U.17 is an Expressive act that conveys the feeling of GMB. Though it may appear empty, semantically, pragmatically, the laughter that precedes the utterance indicates that GMB is indeed overwhelmed with joy. U.18, based on the maxims discussed above, is a direct Directive act.

4.10
U.19 – **GMB:** Thank you very much, Your Excellency.
U.20 - **GEJ:** Congratulations

Fulfilment of CP Maxims
Quantity
U.19 is quite informative. It is GMB's response to GEJ's concession of victory and invitation extended to GMB to come forward for the transition plan. U.20 is informative. GEJ here reinforces his acceptance of the results

of the presidential election, as they were, as at then, with the repetition of the word *'Congratulation'*.

Quality
U.19 is true. GMB thanks GEJ perhaps because apart from the utterance of U.14 by GEJ, U. 18 has removed any doubt about GEJ's sincerity in uttering U.17 and 18.U.20 is also true, as GEJ uses the utterance to reiterate his utterances in U.14 and 18.

Relation
U. 19 is relevant to the contents and theme of the talk-exchange. The greeting form is in appreciation of GEJ's acceptance of the presidential election results, and the invitation extended to GMB to come forward for the transition programme.U.20 is also relevant because GEJ uses it to reinforce his earlier utterances in U.14 and U.18.

Manner
U.19 is courteous, and unambiguous. The inclusion of *'Your Excellency'* shows respect for GEJ's status and power.U.20 is also brief and unambiguous.

Speech Acts Type
On the basis of the maxims discussed above and the grounds commonly shared, U.19 is an Expressive act, while U.20 is a direct Declaration act, but an indirect Commissive act.

4.11
U.21 – GMB: Thank you.
U.22 - GEJ: Ok.

Fulfilment of CP Maxims
Quantity
U.21 is informative, though quite brief. As the conversation is moving towards the end, it is a summary of GMB's feeling.U.22 is informative. Although brief, GEJ's utterance of 'Ok' is a kind of agreement with GMB's cooperation in the telephone conversation, and 'Ok', here, could be interpreted as meaning satisfied.

Quality
U.21 is true because GMB expresses *'Thank you'* for the concession of acceptance of the results, and the invitation by GEJ for GMB to come

forward for the planning of a transition programme. U.22 is also true. Though a word, 'Ok' expresses GEJ's satisfaction with GMB's acknowledgement and the entire telephone exchange.

Relation
Utterances 21 and 22 derive their relevance from the progression of the telephone conversation, as the talk exchange is going to a close. They are relevant to the contents of the previous utterances.

Manner
Utterances 21 and 22 are short, brief and straight to the point.

Speech Acts Type
On the bases of the maxims discussed above and the grounds commonly shared, U.21 is an Expressive act, while U.22 is also an Expressive act.

4.12
U.23 – GMB: My respect, Your Excellency.

Fulfilment of CP Maxims
Quantity
U.23 is informative. It is the last utterance in which GMB pays compliment to GEJ, who is the sitting President of the Federal Republic of Nigeria.

Quality
U.23 is true, as GMB is convinced beyond any doubt that GEJ is sincere in the telephone conversation, hence GMB's use of compliment to address GEJ, whom he also refers to as 'Your Excellency'.

Relation
U 23 is relevant to the conversation. It has a link with all the previous utterances.

Manner
U. 23 is brief and unambiguous. It is also quite orderly.

Speech Acts Type
On the basis of the maxims discussed above and the grounds commonly shared, U.23 is a direct Expressive act, and an indirect Commissive (*My respect*) act.

4.13. Summary of findings

In summary, all the twenty-three (23) utterances analyzed derive their fulfilment of the maxims of quantity, quality, relation and manner from the commonly shared grounds of information about preparation, personalities, conduct, and post-election related activities, including counting of votes, and outcome of the results of .the general elections of March 28 and 29th, 2015.

Table 1
Distribution of Speech acts in the Telephone Conversation

Speech Act Types	Utterances Numbers							Total
Expressive acts	1	12	13	15	17	19	21	22	8
Declaration acts	7	9	11	12	13	14	20		7
Commissive acts	4	6	8	10	14	23			6
Directive acts	3	5	16	18					4
Representative acts	13								1

On the bases of the CP and Common Ground, the distribution of speech acts in the utterances is presented in the table above. There are 9 Expressive acts (Utterances 1, 2, 13, 15, 17, 19, 21, and 22) performed in the telephone conversation. This is followed by 7 Declaration acts (Utterances 7, 9, 11, 12, 13, 14 and 20). Commissive acts come next with 6 occurrences (Utterances 4, 6, 8, 10, 14 and 23). There are 4 Directive acts (Utterances 3, 5, 16 and 18). And there is only one instance of Representative act (Utterance 13). What is significant, here is that in U.13, 3 speech acts are identifiable, since the utterance has three segments.

5.0 Discussion

Discussion and conclusion

Arising from data, the presentation and analysis, we now discuss the findings. All the twenty-three utterances have been analysed on the bases of Grices CP maxims of Quantity, Quality, Relation and Manner., and with the belief that all the speakers in uttering U.1 to U.23 have commonly shared grounds.

5.1. Fulfilment of Quantity Maxim

On the strength of the Quantity maxim, all the utterances are informative. In particular, the mention of names such as '...*General Buhari*...' in U.3, and '...*President Goodluck Jonathan*...' in U.5 is a maximum identifying mechanism to create a common ground. There is also the abundant use of honorific terms to mark politeness, and to suggest acknowledgement of power, as in '*Your Excellency*' in Utterances 1, 7, 9, 11, 12, 13, 15, and 19, used by nearly all the speakers. GEJ's Aide used the expression in U.1, while GEJ used it in Utterances 7, 9 and 12, while GMB used it in Utterances 11, 13, 15, 19 and 23.

All the utterances (1-23) therefore provide enough information to either initiate the conversation, as in utterances 1 and 2; to seek clarification, as we have in Utterances 3 and 12; to provide specific information, as in Utterances 4, 5, 6, 8, 10 and 18; or to confirm situation of things, as in Utterances 11, 12 and 13. Some are even uttered to ask questions, as in Utterances 3, 12 and 16. We equally have some sizeable number of utterances that acknowledged power and status. These are in Utterances 1, 7, 9, 11, 13, 15 and 19.

Common ground is a resource that speakers exploit in inviting and deriving pragmatic inference, as a way to cut costs of speech production by leaving much to be inferred by the listener. This is the situation as in the use of the expressions: '*Your Excellency*', and '*Congratulation*' in many instances in the telephone conversation. Fulfilment of the Quantity maxim in all the utterances largely depends on the common ground that obtains among the speakers, particularly between GEJ and GMB. It is the common ground that GEJ shares with GMB for GEJ and GMB to address each other as '*Your Excellency*...' in the course of the telephone conversation. Common ground also produced the utterance of '*Congratulations*...',despite the non-mentioning of words like election, political parties, etc pertaining to the general election. This is a typical case of the display of an exquisite minimality and efficiency of information, which GEJ and GMB commonly share.

5.2. Fulfilment of Quality Maxim

Common knowledge and ground play a significant role here, as the truth values of all the utterances depend on the shared grounds and knowledge of the presidential election and the results, which are not directly mentioned. Such common grounds are that: GEJ is the sitting president of the Federal Republic of Nigeria; GMB was a former military Head of State of Nigeria; both GEJ and GMB are presidential candidates of their respective parties; as at the time the telephone conversation was going on, GMB was clearly on the lead in the already declared results of a number of states; even if the results of the remaining two or three states being awaited, as at then, were counted in favour of GEJ, GEJ was not likely to be declared the winner of the presidential election; the presidential candidate with the highest number of declared votes cast was to be declared winner of the presidential election; and Nigerians and members of the international community were monitoring the collation and state by state release of the results, either through physical presence or through the television and radio broadcast medium. All the utterances therefore derive their quality from the knowledge of the facts stated above. In other words, the knowledge of all these enhanced the quality of all the utterances.

Apart from the use of 'Your Excellency' by GEJ, his utterance of 'Congratulations' (in Utterances 14 and 20) is a clear demonstration of the acceptance of the outcome of the presidential election, despite the fact that the final results had not been collated. Thus, by uttering 18, the intention of GEJ is no longer in doubt. What is observable here is that as explained by Enfield (2008:223), 'common ground affords economy of expression.' The greater speakers' common ground, the less effort they have to expend to satisfy the informational implicature. They have seen here that an affiliational imperative has compelled the interlocutors to maintain a common degree of interpersonal affiliation proper to the status of the relationship, and again mutually calibrated at each step of an interaction's progression.

In all, the quality of the utterances relies heavily on the economy of expression enabled by common ground. This affords a public display of intimacy; a reliable indicator of how much is personally shared by a given pair of interactants, such as we have in GEJ and GMB's utterances in this telephone conversation.

5.3. Fulfilment of Relation Maxim
All the utterances are relevant to the subject matter of the telephone conversation. This can be drawn through inference in Utterances 7, 9, 12, 14, 18 and 20. Every other utterance derives its relevance from Utterance 18, in which GEJ invites GMB to plan a transition programme. Though we can structurally divide the text into three segments: the opening/introductory part (Utterances 1-13), middle/nucleus part (14-20) and closing/ending (21-23), all the utterances (1-23) are inter related in structure and content.

Though there are instances of outright repletion of expressions, the entire conversation remains a unified text. Textuality in a text is a product of good use of cohesive ties, and these abound in the conversation. Common knowledge is the main key through which some of these cohesive ties are inferred and worked out. The main reason for this situation is that the text is a transcribed speech, and in spoken conversation, presuppositions and implicature abound. Though GEJ and GMB make minimal reference to the past shared experience, listeners and analysts will need to rely on some pragmatic mappings to effectively decode the utterances. Commonly shared ground that is general/central to all the utterances has helped to weave all the utterances together.

5.4. Fulfilment of Manner Maxim

All the participants in the telephone conversation have engaged in conscious use of language. This is attributable to the sensitive nature of the subject of discussion, the temperament of Nigeria as a nation, at that point in time, and the consciousness of the power ratio among the participants in the telephone conversation.

By the economy and brevity of these exchanges, the participants display that they share a great deal of common knowledge, including common knowledge of the status and power of two of the main participants (GEJ and GMB). This may be of immense value for negotiating the vaguely defined level of interpersonal relationship among the speakers. In conversing, they test for, and display common ground, and through the interplay of their contributions to the progressing trajectory of the talk, they demonstrate a hard-to-fake ability to know what is being talked about, even when it is not mentioned directly.

We can see in this telephone conversation that GEJ's information processing mechanism is strategic. This strategic manipulation of information involves the incrementing, maintaining, or presupposing of common ground.

It is in the common ground that GEJ is the current president of Nigeria; GEJ was a presidential candidate of the PDP; GMB was a former Nigerian head of State; GMB was a presidential candidate of the APC that presidential election took place in Nigeria on Saturday 28th March and Sunday 29th March 2015; and that as at the time of the telephone conversation, results of the presidential election were being collated and released to the generality of the public. All these pieces of information shaped GEJ's information processing strategy. He never mentioned any of these directly. It can only be deduced that he has employed formulating reference strategy to communicate some of these unmentioned facts. Thus, the utterance of 'Congratulations' becomes of a more specific reference to concession of victory at the polls.

5.5. Speech Acts performed in the utterances

Given the fulfilment of Grice's maxims, and taking cognizance of the common ground that produced all the utterances, all the speech acts worked out are legitimate acts. While many are direct speech acts, a few are indirect acts. In other words, some of the utterances perform functions that are different from what their surface structures display. Only one utterance (U.13) performs three functions, because structurally, the utterance can be broken into three segments/sequence. Valid as it is that we have used Yule's (1996) classification model, here, it is instructive to state that any other typology such as Searle's, Trauggot and Pratt's, or any uncumbersome classification model can handle the utterances in this telephone conversation.

In terms of distribution, GEJ's Aide produced 3 utterances (Us.1, 3 and 5) with one being Expressive act (U.1), and the other 2 (U. 3 and 5) being Directive acts. This is not a surprise because he is an aide that is merely acting on the instruction of his principal. He was directed by GEJ to put a call across to GMB.

GMB's Aide spoke five times, as we have in Us 2, 4, 6, 8 and 10. Only U.2 is Expressive, while the rest are Commissive acts. All the commissives derive their success from the fact that GMB's Aide is committing himself to connecting GEJ with GMB, on phone, in the 4 utterances.

GEJ contributed eight utterances to the telephone conversation (Us 7, 9, 12, 14, 16, 18, 20 and 22). The volume justifies his role as the initiator of the telephone conversation. While Us.7, 9, 12, 14 and 20 are Declaration acts, perhaps because of his power status, Us 16 and 18 are Directive acts. The only Expressive act is U. 22.It is his contributions that shape the direction of the conversation. All other participants in the telephone conversation rely on the quality of GEJ's contributions to offer responses. He is the driver of the course of the conversation.

GMB contributed seven utterances, with 6 of them being Expressive acts (Us. 13, 15, 17, 19, 21 and 23). Only U.11 is outright Declaration act, while U.13 is a combination of three acts: Representative (*I'm alright...*), Expressive (*... thank you very much...*') and Declaration (*Your Excellency*') acts. The overriding Expressive acts that characterize GMB's contributions is a constitute pleasant surprise (I don't think he ever expected the telephone call, partly due to the hate-campaign that preceded the presidential election)or deliberate minimization of speech. He merely salutes GEJ (Us 11, 13, 15, 19 and 23 where *Your Excellency...*' appear) and thanks GEJ (Us 13, 15, 19 and 21, where the word *'Thank...'* appear) for either putting the call through or for conceding victory. GMB did not provide any new information throughout the telephone conversation.

In all, the entire conversation is not monolithic in terms of speech acts display, rather different types are used.

6.0 Concluding remarks

The analysis has revealed that all the utterances satisfied the maxims of Quantity, Quality, Relation and Manner on the basis of common ground which the speakers and we, the listeners/analysts, share. It is also obvious that Expressive, Declaration, Directive, Representative and Commissive acts characterize the telephone conversation.

The manipulation of common ground serves both interactional efficacy and social affiliation. As seen in this study, richer common ground means greater communicative economy, because it enables greater ampliative inferences on the basis of leaner coded signals. This is so with GEJ's use of the hedge '*Yeah...*' in U.16, and in GMB's use of '*Well...*' in U.17. In a social-affiliational dimension, the resulting streamlined, elliptical interaction has a property that is recognized and exploited in the ground-level management of social relations.

Thus, the choices speakers make will, in general, reflect the level of intimacy and intensity of social relations among speaker, addressee, and referent, and this more directly concerns the common ground of speaker and addressee. In sum, we agree with Enfield's (2008:225) view that 'common ground is a resource that speakers exploit in inviting and deriving pragmatic inference, as a way to cut costs of speech production by leaving much to be inferred...' by other contributor(s) or listener(s). And the text of this telephone conversation has demonstrated this well enough.

Appendix

The Punch, Friday April 3, 2015
The following conversation ensued between Jonathan and Buhari:

Jonathan's Aide: Your Excellency, Sir.
Buhari's Aide: Good evening

Jonathan's Aide: Hope I'm speaking with General Buhari, Sir.
Buhari's Aide: Yes.
Jonathan's Aide: Ok, President Goodluck Jonathan will like to speak with you, Sir.
Buhari's Aide: Ok, ok, I'm connecting you, sir.
Jonathan: Your Excellency.
Buhari's Aide: Hold on.... I'll connect you, Sir.
The phone rings for a moment
Jonathan: Your Excellency
Buhari's Aide: Hold on, Sir
Buhari: Your Excellency
Jonathan: Your Excellency, how are you?
Buhari: I'm alright, thank you very much, Your Excellency
Jonathan: (laughs) Congratulations.
Buhari: Thank you very much, Your Excellency (laughs)
Jonathan: Yeah, so how are things?
Buhari: (laugh) Well ...
Jonathan: So, you'd find time to come one of these days so that we can sort out how to plan the transition period..
Buhari: Thank you very much, Your Excellency.
Jonathan: Congratulations
Buhari: Thank you.
Jonathan: Ok
Buhari: My respect, Your Excellency.

References

Adegbija, E.E. (1999). Titbits on Discourse Analysis and Pragmatics. In E.E. Adegbija, (ed), *The English Language and Literature in English. An introductory Handbook*.Pp186-205.Ilorin, MEL Department, University of Ilorin, Ilorin.

Austin, J.L. (1962).*How to do things with Words*. Cambridge MA: Harvard University Press.

Ayodabo, J.O. (1995).*What Politicians Do with Words: A Speech Act Study of M.K.O. Abiola's June 24 1993 speech*. Unpublished M.A. Thesis, MEL Department of Ilorin, Ilorin.

Bach, K. &Harnish, R. (1975). *Linguistic Communication and Speech Acts.* Cambridge MA: MIT Press.

Clark, Herbert H. 1996 *Using language*.Cambridge: Cambridge University Press.

Crystal, D. (1987).*The Cambridge Encyclopedia of Language*. Cambridge, USA: Cambridge University Press.

Dijk, T.V. (1992).*Text and Context Explorations in the Semantics and Pragmatics of Discourse*.London and New York: Longman.

Enfield, Nicholas J. 2002 Cultural logic and syntactic productivity: Associated posture constructions in Lao. In *Ethnosyntax: Explorations in culture and grammar*. Nicholas J. Enfield (ed.), 231–258. Oxford: Oxford University Press.

Enfield, Nicholas J. 2008 Common ground as a resource for social affiliation.In *Intention, Common Ground and the Egocentric Speaker-Hearer*. Istvan Kecskes & Jacob Mey. (eds.), 223–254. Berlin/New York: Mouton de Gruyter.

Fromkin, V. & Rodman, R. (1983).*An Introduction to Language*.3rd edition. New York: Holt, Rinehart and Winston.

Grice, H. Paul 1975 Logic and conversation.In *Speech acts*.Peter Cole and Jerry L. Morgan (eds.). 41–58. New York: Academic Press.

Grice, H. P 1989 *Studies in the way of words*. Cambridge, MA: Harvard University Press

Kempson R.M. (1996). Semantic, Pragmatics and Natural Language Interpretation. In S. Lappin, (ed.). *The Handbook of Contemporary Semantic Theory*.Cambridge: Blackwell Pub. Inc.

Lawal, A. (1997). Pragmatics in Stylistics: A Speech-Act Analysis of Soyinka's Telephone Conversation. In A. Lawal (ed.). *Stylistics in Theory and Practice*. Ilorin: Paragon Books.

Leech, G. (1983). *The Principles of Pragmatics*. London: Longman.

Levinson, S.C. (1980). *Speech Act Theory: the State of The Art*. Cambridge: Cambridge University Press.

Levinson, Stephen C. 1995 Interactional biases in human thinking. In *Social intelligence and interaction: Expressions and implications of the social bias in human intelligence*. Esther Goody (ed.), 221–260. Cambridge: Cambridge University Press.

Levinson, Stephen C. 2000 *Presumptive meanings: The theory of generalized conversational implicature*. Cambridge, MA: MIT Press.

Lewis, David K. 1969 *Convention: A philosophical study*. Cambridge, MA: Harvard University Press.

Mandelbaum, Jennifer 1987 Couples sharing stories. *Communication Quarterly* 352:144–170.

Moore, Chris, and Philip Dunham (eds.) 1995 *Joint attention: Its origins and role in development*. Hillsdale, NJ: Erlbaum.

Searle, J.R. (1969). *Speech Act Theory*. Cambridge: Cambridge University Press.

Searle, J.R. (1975). Indirect Speech Acts in P. Cole Morgan, J. (eds.) *Syntax and Semantics*. New York: Academic Press.

Searle, J.R., (1976). A Classification of Illocutionary Acts. *Language and Society*. 5. 1-23.

Smith, Neil V. (ed.) 1980 *Mutual knowledge*. London: Academic Press.

The Punch newspaper.Friday April 3, 2015 p. 13.
Tomasello, Michael 1999 *The cultural origins of human cognition.* Cambridge, MA: Harvard University Press.
Traugot, E. & Pratt, M. (1980) *Linguistic for Students of Literature.* New York: Harcourt Brace Jovanovich Press Inc.
Yule, G. (1996). *Pragmatics. Oxford:* Oxford University Press.

Chapter 10

The Discourse of Language of Public Relations (PR): a case study of Nasarawa State University, Keffi

- Adewole Adigun Alagbe

Introduction

Public Relations is a management function in any organization or institution. Public Relations unit plays a vital role of effective information dissemination. It is based on this function that this chapter, therefore, critically looks at how the language of Public Relations is used in an academic environment using Nasarawa State University, Keffi's Information and Public Relations unit as a case study. Data was collected from the Students' Information Handbook and monthly University Bulletin produced by the Public Relations and Information unit of Nasarawa State University, Keffi. The following discourse features: presupposition, Inference and Grice's cooperative principle were used as analytical tools. Finally, the chapter came up with possible solutions.

Public Relation is not new in Nigeria list like other African countries. However, attempt to organize public relations practice in Nigeria began soon after World War I following the establishment of Information office in Lagos by the colonial government.

Today, several organizations in the private and public service/sectors including governments at all level in Nigeria establish Public Relations units that manage their images and relationships internally and externally. Many schools of thought have different ideas and perspectives towards carrying out what public relations entails. Some think it simply means bribery, while some believe public relations is just being nice or friendly to people who come around such person or persons. It is obvious that public relations is viewed beyond such imaginations.

Public relations happens to be one of the functions of the top management. It tends to evaluate public attitudes and behaviour, as well as seeks to identify the policies and procedures of an organization with public understanding and acceptance. Black (1992) states that, the fundamental purpose of public relations practice is to establish a two-way flow of mutual understanding that is based on truth, knowledge and skilful information.

The basic of all human relations is a complex of conflicting self-interest. Every individual and every organization have their own aspirations and hopes. More so, there are tremendous counter demands such as housing, education and leisure on people's aspirations and hopes which they wish to attain. It is in this regard that the services of a Public Relations (PR) exertive are needed.

In our day to day relationships and interactions, we make all kinds of contact and, therefore, we consciously or unconsciously employ public relations techniques, especially when we want to project ourselves or organizations in good light to other people. Public Relations generally involves dealing with members of the public.

Many organizations would want to have a credible image of themselves all the time but as it is, there are good and bad days for an organization, therefore, the Public Relations practitioners must make extra effort to get to the root of the problem through communication flow. The language we use in communication to achieve a credible image for any organization is Public Relations language. It is good to note that every human activity is carried out in a particular language, which suits its purpose to communicate effectively.

It is very sad that Public Relations (PR) in a developing country such as Nigeria has been relegated to the background by many individuals, organizations and institutions. In fact, some establishments do not even have a Public Relations unit or department. Therefore, many issues that are sensitive in nature are left to deteriorate before action is taken.

Basically however, there is great need for Public Relations (PR) to serve as effective link between individuals, organizations, government, institutions and the public. There is also the need for it to truthfully measure up and meet these demands. This will create an atmosphere of mutual understanding with the general public and the world will be a better place where understanding will rule.

This work is geared towards establishing the fact that language is used for communication which is the core unit of human activities. Public

Relations is a unit which uses language for effective communication to a targeted audience, but today this unit is a mere propaganda aimed at influencing people negatively. This poses a lot of problems, especially in the use of sentences, the case of many impostors on the profession, use of language that suits their personal interest, problem of spelling and lack of accuracy to make information complete.

This work focuses on the problem of impostor on the profession, the use of language that suits their personal interest, improper organization of sentences, wrong spelling and lack of accuracy to make their information complete. The need for this work is to look at the major causes of those problems and proffer solutions to them.

The aim of this work is to examine how Public Relations unit of Nasarawa State University, Keffi performs its activities especially that of communication between the management, staff and students. The mode of communication which is the language of Public Relations (PR) and the Nasarawa State University unit (NSUK) will be appraised to see how effectively the unit plays its role of communication.

This is to examine whether Public Relations unit of Nasarawa State University, Keffi (NSUK) is what it claims to be or it is just mere propaganda.

This work is an attempt to contribute to the fact that the language of Public Relations is expectedly persuasive, direct and honest and must always be directed to the targeted audience for the desired impact and to avoid propaganda.

Brief History of Nasarawa State University, Keffi (NSUK) Public Relations Unit (PR)

Nasarawa State University Public Relations unit was established 2001. Public Relations unit came into being under the visionary and able leadership of Professor Adamu Baikie. Muh'd Jamil Zakari is the first Information and Public Relations Officer of the unit.

The objectives of Public Relations unit of Nasarawa State University are:
a. To promote communication between the management, staff and students of Nasarawa State University, Keffi.
b. To carry out effective and informative news of Nasarawa State University, Keffi.
c. To spread information to the various units of Nasarawa State University, Keffi

Nasarawa Sate University Information and Public Relations unit has certain functions to perform. One of the functions of the unit is to establish and maintain mutual understanding between the management, staff and students. It also carries or spreads information among the different units of the University. It educates and informs about social vices, especially cultism. Lastly, the unit promotes or projects the image of the University against any internal and external propaganda.

Conceptualization of Public Relations

Public Relations is a management function of continuing and planned character through which the public and private organizations and institutions seek to win and retain the understanding, sympathy and support of those with whom they are or maybe concerned. This is done by evaluating public opinion about themselves in order to correlate as far as possible, policies and procedures, to achieve by planned and widespread information, more productive co-operation and more efficient fulfilment of their common interest.

Okereke (34) asserts that Public Relations is top management function meant for co-operate planning, positioning of organization, monitoring environmental treads and predicting their consequences. In other words, it is a tool for internal and external communication, crisis management, marketing communication, management of good media relations, shareholders and community relations and for good governance.

In the words of Oyeneye (142), he sees the term 'public' as everyone interested in, or affected by an organization. He identifies different kinds of public as follows:

i) Internal Public
ii) External Public
iii) Special Public
iv) Basic Public

He explains further the four kinds of Public mentioned above.

a. Internal public: These are people within an origination. In Nasarawa Sate University for instance, these refer to students, Staff, provision store owners, etc.
b. External public: These are publics outside an organization e.g. community members, government officials and agencies.

c. Special public: These are very important elements to the survival of any organization. Relating this to Nasarawa State University, this includes students, staff both academic and non-academic.
d. Basic public: This is a general term that applies to the people associated with most organizations regardless of the nature of their services, e.g. staff, contractor, government and private agencies etc.

On the other hand, Okereke (148) opines that Public Relations varies according to authors its descriptiveness, prescriptiveness or functional or a combination of all or any two. He says Public Relations includes planning, continuity, Honesty and mutual communication, understanding, mutual benefits, tools and recognition.

Similarly, Lasswell (23) views Public Relations as the management function which evaluates public attitude, identifies the policies and procedures of an organization with the public interest and executes a programme of action to earn public understanding and acceptance.

Furthermore, De-fleur and Ball Rokeach (192) argue that Public Relations is

> the distinctive management function which helps to establish and maintain mutual lines of communication, acceptance and co-operation between organization and the public. It involves the management of problems or issues: helps management to keep abreast of and effectively utilize change, serving as an early warming system to help anticipate trends; and uses research and sound ethical communication techniques as its principal tools.

A close look at their argument suggests the following attributes of public relations as

(i) Public relations involves planned and deliberate activities.
(ii) Public relations is a continuous and sustained action, not adios nor tied to the expedient.
(iii) Public relations is mainly proactive, not merely reactive.
(iv) Public relations is primarily for a management function, though like other management functions, it has its "technician" operations.
(v) Public relations activities are directed as varied "publics" not at the "the public".
(vi) Public relations thrives on dialogue or multi-way communication, not on monologue or one-way communication.

(vii) Unlike propaganda, public relations seeks to satisfy the mutual interest of the patro-organization and her publics, not the single-minded Interest of the former.
(viii) Basically, public relations employs a fundamentally persuasive not threatening mode of communication.
(ix) Public relations respects public opinion as a matter of life and death, although it does not ponder on every opinion without due examination.
(x) Public relations is at once forward-looking or predicative, and backward-looking or evaluative.

A theory by International Institute of Public Administrations (4), argue that Public Relations Association sees public relations practice as:

> The Arts and Social Science of analysis trends predicting the consequences, and implementing planning programmes of action which will serve both the organization and public interest.

In like manner the British Institute of Public Relations (13) comes up with their own definition of PR as:

> the deliberate, planned and sustained effort to establish and maintain mutual understanding between an organization and its products.

The above definition sees public relations as an organized activity that is goal-oriented and very tangible. It is also a process that is continuous, especially the communication aspect. In response to this definition, Oyeneye, (20) looks at "mutual understanding" as communication effort which should be a two-way issue and will result in a two-way understanding". In other words, an organization has to send out information and also receive feed backs from its public. To him, The term "organization" refers to all kinds of organization, refers to commercial and non commercial, manufacturing sectors, educational and religious organizations, etc. The term "publics" here means all human activities which are sub-divided into common fields of interests, problems and aspirations. These divisions are for different publics and not the general public.

Similarly, Jefkins (32) sees public relations as:

> ...consists of all forms of planned communication, outwards and inwards, between an organization and its publics for the purpose of achieving specific objective that concerns mutual understanding.

Here, Jefkins is of the view that public relations for organization means to map out programme and policies for organization, institutions so that specific set goal would be achieved.

In view of the explications on public relations above, it is much more reasonable to agree with Oyeneye (32), that Public Relations (PR) should be defined with a set of guidelines which include: public relations is a planned and continuous communication process; it is a two–way communication activity; it is for the mutual benefit of both organization and the publics: the goal of public relations is to achieve good will and mutual understanding: it applies to both commercial and non commercial organization; public relations (PR) is a management function, favorable image and reputation can only be achieved through good deeds and responsible performance; research is employed at the beginning, during and after public relations programmes; public relations (PR) is tangible activity because objectives can be regarded as the relationship between an individual and another or with the general public, an organization or government with another and this incorporates the area of international relations.

Public relations is based on truth and does not mask reality. It is a profession and business that is at the moment world wide in scope. For purpose of clarity, certain prominent and recurring terms like language and propaganda are defined below as used in this work.

Propaganda

Most people are of this view that Public Relations (PR) is mere propaganda, but most public relations practitioners insist that the term is the exact opposite of public relations.

Jefkins (7) re-asserts this view of public relations practitioners where he says:

> Propaganda is biased information to gain support for a cause, belief, but public relations is concerned with achieving mutual understanding.

In the same vein, Celvin (36) agrees with the above view. He says propaganda seeks to present part of the factors, to distort their relations, and to force conclusion which could not be drawn from a complete candid survey of all the facts. He further emphasizes his point by describing propaganda as "half truth, lies, ambiguities, evasions, calculated silence…"

Similarly, Oyeneye (19) seems to agree with the concept of his predecessors above when he asserts that.

> Let it be emphasized that public relations does not need to apply any form of propaganda to succeed. They are two parallel lines and should not meet at any point. The moment a public relations practitioner introduces or embraces propaganda, he has taken his first step towards failure.

Review on Discourse Analysis

The approach being adopted for this work is Discourse Analysis. Discourse is simply language in use. In the opinion of Osisanwo (15), language is an instrument of communication among human beings. He believes that human beings interact through language by taking on one another. He further says, this talk is termed "discourse" and its organizational structure has to be accounted for and studied. Hence, the meaning of Discourse Analysis emanates from such talks which are eventually analyzed. He also says that, for meaning to be relevant, the context and situation must be established and how this situational context is used for specific purpose so as to convey specific message.

On the other hand, Stubbs (31) sees Discourse Analysis as language in use in social contexts, and in particular with interaction or dialogue between speakers. In essence, Discourse Analysis is concerned with what language is used for and not the formal properties of a language. The concern here is with the different parts of a conversation. He focuses on the different social contexts, their organization and the process of encoding and decoding meaning in talk or in an utterance.

More so, John (21), sees Discourse Analysis from two points of view. He reveals that the divisions are oral and written discourse, though he views written discourse as a 'text'.

Akwanya (31), on the contrary sees written discourse in three different perspectives:
(i) Discourse is realized through event and meaning of a text.
(ii) In written discourse, specific individuals are linked to a predicate, which can be a   quality, a class, a relation or an action.
(iii) He also says, any written discourse must have sense and reference.

In the same vein, Osisanwo (7) views written discourse as text aspect of discourse analysis. He furthers says, for the meaning of a text to be relevant, the context and situation must be established and how the situation context is used for the specific purpose to convey specific message. More so, He identifies some certain features as follows: speech act, contexts, inference, presupposition and implicative.

Framework of Analysis

The linguistic framework that the researcher has selected for this research work is functionalism. Functionalism deals with meaning and interpretation than the language itself. The linguistic theory of functionalism also centres on the relationship between a meaning and the wording by reference to what it means. The major proponents of this linguistic theory are Andre Martinet and M.A.K Halliday. According to Martinet (30), function of language is translated simply as meaning. In his view, grammar of language is functional in three different senses:

(i) It aims at accounting for how language is used; and postulates that this is what shapes the system itself.

(ii) It seeks to understand the role of language in bringing out the meaning.

(iii) It studies each linguistic element in terms of the function in the whole. This means that the function of a word is determined within the sentence.

For example, it maybe analyzed by examining the meaning which the sentence intends to convey. In this view, linguistic phenomenon permits the dissolution of the tension between thought and speech. He also says language may in fact be seen as a means of or for thinking and acting.

More so, Halliday (xvii) similarly accounts that functionalism deals with how meaning functions in a sentence. Hence, there is a clear line between semantics and grammar, and a functional grammar is one that is pushed in the direction of semantics.

Akwanya (46), like Martinet (30) and Halliday (xvii) sees functionalism as a theory that is very productive in Discourse Analysis as it is highly attentive to the relationship of language and the light. It focuses on language structure which is known as functional linguistic. He says the two main approaches are within functional linguistics. One approach emphasizes on the relationship between language and thought, while the other approach is on the basis of the meaning.

Methodology

The data collected for this work was obtained from the Students' Information Handbook and the Official Bulletin produced by Public

Relations unit of Nasarawa State University, Keffi. These written documents were critically studied in order to identify the language of public relation in an academic environment and to identify the discourse of such 'language in use'. The analysis was done using the Grice's Co-operative Principle. This Co-operative Principle has its maxims which the participants use as guide in a written discourse. They are:

Quantity: This maxim states that one should make his contribution as informative as required and do not make contribution more informative than necessary.

Quality: One's contribution should be on truth. One should not say what he believes to be false and do not say that for which he lacks adequate evidence.

Relative: One should be relevant with you contribution.

Manner: One should be clear and avoid obscurity of expression; be brief and be orderly.

The second step taken has to do with inference. The hearer of an utterance or the reader of a written text has no direct access to the meaning which the speaker or writer has in mind. Inference therefore, is that process which the hearer or reader goes through and what he understands from the literal meaning of what is said (or written) to what the speaker (or writer) intends to convey. It is closely tied to the utterance context.

The third step is presupposition: in writing, there are some basic assumptions which the speaker or writer must make concerning the hearer or reader in relation to the subject matter on ground. Such assumptions are made without any challenge from the interlocutors because they are built on assumed common ground.

Data Analysis and Discussion

The analysis is done based on the following discourse features: presupposition, inference and Grice's cooperative principle.

Presupposition

Most of the discourse (language use) at public relation information unit is based on assumptions. These assumptions are used by the hearer or reader in relation to subject matter on ground. The following are some extracts from the Students' Information Handbook, 2006/2007 edition on page xi titles:

> *Message from the Dean of Students' Affairs, "... but growing fast. There is, therefore, the need for your tolerance, dedication and ..."*

(Source: Students' information Handbook 2006/2007 edition)

This means that the students are expected to contribute to the progress and development of the University because the university is still at the growth level.

The second paragraph presupposes students to study hard and come out with good result and to avert corruption, examination malpractice, cultism and any other act of indiscipline that will incriminate them on campus and in their communities at large.

Thirdly,

"Attendance of lectures and continuous assessment"

(Source: Student's information Handbook 2006/2007 edition)

Students are expected to attend lecture always and lecture attendance of 75% is necessary for every student before taking examination.

Fourthly,

"Student project"

(Source: Students' information Handbook 2006/2007 edition)

The above presupposes that students at final year will write and present project, if not, after last the date of submission, it shall be rejected or not collected for that particular academic session.

"Placement of Posters & Bills"

(Source: Nasarawa State University, Keffi. Official Bulletin Vol. 12 No. 17. January - March, 2008)

Students and staff presuppose that the Information Unit is warning students and academic staff against displaying posters and bills on walls and this placement should only be displayed on the schools notice boards.

"APPRECIATION"

(Source: Nasarawa State University, Keffi. Official Bulletin Vol.012 No17 January – March, 2008)

The university Students, academic and non-academic staff presuppose that the family members of the late Alhaji Abdullahi Al-Amins express their appreciation to them for their condolences.

(Source: Nasarawa State University, Keffi. Official Bulletin Vol. 12 No17 January – March, 2008)

"Two dons present papers in international conference"

Academic, non-academic Staff and students assume that two lecturers from Faculty of Education presented papers at the international conference held in Liege, Belgium. The names of the lecturers are Prof. A.A. Eniayeju and his title of the paper is "Women and Sustainable Development in Nigeria: Empowering the Girl-child Mathematically" and Ngozi P. Nwosu and her title of presentation is "Education for all Women by Year 2015: Women Centre for Continuity Education, Sokoto as a Case Study". These presentations are indeed great achievement for the Nasarawa State University, Keffi.

Inference
The hearer of an utterance or the reader of a written text has no direct access to the meaning which the speaker or writer has in mind. He (the reader or hearer) has to go through a process of arriving at an interpretation of such an utterance or a chain of utterance. In relation to this, Wales (248) defines inference as the deductive process through which something is worked out or made explicit in terms of what is spoken or written. To him, therefore, inference is that process which the hearer or reader goes through to get from the literal meaning of what is said (or written) to what the speaker (or writer) intended to convey. He also says that it is closely tied to the utterance context.

"DRESS CODE" ... be properly dressed otherwise you may not be allowed into Examination Halls, Lecture Halls and other formal places:
What students deduce from the above information is that anybody who refuses to dress properly will not be allowed to sit for exams and will not attend lecture and will not be attended to in offices, etc. In addition,

> "...All staff should actively help in the enforcement of dress code...."

Students also infer from the above that both academic staff in their offices and non-academic staff at the Administrative block will also aid to stop indecent dressing.

Nasarawa State University: NSU Anthem
1. NSU we hail thee, we love our great citadel of learning we call on God to help us to acquire knowledge for development
2. As a mark of our love for thee, we pledge to shun all forms of vice. So that our institution can be a reference point in our nation.
3. All hail the vision of our founding fathers, to establish on solid minerals a great University of note to take our state to enviable heights.

(Source: Official Bulletin, Vol. 13 No. 18 March, 2008)

"NSU we hail thee"

What the academic staff, non –academic staff and students deduce from the NSU Anthem above is that they come to Nasarawa State University with love.

"Our great citadel of learning"

What they deduce from this above is that Nasarawa State University is their great institution where they acquire knowledge..

"We call on God to help us to acquire knowledge for development".

They also infer here that they should ask God to help them in their endeavours.

"Acquire knowledge for development"

Students are also informed here to procure knowledge for progress.

"As a mark of our love for thee"

The academic staff, non-academic staff and students deduce that Nasarawa State University is worthy to be appreciated. Therefore, we should work against all forms of social disorder. We pledge to shun all forms of vice".

"So that our institution can be a reference point in our nation"

They deduce that everyone should go against social vices in order to make our University a great centre of education in our country.

All hail the vision of our founding fathers.

Everyone should work towards actualizing the vision of the University founders.

To establish on solid minerals

Everyone should build on the standard ground.

A great university of note to take our state to enviable heights.
Lastly, the management, academic staff and students deduce from this line that with a great University, this state will be taken to a higher level.

"Why students fail exams"
First, students deduce meaning that a lot of them fail exams because they don't start preparation at the beginning of a semester "... Student fail to star ..."

Second, students infer that they fail to understand the group of which they belong. This group is classified into two: "Quick learners" and "Slow learners" because some students just understand or assimilate through listening to their lectures while others must go through the process of reading their notes more than once in order to understand what it means.

Third, many students fail because they don't know which group they belong, that is, their level of understanding or learning, "the inability of students to know which group they belong brings failure in their exams."

Lastly, students fail because they don't understand the question properly before answering. "... When they find it difficult to understand the questions being asked in an examination, they will fail."
(Source: Nasarawa State University official bulletin October – December, 2007 Vol. 11 No.16)

General conduct and discipline of students in the University.

A Student shall not:
- "Be insubordinate to university officials" - Students are not to disobey university officials.
- "Keep guests and visitors in their rooms" - Student infer from this quotation that they are advised not to accommodate guests and visitors in their hostel rooms.
- "Organize parties in hall of residence without official permission of the hall warden" - Students infer that they can organize parties only with official permission or if it is officially accepted.
- "Engage in betting and gambling activities" - Students also infer that they are advised to disengage from any form of betting and gambling activities.
- "Steal" - Students also infer from this they should abstain from stealing.

- "Engage in drug abuse" - Students also infer that they are advised to stay away from any form of drug abuse.
- "Engage in drunkenness and smoking in public places" - Student infer that they should abstain from drinking and smoking of any kind around the school premises.
- "Engage in sexual assault and abuse" - Students are to disengage from all forms of sexual harassment and abuse.
- "Constitute a threat to the life of their fellow students" - With this, students infer that what so ever may be the reason, they should not be a threat to one another.
- "Be a member of any prescribed organization" - Here, students infer that they are expected to associate with only the permitted associations.
- "Participate in any illegal or secret meeting organized by secret societies / organizations…" All unregistered societies /organization are prohibited for students' participation.
- "Engage in any act that constitutes a nuisance" - Students are advised to avoid any from of disturbance or social unrest in the University.
- "Discharge human waste…" - Disposal of human waste in an unauthorized place is prohibited. Here, students are expected to pass out waste excretion in an authorized place like the toilet.
- "Use bathrooms and toilets indecently" - Students should use toilets and bathrooms neatly instead of littering the environment with human waste.
- "Wash or spread clothes on the veranda" - This means that students are not to wash or spread clothes on the hostel veranda.
- "Destroy ornamental plants" - Students are advised not to damage any plant that has been planted by the University which is meant to beautify it.
- "Create unauthorized entrances in the halls" - Student should not make or provide illegal entrances in the halls.
- "A student who is rusticated or has been advised to withdraw from the University for any reason shall neither attend lectures nor live in any hall of residence" This infers that any students (s) that has been expelled from the University must not receive or attend lecture and should not be found around or within the University premises.
- "A students' organization /association shall not invite nor accommodate any outside who is not cleared by the vice chancellor, or

any other authorized University functionary". Students infer that they should not invite any body that is not a student and not officially invited by the University.

(Source: Students' Information Handbook 2006/2007 Edition)

Paul Grice's Cooperative Principle

Grice (45) asserts that conversation takes place by reason of what is called the Co-operative Principle, which comprises the tacit agreements holding between the speaker and hearer. This Co-operative Principles has its maxims:

Quantity

The first is, make your contribution as in formative as is required (for current purpose of the exchange).

The second is, do not make your contribution more informative than required.

Quality

Do not say what you believe to be false, and do not say that which you lack adequate evidence.

Relation

Be relevant at all times.

Manner

This maxim has an overall instruction: "be perspicuous": but this is further divided into four maxims which are; be brief, be orderly, avoid obscurity and avoid ambiguity.

While addressing the issue of admission, the University Vice –chancellor has violated the maxim of Quantity which states that a speaker's contribution should be as informative as required.

> "Noting the Concern of government on admission, the Vice–Chancellor explained that for 2007 / 2008 academic session, more than 11,000 Candidates applied whereas the NUC's Quota (based on carrying capacity of programme audit) has put the ceiling of intake at 1,330..."

The above conversation has violated the maxim of quantity because the Vice-Chancellor is only expected to meet up with the interest of the Governor, who is The Visitor by meeting or giving the indigenes high quota of admission than non-indigenes. Hence, the Vice-Chancellor rather tells long story about NUC'S Quota, Senate's belief on admission, school fees issue, etc. which make his contribution more than required. While responding to the Vice-Chancellor's speech, The Visitor has violated the maxim of quality too by responding to more than what the Vice-Chancellor said.

Below is one of the expressions of The Visitor:

> "He pointed out that three issues of utmost priority to his government are funding, provision of infrastructure and basic facilities and strategic planning..."

A critical look at the above expression by The Visitor as shown above reveals that it violates maxim of relation which states that the exchange must be relevant to the conversation in context but the above expression goes in contrary to it. In the same vein, the above expression also violates the maxim of manner which states that exchange must be orderly and brief.

Likewise, the Vice-Chancellor while addressing the issue of admission violated the maxim of relation which indicates that exchange must be relevant to the conversation:

> Baikie expressed delight and appreciation to His Excellency for granting the University management audience...

(Source: Official Bulletin Vol. 12 No. 17 January-March, 2008)

Conclusion

It has been discovered that language use is a common problem at the Public Relations Information unit. It is also discovered that academic staff, non-academic staff and students find it difficult to understand the language use of the (PR) information unit based on the fact that meanings of language use in the Students Information Handbook and the University's Official Bulletin are usually deduced and presupposed. Thus, making it difficult for them to understand the direct meaning from the expressions and conversation due to Grice' maxims principle of co-operation of exchange in the course of conversation which are violated. Though the language use in the Students' Information Handbook shows simplicity and easy to comprehend, the students and staff members who are meant to act on the language rather act in assumption. The work also concludes that maxims of Grice's Co-operative Principle are violated or flouted on exchange, in the course of conversation in the University's Official Bulletin.

Works cited

Akwanya, A.N. *Semantics and Discourse Theories of Meaning and Textual Analysis*. Enugu: ACENA Ventures Limited, 2007,

Brown, G. and Yule G. *Discourse Analysis*. Cambridge: Cambridge University press, 1983.

Cutlip and Center. *Effective Public Relations* London: Prentice Hall, 1964.

Frank, Jefkins, *Marketing Advertising and Public Relations*. London: Heineman, 1987.

Halliday, M.A.K An Introduction to Functional Grammar. London: Arnold, 1985.

Lasswell, H.D. *The Structure and Function of Communication in Society*. Hoit; Rinehart & wins to, 1998.

Martinet, Andre. *A Functional View of Language*. Oxford: Clarendon, 1961.

Osisanwo, Wale. *Introduction to Discourse and Analysis and Pragmatics*. Lagos: Femolus –fetop publishers, 2003.

Oyeneye, P.D. *Concepts and Principle of Public Relations*. Lagos: Media Gate, 1997,

Stubbs, M. Stubbs, M. *Discourse Analysis: the Sociolinguistic Analysis of Natural Language*. Oxford: Blackwell, 1995.

Chapter 11

Critical Discourse Analysis: An Overview

- Peter Okpeh

1. Introduction

What is now known in discourse studies as *Critical Discourse Analysis* (henceforth CDA) is the cumulative outcome of a series of developments in discourse studies, arising from varying theoretical conceptions of linguistics and a range of influences from numerous disciplines. The divergent nature of the linguistic theories and the multi-disciplinarity of the influences that have historically shaped the eventual emergence of CDA as an approach to discourse studies are informed by the scope and complexity of the questions that CDA itself sets out to investigate regarding the human society. Furthermore, since theoretical concepts in scholarship are usually never considered sacrosanct, the differing conceptions of linguistic theories that have influenced CDA are also the result of a sustained tradition among linguists whereby existing theories are constantly being challenged and subjected to critical evaluation, consequently leading to either the modification of such theories or the formulation of new ones. Commenting on this in relation to the necessity of the emergence of Critical Linguistics (CL), the theoretical precursor of CDA, Fowler (1989) argues as follows:

> The prevailing orthodoxy of linguistics is that it is a descriptive discipline which has no business passing comments on materials when it analyses; neither prescribing usage nor negatively evaluating the substance of its enquires. But I see no reason why there should not be branches of linguistics with different goals and procedures, and since values are so thoroughly implicated in linguistic usage, it seems justifiable to practice a kind of linguistics directed towards understanding such values, and this is a branch which has become known as critical linguistics...the familiar transformational – generative linguistics invented by Noam Chomsky ... is in general terms unsuitable, because its aim is to refer to linguistic structures

to the set of structural possibilities that are available to human language as a universal phenomenon... Chomsky is not interested in the role of language in real use (and indeed will not allow such matters to be a valid concern of linguistics).

Apart from the fore going, CDA has such broad connection with several theoretical concepts and disciplines because it focuses, among others, on three indispensable indices of the human society, namely, *discourse, power* and *ideology*. This, Wodak (1996) argues, is why CDA scholars should work with other researchers in fields such as sociology, psychology, sociolinguistics, anthropology, and other domains of human interest where discourse either constitutes or is constitutive of social structures. This further buttresses the view that CDA, whether as a methodology or a theory, is a multi-faceted approach to the exploration and analysis of power relations on various social domains. In what follows, attempts are made to examine CDA as a theoretical/ methodological approach to discourse studies. Specifically, the chapter centres on:
a. theoretical antecedents of CDA
b. conceptual focus of CDA across models
c. Perceived Weaknesses of CDA

2. Theoretical Antecedents Of Critical Discourse Analysis

Before the emergence of what is now known as Critical Discourse Analysis, there had been attempts by philosophers and social scientists to evolve theories that should provide a comprehensive evaluation of the society by digging beneath the surface of social life to uncover those assumptions that keep people from a full and true understanding of how the world operates. On a broad scale, these theories include anti-foundationalism, social critical theory, post-modernism, feminism, Foucaudian discourse theory and critical linguistics. Although all these theoretical traditions have directly or indirectly influenced CDA, this study focuses on only three of them:
(a) Critical Social Theory
(b) Foucauldian Discourse Theory
(c) Critical Linguistics

This selection is informed, not just by the profound impact these theories have made on the philosophical orientations and analytical goals of CDA, but also because of their seeming collective concern with the notions of *power, discourse* and *ideology* on the one hand, and the interconnectivity among these three social constructs, the deconstruction of which is the overriding goal of CDA as a theoretical model.

i. Critical Social Theory

Rooted in Marxist ideology and the literary traditions of literary criticism, critical social theory, according to Leonard (1990), attempts to critique historically based social and political institutions that oppress people, while at the same time having a situated practical intent to decrease such oppression. The theory, according to Powers and River (1980), emerged from the Marxist studies of social research established in Frankfurt in 1923, which later became known as the Frankfurt School. Although the theory, in Held's (1980) opinion, is most associated with Jurgen Habermas, its primary authors are Horkheimer, Adorno, Marcuse, Lowenthel and Pollock. Multi-displinary in contents, the theory has as one of its chief goals, the advancement of the emancipatory role of knowledge. Leonard (2003) opines that when the theory is applied to classroom discourse, it will help to broaden students' horizon of possibility and expand their sense of a larger humanity, consequently liberating them from the confines of their common sense. Adorno (1979) remarks that *criticalness* of the theory hinges on its commitment to "expose the dialectical tensions in modernity, such as between authoritarianism and enlightenment. Powers and Rivers (1980) note that critical social theory describes how people groups exist in relation to the historically based dominant ideologies that structure their experience. This, perhaps, is why the theory advocates the bringing about of self-liberating practices among people, using awareness of oppressive conditions, brought to light through research. Horkheimer, one of the founding fathers of the theory notes, concerning its critical nature, that it seeks to liberate human beings from the circumstances that enslave them.

One of the ways by which the theory hopes to facilitate this liberation is by challenging the representation that encourages oppressive ideologies, and so make people the victims of exploitation. The influence of critical social theory on CDA is seen in the former's commitment to the liberation of people from ideological bondage, imposed on them by society, by presenting them with a more objective and realistic interpretation of social realities which is the goal of CDA.

ii. Foucault Theory on Discourse

The Foucault Theory on Discourse also known as Foucauldian Discourse Analysis is credited to Foucault (1969). The theory, as Foucault himself puts it, "sets out to address the relationship between power and knowledge and how they are used as a form of social control through societal institutions". In Foucault's opinion, the analysis of discourse should be done with recourse to, not just present social realities, but the power and historical components of such discourse over periods of time. To him, power relations in modern western civilizations can be represented as resulting from several key conceptual changes in social thought (Drefus and Rabinow 1983).

Kendell and Wicham (1999) outline five steps in using Foucauldian Discourse Analysis. The first step, according to them, is a simple recognition that discourse is a body of statements that are organized in a regular and systematic way. The remaining steps are based on an identification of rules on:
1. how those statements are created.
2. what can be said (written) and what cannot.
3. how spaces in which near statements can be made are created.
4. making practices material and discursive at the same time.

A review of the theory shows that besides focusing on the meaning of discourse, its distinguishing characteristic is its emphasis on power relationship which, according to Foucault, is expressed through language and behaviour on the one hand, and the relationship between language and power on the other. The theory is concerned with the analysis of how the social world expressed through language is affected by various forces of power. In this connection, the theory enables the researcher to understand how society is being shaped (or constructed) by language, which in turn reflects existing power relations.

Like critical social theory, Foucauldian Discourse Analysis is often used in the analysis of politically oriented data and is preferred by scholars who are critics of traditional forms of discourse analysis (such as Courlthard and Sinclaire's analysis of classroom discourse) because of the latter's failure to account for the political implications of discourse and the ideological basis of such implications.

The theory's influence on CDA is in connection with the foregoing, plus its conceptualization of dominance and marginalization as inevitable parts of power relations which is the motivation for resistance.

iii. Critical Linguistics

Critical Linguistics started in the late 1970s with a group of scholars from the University of East Anglia who set out to advocate the need to investigate the centrality of language in the way individuals are perceived as social subjects (Fowler, 1979). Critical Linguistics, according Johnson (1999), attempts to explore relationships between language use and the social conditions of that use. The word "critical", according to him, is associated with "critique" and agrees with Fairclough's (1985) notion of "making visible the connectedness of things", particularly exploring (more than the traditional descriptive linguist would do) the wider social connotations of language use. The critical linguist, according to him, views the world as social structures manifesting different ideologies, and studies the way language use reflects these. Based on Halliday's (1985) system functional linguistic theory, Critical Linguistics seeks to unveil the connection between linguistic choices and ideological processes. Like in CDA, the goal of critical linguists is to examine the linguistic strategies and apparatus through the use of which people are kept under dominant forces. Its basic assumption, according to Lemmouch (1987) is the need for its practitioners to analyze a large set of linguistic features in context and examine the aggregate ideological mediation of these features. In other words, in analyzing a text, one should not look at isolated linguistic items to read off social meaning. Fowler (1970), the leading proponent of the theory, remarks as follows:

> There is no predictable one-to-one association between anyone linguistic form and a specific social meaning. Speakers make systematic selections to construct new discourse, on the basis of ideas – ideologies – and complex purposes of all kinds. To isolate specific forms, to focus on one structure, to select one process, in fact to list components of a discourse out of their context.

Concerning the analytical goal and philosophical orientations of Critical Linguistics, Wodak (1996) outlines a number of questions, some of which are:
i) How does the naturalization of ideology in discourse come about?
ii) Which discursive strategies legitimate control or naturalize the social order?
iii) How is power linguistically expressed?
iv) How are consensus, acceptance and legitimization of dominance manufactured?
v) Who has access to which instrument of power and control
vi) Who is discriminated against and what way?

Conceptual Focus of CDA

A multi-disciplinary approach to the study of discourse, CDA is an analytical research model that views language as a form of social practice in which all forms of linguistic usage are believed to encode the ideological dispositions of language users (Fairclough 1985). It was originally known as Critical Language Studies (Billing 2003), and scholars like van Dijk(1999) prefer to call it *Critical Discourse Studies*, suggesting that it is a combination of theory, application and analysis. As an institutional research programme, CDA traces its origin to a Symposium held in Amsterdam in 1991 when its founding practitioners – Teun Van – Dijk, Norman Fairclough, Theo Van Leunsen, Gunther Kress and Ruth Wodak – met to deliberate on the different theories, approaches and methodologies in Discourse Analysis, and the need to formulate a model that will not just be interdisciplinary, but will also integrate other linguistic grammatical theories that are relevant to the analysis of language use. (Wodak, 1996). Consequently, besides sharing interest and methods with disciplines that study social groups and structures, such as anthropology, philosophy, sociology, psychology, ethnography and ethnomethdology, CDA usually relies on insights from such branches of linguistics as pragmatics, sociolinguistics, text linguistics, cognitive linguistics, literary studies, conversation analysis and semiotics.

From its inception, CDA was designed to question the status quo by detecting, analyzing, and also resisting and counteracting enactments of power abuse as transmitted in private and public discourse, and herein lies its *criticalness*, which according van Leeumen (1996) is viewed in terms of its explicit and unapologetic attitude towards the forces of oppression and dominance in the society. In doing this, CDA is seen by Wodak and Fairclough as seeking to expose the manipulative nature of discursive practices in the society which manifest as class conflict, false consciousness, exploitation, or power relations conceived and perpetrated through the habitualization of unquestioned and long held ideological beliefs and attitudes which are concealed in the language behaviour of the members of a society.

As a research programme, CDA accomplishes this by creating a liberating consciousness through a systematic demystification and explanation of texts that are ideologically shaped by relations of power in the society. This text – demystification process is aimed at eradicating the social barriers and oppressive structures enforced by these ideological beliefs. Since language serves as the ideological anchorage of these oppressive and social structures, the critical linguist must seek to establish through the process of analysis, the connection between language choices reflected in texts and talk and the social and cultural contexts in which such texts and talks are produced and consumed. This is possible by unveiling and bringing to the fore the linguistic strategies that serve as evidence of these oppressive tendencies .And herein lies the social intervention mission of CDA.

Approaches to Critical Discourse Analysis

According to Billey (2003) CDA has become an established academic discipline with the same rituals and institutional practices as all other academic disciplines. Consequently, its proponents and practitioners differ, in spite of many areas of similarities, on issues relating to theoretical foundations methodology and analytical goals and focus. In what follows, attempts are made to examine these differences as "approaches" under the names of its key founding authors, among whom are Fairclough, Van Dijk, and Wodak,.

CDA Model by Fairclough

Essentially Marxist in orientation Fairclough's Dialectical – Relational Approach to CDA is one of the most significant theoretical contributions to CDA. According to Wodak and Meyer (2009), this approach to CDA highlights the semiotic reflection of social conflict in discourses, which translate into the author's interest in social structures, practices and events.

Fairclough's model of analysis, according to Rahimi and Riasati (2001), has gone beyond the "whatness" of the text description towards the "how" and "whyness" of the text interpretation and explanation, consequently making the underlying assumptions behind selections of discourse to be ideologically driven and motivated. Through this model therefore, the social processes and ideology embedded in a discourse can be unveiled by analyzing the forms of language used in the discourse. Terminologies such as dominance, resistance, hybrid action of discursive practices, technologization and conversationlization of discourse are commonly used by CDA practitioners that employ this model in their analysis.

A very significant aspect of Fairclough model is its inclusion in the structural analysis of the context of a text, the analysis of agents, tense, transitivity, modality, visuals images or body language. Also, Fairclough believes that one single way of analyzing a problem does not suffice.

CDA Model by van Dijk

Known as the *socio-cognitive* model van Dijk's (1991) approach is characterized by the intersection between cognition, discourse and society. The model began with informal text linguistics and subsequently incorporated elements of the psychological model of memory, together with the idea of frame taken from cognitive science (Hidalgo 2005). Van Dijk's approach essentially focuses on stereotypes, the reproduction of ethnic prejudice and inequality, power abuse by elites and resistance by dominant groups. Among these variables the most widely quoted and referenced by CDA scholars are power abuse and dominance.

Dominance in van Dijk's opinion is the exercise of social power by elites, institutions or groups, which results in social inequality including political, cultural, class, ethnic, racial and gender inequality (van Dijk, 1991). This reproduction process, in van Dijk's opinion, may involve different "modes" of discourse – power relations as the more or less direct or overt support, enactment, representation, legitimization, denial, mitigation or concealment of dominance, among others. CDA scholars who lean towards van Dijk's approach want to know the structures, strategies or other properties of text, talk, verbal intervention or communicative events that play a role in these modes of reproduction.

Although most CDA research according to van Dijk(1991)pay attention more to "top-down" power relations of dominance, than 'bottom–up relations of resistance, compliance and acceptance, power and dominance are usually not unilaterally imposed on people. Most times, according to him, power abuse are usually 'jointly produced. A very apt example of this is the religious domain where the faithfuls are taught to accept the fact that "dominance" and "inequality" which manifest as "virtues" of "submission" within the context of religious practice, are "natural", and so should not be opposed or challenged. The basis of this understanding hinges on the long held ideology in religion that religious leaders are God's representatives on earth, to whom their followers must give an unquestionable submission in matters relating to the tenets of their faith. By its very nature, therefore, religion, especially Christianity, abhors all forms of resistance and opposition to constituted authorities, either in the church or the secular world. This ideology finds its clearest most potent portrayal in such metaphorical expressions as *sheep, children, weaker vessels* used to refer to the members of the congregation and *men of God, God's oracles, and God's spokesmen* used to describe the clergy.

The naturalization of this type of dominance is, according to van Dijk, possible through a socio-cognitive process of *mind-control* which to him is facilitated when members of a discourse domain accept beliefs, knowledge and opinions from those they consider authoritative, trustworthy, or creditable sources, such as scholars, experts, professionals or the media (Nester et al. 1993). Mind control, according to him, is also facilitated in discourse when in some situations, participants are obliged to be recipients of discourse, such in education or a work place situation. Situations where lessons, learning materials or job instructions are interpreted and learned as intended by institutional or organizational authors (Giroox 1981). This means of mind control is, again, highly manifest in especially religion where the interpretation of the sacred texts are highly subject to the opinion of the clergy which, as earlier stated, must not be challenged as they are considered to be "God's representatives" to the other adherents and followers of the religion. Thus, most of the members usually swallow, hook *line and sinker,* whatever issues from their religious leaders, because they lack the knowledge and beliefs needed to challenge the discourse or information they are exposed to.

Besides these contextual means of mind control, van Dijk's approach is also inclusive of other structures of mind control which are essentially discursive. These structures, which bother essentially on the use of persuasive strategies, include the highlighting of topics in a newspaper headline, argumentation and manipulation in discourse which manifest in implicit communication of beliefs to recipients without actually asserting them, and by so doing minimizing their chances of being challenged.

To van Dijk, socio-cognition, the "system of mental representations and processes of group members" **(P. 8)** mediates between society and discourse. These mental representations manifest ideologically along the *Us* versus *Them* dimensions, or the *in group* and *out group* ...Members of one group usually present themselves or their own group in positive terms, and the other group in negative terms (van Dijk 1993, 1995, 1996,). According to Jaffer Sheyholisami (1988:61) van Dijk believes that any CDA scholar who desires to make transparent such an ideological dichotomy in discourse needs to analyze discourse in the following way:
(a) Examine the context of discourse; historical, political or social background of a conflict and its main participants.
(b) Analyze groups, power relations and conflicts involved.
(c) Identify positive and negative opinions about US verses Them

(d) Make explicit the presupposed and the implied
(e) Examine all formal structure: lexical choice and syntactic structure, in a way that helps to (deemphasize polarized group opinions.

Also included in van Dijk's approach is the difference he makes between the Macro and the Micro social orders. Whereas, according to him, power, dominance, and inequality between social groups fall within the Macro level of analysis, language use, discourse, verbal interaction, and communication belong to the micro level of analysis. These two levels of social order and analysis, according to him, form one unified whole in everyday interaction and experience.

CDA Model by Wodak

Wodak's approach to CDA is known as the Discourse-Historical Approach (DHA). The approach attempts to describe and analyse those cases where language and other semiotic practices are used by those in power to maintain domination (Reisigl and Wodak 2009). Hidalgo (2011) notes that although initially the approach was concerned with prejudiced utterance in anti-Semitic discourse, recent developments in its analytical postulations include the discursive construction of national sameness and the social exclusion of out groups through the discourses of difference, and the reconstruction of the past through sanitized narratives. Drawing roots from socio-linguistics and ethnography, the approach gives an important place to strategic communication oriented to understanding. Its central tenets according to Hidalgo (2005), is the need to bring together the textual contextual levels of analyses. Consequently, the model of context used in it invokes historical knowledge understood in terms of four layers: (a) the linguistic co-text (b) the inter-textual and inter-discursive level (c) the extra-linguistic level, and (d) the socio-political and historical level (Wodak and Meyer 2009).

In the model, the interconnection between various texts and discourses leads directly to the notions of de-contextualization and re-contextualization; processes in which elements typical of a particular context can be taken out of it and inserted into a new context with which it has not been conventionally associated (Hidalgo, 2011).

Conceptualizing CDA within the context of her own model, Wodak (2005) herself considers CDA to be fundamentally interested in analyzing opaque as well as transparent structural relationships of dominance, discrimination, power and control as manifested in discourse. The *critical* component of CDA in her view is in its commitment to investigating social inequality as it is expressed, constituted and legitimized via language use.

One of the defining features of CDA within this model is its concern with power, as a central condition in social life, and with how language indexes and expresses power, at the same time mediating where there is contention over, and challenge to, power. The texts that form the data for discourse analyst using this model are usually sites of struggle in that they often show traces of differing discourses and ideologies contending and struggling for dominance (Wodak, 1996).

Perceived Weaknesses of CDA
In spite of its increasing popularity and its visibility on the intellectual landscape, CDA has been perceived by some critics as possessing weaknesses that undermine its status as a recognizable approach to discourse analysis. Breez (2011) summarizes the barrage of criticisms against CDA under three perspectives. The first according to her bothers on the underlying premises of CDA as an approach to discourse studies. Here the focus is on what Hammersley (1997) perceives as the ambitious claim of CDA practitioners to offer a comprehensive view of society and how it functions, which is superior to other positions, because it is conducted in a spirit of reflexive critique. CDA practitioners are often quick to talk about their goal of creating "a world where people are not discriminated against because of sex, colour, creed, age or social class"(Caldas-Coilthard& Coulthard,1996) Operating from such a premise, CDA practitioners seem not just to be biting off more than they can chew, but appear committed to a utopian agenda that is not realistic in real life.

Another perspective from which the weakness of CDA is viewed relates to its *critical* perception of society. By the very premises of its historical antecedents. CDA was designed to challenge and oppose the status quo, and this, its proponents claim, is with the intent of liberating the victims of hegemonic influences and oppressive power relations in the society. Given this preconceived objective, CDA scholars always have a suspicious view of society. Consequently, CDA- based studies are always revolutionary focusing on textual evidences of power imbalances and exploitative ideologies, the unveiling of which should encourage resistance which will in turn facilitate liberation. In contrast to this, Martins (2004:186) advocates a more constructive and complementary evaluation of society which will take into account '…how people get together and make room for themselves in the world in ways that redistribute power without necessarily struggling against it.'

The heterogeneity of its theoretical antecedents makes some critics to view CDA as being uncertain about it exact preferences for a particular social theory. Regarding this, Breez (2011) remarks that CDA draws from a vast and somewhat contradictory panorama of ideas about society, encompassing thinkers from Marx, through Gramsci and Horkheimer to Giddens and an enormous diversity of approaches to language and communication without ever perceiving the need to justify this eclecticism or to systematize its intellectual base. Although scholars like Fairclough and Chouliaraki (1999) believe that this liberality and flexibility of CDA to other disciplines is a strength rather than a weakness, its consequences leads to lack of coherence, indiscriminate mixing of incompatible concepts, and unsystematic application of methods (Breez, 2011).

Conclusion

In spite of the barrage of criticisms levelled against it, CDA has fast arisen as a huge and recognizable approach to the analysis of discourse. Heterogeneous in its historical antecedents and liberal in its methodological applicability, CDA is concerned with issues of ideology, power, dominance and inequality as they manifest in discursive practices.

References

Billig, M. (1991) *Ideology and Opinions*. London: Sage.
Chouliaraki, L., and N. Fairclough (1999) *Discourse in Late Modernity. Rethinking Critical Discourse Analysis*. Edinburgh: Edinburgh University Press.
Foucault, M. (1969) *The Archaeology of Knowledge*. London: Routledge.
Fairclough, N. (1985) *Critical Discourse Analysis*. London: Longman.
Halliday, M.A.K. (1985) *An Introduction to Functional Grammar*. London: Edward Arnold.
Hammersley, M. (1997) *The Foundations of Critical Discourse Analysis. Language and Communication* 17: 237-248.
Hildago,T. (2011) *Critical Discourse Analysis: An Overview*. In Nordic Journal of English Studies, Vol.10,No.1 (pp.86- 100)
Reisigl, M., and R. Wodak (2009) "The Discourse Historical Approach". In R. Wodak and M. Meyer (eds.) *Methods of Critical Discourse Analysis*. London: Sage. pp. 87-121.

Van Leeuwen, T.J. (1996). "The Representation of Social Actors". In C.R. Caldas-Coulthard, & M. Coulthard (Eds.), *Texts and Practices. Readings in Critical Discourse Analysis*. London: Routledge.

Van Dijk, T. (1991) *News as Discourse*. New Jersey: Erbanum.

Wodak, R. 1996: The genesis of racist discourse in Austria since 1989. In R. Caldas- Coulthard and M. Coulthard (eds). *Texts and Practices: Readings in Critical Dis- course Analysis*. London: Routledge. 129-49.

Wodak, R. & Meyer, M. (2009). "Critical Discourse Analysis: History, Agenda, Theory and Methodology". In R. Wodak & M. Meyer (eds.), *Methods of Critical Discourse Analysis* (pp. 1- 33). Los Angeles, London: Sage.

Chapter 12

Contextualizing an African Brand of Terrorism in the Eye of Critical Discourse: a Case of Nigeria's Boko Haram Islamic Sect

- Oladimeji Olaniyi & Abiodun Jombadi

1.0 Introduction

The recurrent grave impact of terrorism on the world's affairs has necessitated the deconstruction of the nature of terror speeches and by extension terror actions with specific consideration for analysis that bothers on the remote and immediate causes of terrorism, the underlying ideologies which propel it and the solutions necessary to nip it in the bud. The chapter investigates the ideological contents inherent in the selected translated speeches of Abubakar Shekau, the self-acclaimed leader of the Nigerian Boko-Haram Islamic sect. The chapter adopts Critical Discourse Analysis, a methodological procedure that hinges on a multidisciplinary theoretical approach to unravel the ideology within the text. It draws insight from systemic functional grammar (Halliday, 1985), critical pragmatics (Mey, 2006), semiotics (Barthes 1994) and van Dijk's theory of socio-cognition (2002).Our data consists of the speech delivered by Abubakar Shekau in admittance of the abduction of the Chibok school girls. The findings reveal that Boko-Haram's activities are instigated by three ideologies: the need for restoration and sustenance of Islamic faith and its spiritual order; need for self-determination and a vision to institutionalize Islam. The system of meaning embedded in the linguistic structures of the text foregrounds violence as the only method the sect finds admissible to actualize its mandates. Demolition of educational and democratic institutions, vehement persecution of Christians and Muslims who oppose fanaticism in Islam and secular constitutional frameworks are the major targets for onslaught. The chapter concludes by reiterating the nature of the group's dominance which is anchored on two factors. The sect seeks to perpetually gain dominance through destructive actions of high magnitude. This is usually followed by the attempt to psychologically control and influence the mind of the populace by asserting such dominance through speech.

Language serves expressive purpose in so much as it mirrors the thought of the user. Discourse (any given instance of language use) frames the world in meaning by words, that is, only in discourse is the world made meaningful. This position draws on a key insight of Foucault's (cited in Locke, 2004, p.6) that 'discourse is in an active relation to reality, that language signifies reality in the sense of constructing meanings for it, rather than that discourse is in a passive relation to reality, with language merely referring to objects which are taken to be given in reality' (1992, p.1-2). This insight propels our attempt at deciphering hidden ideological load in the speech delivered by the imperial leader of Boko Haram sect after the kidnap of Chibok schoolgirls.

Boko Haram, a dreaded terrorist sect began its uprising in Bauchi State, Nigeria, instigating a riot and attacks on security agents. Its first major onslaught took place on April 22, 2011 in Yola, Adamawa State of Nigeria where it attacked a prison and freed 14 inmates. It has subsequently launched further diverse attacks on churches, mosques, public places, educational and governmental institutions as well as on Islamic clerics. The climax and the most embarrassing of all these was the abduction of 279 female students from their school's dormitories in Chibok town, Borno State on April 14, 2014. On May 5, 2014, the leader of the sect, Abubakar Shekau, surfaced on the internet and claimed responsibility for the abduction on behalf of the sect. The speech he delivered on that platform as well as other previous speeches is what this study uses as a resource for deconstructing the ideologies inherent in the texts.

In the context of this investigation, the research posits language as a system that constitutes meaningfulness on its own term far beyond the notion of language as a medium for expressing meaning. In the last thirty years, language has shifted from a notion of representation as a direct or mediated reflection of reality to a conceptual and methodological account of representation as a form of signification (Parker, 1999, p. 4-5). Shekau's speech under focus is conjectured as a representation of a discursive event with embedded signification that can be analysed using critical discourse analysis (CDA), a procedure aimed at discovering the underlying ideological contents instantiated in the text by engaging in textual analysis appropriated within the purview of multidisciplinary theoretical constructs. This analysis rests on the assumption that the speaker uses language to shape ideological positions that crystallize the belief, the orientation and the identity of the sect whose activities have drawn the world's attention since early 2011. This foray is in tandem with Owala et al's (2013,p. 284) position that "a text is a choice of syntactical forms whose structures show ideologies of specific societies. The choice of language manifests itself in text in a manner that preserves and perpetuates these ideologies". The chapter therefore explores the selected texts for analysis in order to detect the extent linguistic forms have been able to represent ideological constructs. Our underlying assumption relates to the position of Hunjo (2009, p.3) that 'linguistic forms contain social realities made to exist by social actors within contexts.

2.0 Terrorism and Language Use

Terrorism has been defined as an action or movement motivated by objectives, where such objectives could be rooted in religion, governance, economy, inheritance, etc. It is a phenomenon that grows out of conflict and discord, an action against a discomforting status quo (Chukwu *et al.*, 2014, p. 80). Terrorism is as old as human struggles, actions and inclinations. From a positive perception, it has "historically remained part of the management tools for addressing violent conflicts" (Imobighe and Eguavon, 2006,p.8). However, within the confine of recent global discourses and experiences where attacks, maiming, killings and destruction trail various acts of terrorism, it has become inimical especially in the face of its destructive tendencies. The attendant consequences of terrorism, whether as a liberation struggle or criminally intended attack, take away from it any form of justification.

Chukwu (ibid: 84) proposes that "terrorism is a type of organised violence motivated by instinct to protect and propagate ideological interest, be it political, religious or economic". This chapter maintains that the ideological interest that instigates terrorism can be unravelled by investigating the way language is used especially as it affects the interest of the terrorist who uses language as an instrument of social control.

3.0 Theoretical Orientation

The chapter leverages on the facilities of Critical Discourse Analysis (later referred to as CDA) to comb the ideological loads in the selected text. CDA is an interdisciplinary approach to the study of discourse that views language as a form of social practice and focuses on the ways social and political domination are reproduced in texts – spoken or written. The idea is to illuminate ways in which dominant forces in the society construct versions of reality that favour their interests (Owala et al., ibid., p. 286). Prominent critical discourse analysts are van Dijk (2002), Fairclough (1989), Wodak (1997), van leeuwen (2002) and Bloomaert (2005). Hunjo (2009, p.6) elaborates on the highpoints of CDA to include: analysis of textual function in relation to life as a social action; application of interdisciplinary tools of scientific study of text which cuts across the use of tools of linguistics and the social sciences; and the ability of each critical discourse analyst to demonstrate "some understanding and closeness to the society his or her data represent."

As a tradition, CDA draws on distinct schools of social enquiry: the neo-Marxism of the Frankfurt school, the Foucaultian archaeology, poststructuralist deconstruction and post-modernism (Denzin and Lincoln, 1994, p.140, van Dijk, 1993, p. 251). It crystallizes the nexus between discourse practices, social practices, and social structures. CDA is concerned with the ways in which the power relations produced by discourse are maintained and/or challenged through texts and the practices which affect their production, reception and dissemination (Locke, ibid, p. 38). As Wodak (2001, p.11) puts it, CDA takes an interest in the ways in which linguistic forms are used in various expressions and manipulations of power.

Reading a text critically relates to a means of 'developing an awareness of how texts mediate and sustain particular discourses and power relations' (Lankshear, 1994, p. 10). Such ample discussion of power relations should, moreover, indulge and highlight the potential social effects of the meanings that a reader of a text is positioned or called upon to subscribe to in the act of reading. CDA supports the quest of Mey (2006, p. 320) for a critical analysis that relates language mechanisms to the powers of society that operate in discourse. This may include its embedded ideological constructs. Writing on CDA, Wodak (1996 cited in Olateju, 2004,p.17) posits that "Language use may be ideological. To determine this, it is necessary to analyse texts to investigate their interpretation, reception and social effects."

4.0 Methodology

The chapter rests on the fact that meaning is not a monolithic construct; it is a multidimensional and slippery concept with amazing complexity for understanding silent meanings of texts. It draws insight from critical pragmatics (Mey, 2006), systemic functional grammar (Halliday, 1985), semiotics (Barthes 1994) and van Dijk's theory of socio-cognition (2002). This method of analysis favours the multidisciplinary approach of CDA to language study and avails the chapter a balanced consideration for contexts of culture and situation as well as the assessment of the significance of the linguistic structures in terms of their functions/purposes. The analysis therefore draws on the (linguistic) analytical resources that are available in other fields in order to achieve the objective of deconstructing the inherent ideological orientation of our select texts in use.

The selected speeches have been carefully chosen for their suitability in mirroring the salient ideological stance of Boko Haram terrorist sect as the speaker opened up on what he perceived as the justification for various terror actions which drew the entire world into a mixture of astonishment and fury. According to him, the incident was necessary to force the world and Nigeria in particular to give attention to its agitations propelled by its ideologies.

5.0 Data Presentation and Analysis

This section examines the data closely by analysing and presenting the discussion of relevant parts of the texts with the methods mentioned above. The texts exemplify instances of linguistic structures that shroud the inherent ideological engine that propels the actions of the sect.

5.1 The need for restoration and sustenance of faith and spiritual order

A careful analysis of the lexical selection and intertextuality embedded in Shekau's speeches portends an absolute determination to defend a sacred course rooted in spiritual values. The text below begins with a simple sentence comprising a pronominal subject and a complex complement:

> We need to break down infidels, practitioners of democracy and constitutionalism, voodoo and those that are doing Western education in which they are practising paganism.

This data demonstrates an ideational function of language with transitivity structure containing an actor (we), a material process (need to break down), and three beneficiaries (infidels, practitioners of democracy and constitutionalism, and those that are doing Western education...) all in an awry relationship. The lexical choice 'we' asserts van Dijk's(1993 : 355) submission that "not all members of a powerful group are always more powerful than all members of dominated groups: power is only defined here for groups as a whole." The semiotic significance of the pronominal subject therefore underscores Shekau's speeches as embodiment of the collective grievances of all the members of Boko Haram. The deconstruction of the group's ideological load then becomes feasible with the belief that the group's power has been vested on Shekau. This radical identity epitomized in the shared socio-cognition which informs the loyalty of the sect members towards their ideology is steeped in the mental process of the transitivity system of the ideational metafunction: "We know what is happening in this world,, it is a Jihad war..." This is further corroborated by the excerpt below:

> I am not Boko Haram; I am Jamaatu Allussunna
> lildaawatiwal Jihad. I don't care what you call me;
> you are in trouble...

The speaker's dominance is heightened by two observable actions. First, the predominance of four short independent clauses of the ideational and interpersonal function category with selected relational and material process is reminiscent of two events. The relational process, on the one hand, demonstrates the text producer's tinge with identity. The material process, on the other hand, reveals the speaker's attempt to depict his superior perception of himself as well as his inferior perception of his perceived enemies. Bloor and Bloor (1995, p. 9) identify ideational function as a process of using language to organise, understand and express our perceptions of the world and of our consciousness. Second, the deliberate appropriation of the insignia of name-calling as a social code which favours Jamaatu Allussunnalildaawatiwal Jihad as against the popular name Boko Haram foregrounds a religious course by showcasing loyalty for Arabic, the sacred language of Islam. Shekau knew that a word with religious appeal was more suitable in sustaining his movement. This subtle manipulation is similar to what the late Osama Bin Laden's letter published under the heading: "Osama feared disintegration of group" in a

Kenyan newspaper Taifa Leo of 25th June, 2013 sought to achieve. Bin Laden was quoted as saying:

> The problem with the name Al-Qaeda is that it did not have a religious theme that appeals to Muslims worldwide that they are in a holy war against America. May be a name like Taifat al-Tawhedwal Jihad which means one religion with Jihad would be better or Tamaatl'Adat al Khalifat al-Rashida which means the return of Khalifa.

Owala's *et al.* (ibid, p. 289) analysis of this text demonstrates the significance of deliberate code-mixing as a subtle attempt to manipulate the minds of people in issues of terrorism. The selected (mixed) code being the sacred language of a religion understood worldwide as a religion of peace cannot conform to the ruthlessness ingrained in the statement: *"I don't care what you call me; you are in trouble."* In addition, the semiotic relevance of the name-calling relates to the text producer's confirmation of his outright loyalty to the ideology of the sect. It is said that social actors often express their socio-cultural and psychological assessments of themselves or other players in their socio-cultural space through such insignia as name-calling: "I am JamaatuAllussunnalildawaatiwal Jihad."

5.2   Need for Self-determination
A critical assessment of the data below points to a secession ideology:

> We said we will worship our Allah and stick to what he said. We left your sight and you are still fighting us.
>
> Go and form your own land; we are in Allah's land and don't know Nigeria. We don't know Cameroun or Chad...
>
> I don't have a country. Islamiyya is what I have.

The text foregrounds ten clauses in a paratactic relationship. It involves linking the clauses together on an equal footing. The text producer reflects these parallel relationships within the confine of a transitivity system of predominantly ideational metafunctions to construct an ideology aimed at secession. The persistent material processes of the verbal groups spark off a radical thought about legitimising secession from Nigeria and by extension other neighbouring African countries such as Cameroun and Chad. The paratactic relationship among the clauses indicates a consensus ideology shared among all members of the sect which symbolizes a common identity.

5.3   A Vision to Institutionalize Islam

Another ideological load embedded in the select texts is the attempt by the sect to institutionalise its brand of Islamic ideology as a substitute to formal education. This, it hopes to achieve, by persecuting students of secondary schools and higher institutions of learning. The text producer begins by making a selection for a modality and transitivity systems of the ideational metafunction to indicate an intention by the speaker to trade the captives (who are symbols of Western education) with religious rite of marriage. Marriage, here, is intended to serve as a method of perpetuating adherence towards this brand of Islamic ideology:

> I will marry out a female at 12...Just because I took girls in a Western school, they are worried. I said they should desert the school, they should go and marry...I am selling the girls like Allah said until we soak the ground of Nigeria with the blood of infidels and...This is our differences and that is where I detect that Western education is infidel...

The speaker pontificated his radical approach for instituting his ideology by utilising pronominal as a cohesive device. All the pronouns function in the endophoric anaphoric forms to reiterate the commitment towards institutionalising the sect's brand of Islamic ideology. In keeping faith with this ideology, the sect captured few local government areas in Adamawa and Yobe states of Nigeria and hoisted their flags while announcing a regime of its form of sharia legal system.

6.0 Material process as representative of violent approach

The import of the imbalance between the subject and the complement can be understood in the light of the symbolic weight of the material process of the predicator: "...*need to break down*" which portends an angry individual with a brutal determination to grapple and physically crush an opponent. This lexical structure highlights the relationship between the process and the participants within the clause process.

The structure above represents the method which the group adopts to advocate its interest. Osisanwo (1999, p.72) maintains that language users construct sentences by taking decisions and making selections or choices. These selections are useful to express intended meanings in their texts –

spoken or written. The instance of the verbal group above signifies a defiance of conventional method of conflict resolution within a democratic process. It infers the sect's crude means of advocating their grievances.

7.0 The functions of reference and intertextuality in the representation of Boko Haram's targets

In the context of the Systemic Functional Analysis, the beneficiaries (targets) of the sect's warfare can be categorised into three: (1) infidels, (2) custodians of democratic institutions and by inference the institutions themselves; and (3) regulators of educational institutions.

The speaker is on a mission to rescue sacred religious values from complete desecration; therefore, all individuals and institutions who have hitherto contributed to such perversion must be annihilated. First among those who constitute this sect are the infidels, those individuals who donot believe in what is considered by others as a true religion. It may be safe to assume that the speaker here refers to any individual who is not a Moslem since the speaker is a Moslem. Second beneficiaries are custodians of democratic institutions. It can thus be inferred that the sect holds democratic practices such as electioneering, peoples' representations, secular judicial system, legislative process and all recognised constitutional frameworks as inimical to faith and tantamount to desecration of spiritual order.

The elements of intertextuality in the speech allude to democratic and constitutional practices as voodoo and western education as paganism. The following text reiterates social actions that the speaker refers to as paganism:

> If you say, 'I pledge to Nigeria, my country', it is wrong and an act of paganism. For me, I pledge to Allah, my God, to be faithful to my Allah, and you to your country. With all your strength, you said you will worship a land.

The speaker made anaphoric reference to the pledge citizen make to the nation as being wrong thus establishing the basis for general bombings. This doesn't exhaust the list of its targets: *"All those clerics are to be killed for following democracy, all of them are infidels..."* Here, reference is made cataphorically to Islamic clerics who are likewise perceived as infidels. They also form part of the targets for the onslaught.

The speaker, however, opted for a relational process of the ideational metafunction when referring to Christians and those who may have derailed from the Moslem faith. Though, the semantics of Relational Processes is very complicated (Bloor and Bloor 1995: 120), it is , nonetheless, decipherable within contexts. Thus, within the given context, they are also regarded as infidels who deserve to share the fate of Islamic clerics: *"We are anti-Christians...infidels."*

Shekau further deployed imperative option of mood system of the interpersonal metafunction of language to include President Goodluck Jonathan, Kashim Shettima (Borno State Governor) and other world leaders in the list of the sect's targets: *"Harvest Jonathan's neck, harvest Kashim's neck..."* The word harvest, sourced in agriculture, naturally conveys a rewarding system that follows a rigorous and persistent energetic investment in ploughing, planting and weeding. An analysis of the excerpt therefore portends that the sect's assignments are not hastily carried out. There are precursory plans and underground machinations that precede every attack it unleashes on the populace.

8.0 Conclusion

The chapter has attempted to analyse Shekau's select speeches bothering on various terror attacks. The chapter conceived the text's linguistic structure as a form of social practice and discursive events loaded with ideologies. To unearth the inherent ideological constructs, we linked its meaning network to context-sensitive situations and social structures and arrived at the deconstruction of ideologies that instigate actions by the Boko-Haram sect.

From the perspective of a complex philosophical and social analysis, we view the texts producer's intention for delivering the speeches as acts aimed at controlling the acts and minds of citizens of Nigeria. This is in consonance with a vital part of terrorism which thrives in unleashing trepidation by means of a power base rooted in a privileged access to brute force. Boko-Haram reinforces its dominance by repeated bombing actions. This way, it successfully secured control over few local government areas in North-East States of Nigeria. van Dijk (ibid., 355) rightly posits that "the power of dominant groups may be integrated in laws, rules, norms, *habits*...and thus take the form of what Gramsci (1971) called hegemony. Every successful terror action by the sect entrenches itself in further dominance over the Nigerian nation in general and the North-East in particular. This is a form of physical terror; the second form is the one expressed through speech which this chapter conceives as a psychological terror.

The speech is understood in the context of a shared ideology and not an isolated opinion of the text producer. CDA works with the assumption that power is only defined for groups as a whole. Shekau's speeches, therefore, being representative of the sect's opinions are understood as consensus views loaded with shared ideologies.

Appendix

"*[We]* need ... to break down infidels, practitioners of democracy, and constitutionalism, voodoo and those that are doing Western education in which they are practicing paganism."

"If you say, '*I pledge to Nigeria, my country,*' it is wrong and an act of paganism. For me, I pledge to Allah, my God, to be faithful to my Allah, and you to your country. With all your strength, you said you will worship a land."

"*[Nigerian government]* would defend indivisibility of the country and its oneness. For me, I will defend only what Allah said and you are only defending country."

"We said we will worship our Allah and stick to what he said. We left your sight and you are still fighting us. Go and form your own land, we are in Allah's land and don't know Nigeria. We don't know Cameroon or Chad. ... I don't have a country. Islamiyya is what I have.

"There is no President in Nigeria ... No President in the world, only Islam."

"I am not Boko Haram, I am JamaatuAllussunnalildaawatiwal Jihad *["People Committed to the Propagation of the Prophet's Teachings and Jihad"]*. I don't care what you call me, you are in trouble. I am against government of the people by the people."

"I am nothing if Civilian JTF kills me. Even a small person can kill me. You killed Mohammed Yusuf *[Boko Haram founder and original leader until his death at the hands of Nigerian military in 2009]*, are you not saying he is even better than Shekau? Even if you kill me, other fighters will rise better than me, I am nothing and worthless before God."

"We know what is happening in this world, it is a Jihad war against Christians and Christianity. It is a war against western education, democracy and constitution. We have not started, next time we are going inside Abuja; we are going to refinery and town of Christians."

"All those clerics are to be killed for following democracy, all of them are infidels. I will tell Muslims what Allah wants them to do. We are anti-

Christians, and those that deviated from Islam, they are forming basis with prayers but infidels.

"You are dying because of money and I will die believing in Allah."

"Harvest *[President Goodluck]* Jonathan's neck, harvest Kashim's*[Borno State Governor]* neck, Allah said ..., even in Ka'aba, if some is doing salat*[prayer]*, for so long as he is deviating from what Allah said, he is infidel.

"After we have killed ... and get fatigue, wondering on what to do with their smelling corpses, smelling of Obama, Bush, Putin and Jonathan, then we will open prison and imprison the rest.

"It is Jonathan's daughter that I will imprison. Nothing will stop this until you convert. If you turn to Islam then you will be saved. We will kill and imprison and never get tired. Bring your trillion, there is nothing we can do with your money, if you know us you will not think that of us.

"What I will want you to know is, there is slavery in Islam, don't be deceived about the United Nations, it is useless thing and I call them United Nations of Absurdity led by Ban Ki-moon.

"Prophet Muhammed took slaves himself during Badr war. He killed many and because of this. I will also kill Obama if I catch him. I will kill Jonathan, if I catch him. Just like you want to catch me and kill me.

"All those with turbans looking for opportunities to smear us, they are all infidels. Betrayers and cheats like them, like Israel people, Rome, England, they are all Christians and homosexuals. People of Germany, *[people]* like Margret Thatcher, Ndume are all infidels."

Speaking on the subject of captured girls, Shekau, however, did not disclose any further infomation as to the precise number of girls they are holding or the reasons for their kindap.

"I will marry out a female at 12. I will do same for a 9-year-old girl, like it was done on my mother Aisha and wife of Prophet.

"Just because I took girls in a Western school, they are worried. I said they should even desert the school, they should go and marry. I am the one that captured your girls, and I will sell them in the market. I have my own market of selling people; it is the owner that instructed me to sell. I am selling the girls like Allah said until we soak the ground of Nigeria with *[the blood of]* infidels and so-called Muslims contradicting Islam.

"This is our differences and that is where I detect that Western education is infidel. This is a message to Muslims to wage war against infidels who are not doing what Allah said.

Received 17th October, 2014 from www.naij.com/65903.html

References

Bloor, T & Bloor, M. 1997. *The functional analysis of English: A Hallidayan Approach.*
New York: Arnold

Chukwu, K, et al. 2014. 'Language use, communication and terrorism in Nigeria: a critical discourse analysis'. In Global Journal of Arts, Humanities and Social Sciences. 2 (4), 84. Retrieved from 4th Nov., 2014 from www.ea-journals.org.

Denzin, N. & Lincoln, Y. (eds). 1994. *Handbook of qualitative research.*Thousand Oaks:
CA: Saga Publications, Inc, pp 138-57.

Hunjo, H. 2009. 'A critical discourse analysis of Wole Soyinka's postcolonial non-fictional Political texts'. Unpublished Ph.D Dissertation. English, Arts. University of Ibadan. Pp 6-7.

Lankshear, C. 1994. *Critical literacy.* Belconnen, ACT: Australian Curriculum Studies Association.

Locke, T. 2004. *Critical discourse analysis.* London: Continuum International.

Mey, J.L. 2006. *Pragmatics: an introduction.* UK: Blackwell Publishing

Olateju, M. 2004. *Discourse analysis: analysing discourse in the ESL classroom.* Ife: Obafemi Awolowo University Press Ltd.

Oloruntoba-Oju, T. 1999. 'Sociolinguistics: An Overview'. In Adegbija, E. (ed) *The English Language and Literature- in-English: an introductory handbook.* Ilorin: The Dept of Modern European Languages. pp 135-6

Osisanwo, W. 1999. *An introductory analytical grammar of English for undergraduate: a systemic approach.* Lagos: Femolus-Fetop Publishers.

Owala, et al. 2013. 'A study of terrorism discourse in TaifaLeo Newspaper of Kenya'. In Mediterranean Journal of Social Sciences. 4 (4) Retrieved 11 th Nov., 2014.

Parker, I. & The Bolton Discourse Network. 1999. *Critical textwork: an introduction to varities of of discourse and analysis.* Milton Keynes: Open University Press.

van Dijk, T. A. 1993. 'Principles of critical discourse analysis'. *Discourseand Society 4(2),* 249-83.

Wodak, R. 2001. 'What CDA is about – a summary of its history, important concepts and its developments'. In Wodak, R. & Meyer, R (Eds). *Methods of critical discourse analysis.* London: Sage, p 11.

Chapter 13

Forensic Linguistics

-Olaoluwa Duro-Bello

Introduction

The last decade has witnessed the coming of age of forensic linguistics amongst the other sub-disciplines of linguistics. It is no longer a specialization practiced by a handful of scholars who just happen to have language and law interests, but rather it has metamorphosed into a sound multidisciplinary field that interfaces law and linguistics in areas such as legal language, courtroom discourse, authorship identification or attribution, libel, trademark disputes, plagiarism amongst others. Its rise to prominence is hardly surprising given the centrality of the use of language to life in general and the law in particular. This chapter offers a concise introduction to this multidisciplinary field of linguistics, its development and application to the justice system.

The Big Question

There has hardly been a time when I discuss my fond interest in forensic linguistics that I don't get hounded in my tracks to answer the big question: What is Forensic linguistics? My presumptuous stance that the popularity of the discipline has permeated even the discourse of laymen is usually put in check when I get this question, and to my surprise I have even been asked same by students of linguistics. My one-liner for many years has been 'forensic linguistics is the application of linguistics to legal issues', but like all answers this has often served as an invitation for more questions. For example, 'the application of linguistics, how?' or the occasional disdainful 'when did you start doing law, I thought you are a linguist?'

To answer the former, I would usually make it clear that it is only in the application of linguistic knowledge that the rigor of any linguistic analysis is complete. Therefore, *application* here refers to the use of linguistic knowledge to examine the ways that language is being used in legal settings. This covers who is using language, how they are using it, why they are using in a particular manner and what is being accomplished by its use amongst other things. Olsson (2004) provides further clarity on the subject of *application of linguistics* by stating that 'the word *applied* is not necessarily being used in the same sense as, for example, in the phrase *applied statistics*, where what is being applied is a theory underpinning a particular science to the practice of that science, rather it is the application of linguistic knowledge to a particular social setting, namely the legal forum.

As for the second question, I remain a linguist, but to understand law one must understand language. The field of law provides an excellent opportunity for forensic linguistics to thrive especially since lawyers, judges, courtroom staff and law-enforcement agencies directly engage speech and writing in nearly everything they do. Mellinkoff (1963:vii) captures this aptly thus 'the law is a profession of words'. Furthermore, the domain of law has received attention from scholars in non-legal fields in the past; these include anthropologists, psychologists, sociologists and political scientists. It is therefore not too strange an occurrence to have linguists examine matters of law and offer their expertise as supporting evidence in the pursuit of justice. This interface has thus enabled linguists make positive contributions to the operation of the law by applying the rigorous scientifically accepted principles of linguistic analysis to corroborate other tenable legal evidence in court.

The big question has also been addressed by linguists over the years. For Gibbons and Turell (2008:1) forensic linguistics is 'the interface between language and the law'. Rock (2011:139) defines it is as 'an umbrella term for all forms of language-based research on matters legal. Turell (2008:155)opines that 'it is an established discipline which seeks to uncover and establish the existing interplay between linguistic and legal issues'. Coulthard *et al.* (2010) define the discipline in its broadest sense as 'the application of linguistics to three principal domains: written legal texts, spoken legal practices and the provision of evidence for criminal and civil investigations and courtroom disputes.

It is clear from the foregoing that the law and language are inseparable. We need language to enact/frame the law, understand the law and effect the law. It is perhaps for this reason that as linguistics developed throughout the course of the twentieth century, linguists have taken an increasing interest in the relationship between the two, especially in the area of the language of the law, the use of language within the law, and language in the judicial system.

Historical Retrospect on Forensic Linguistic Research

Like almost all sciences it is difficult to say that Forensic Linguistics began at a specific moment in time. The case of forensic linguistics is further peculiar because official documentation of the earliest consultations between linguists and the law are considerably sparse. Thus, before becoming a recognised sub-discipline of linguistics, the participation of linguists on civil and criminal cases was isolated and their methodology was not established within parameters of validity and reliability (Turell, 2008). At different times within the last half a century, linguists had been called upon by lawyers, police and other law enforcement agents, to use their expertise to provide language based evidence. Shuy (2001:438) asserts that, linguists who engaged in such work did so as aside-issue application of their primary work as dialectologists, phonologists, syntacticians, or, in some cases, applied linguists in the most general sense. There were several phonologists doing forensic work in voice identification (Tosi 1979), butthere is no record of any linguists referring to themselves as forensic linguists before 1968(Turell, 2008; Olsson, 2004 and Shuy, 2001). Coulthard *et al.*, (2010) record that the earliest well-documented casework comes from the 1970s and includes: Hannes Kniffka's contributions in the German legal system (Kniffka,2007); Raven McDavid's involvement in a trademark dispute (McDavid (1977) in Butters, 2008); Michael Gregory's evidence on a disputed confession statement (Gregory, 2000); and Roger Shuy's evidence in a case of solicitation to murder (Shuy,2005).

The phrase *Forensic Linguistics* is also a recent coinage which dates back to the publication of The Evans Statements: A Case for Forensic Linguistics, by Professor Jan Svartvikin 1968. He presented an analysis of statements given by Timothy John Evans, suspected of murdering his wife and baby, to police officers at Notting Hill Police Station in 1953. In his presentation, Svartvik demonstrated that the disputed parts of the statement allegedly given to police following Evans' arrest had a grammatical style measurably different from the style of uncontested parts. Along with other evidence collected in the course of different threads of investigation, the findings of Svartvik showed that Evans could not, as had been claimed at his trial, have dictated the statements attributed to him. Evans was executed in 1950 but Svartvik's now famous forensic linguistics contributed to his posthumous pardon 16 years later (Coulthard and Johnson, 2007; Olsson, 2004; Coulthard et al., 2010).

There were, of course, instances of the application of linguistics to law much earlier than this. Coulthard and Johnson (2007:5) mention that almost 20 years before Svartvik's coinage of the phrase, the term *forensic English* had been used by F.A. Philbrick (1949) in the title of his book on legal English, Language and the Law: The Semantics of Forensic English, but the phrase was never taken up. Olsson (2004) traces its history even further back, to attempts by British and American mathematicians and statisticians in the nineteenth century to develop methods of authorship attribution. Notable amongst them were Augustus de Morgan, in 1851, TC Mendenhall (1887 and 1901) and in the earlier part of the twentieth century Udney Yule (1938 and 1944). These studies tended to concentrate on easily measurable attributes like word length average, mean sentence length, and so on, to link texts to the same author. Coulthard et al. (2010) record the earliest interest in how, and to what effect, language is used in legal and forensic contexts as dating back to at least ancient Greece and Rome. They claim that in the fourth century BC, Aristotle produced a typology of rhetoric according to the occasions it served, distinguishing between political, ceremonial and forensic oratory; the latter he (Aristotle) associated with the courtroom.

The history of forensic linguistics can further be traced from several directions across the globe. In Europe pioneer studies on forensic linguistics can be traced back to 1985, primarily in Birmingham, when experts were called into court to contribute their expertise in handwriting analysis and authorship attribution of both spoken and written texts. Prior to the founding of the International Association of Forensic Linguists (IAFL) forensic linguists met at conferences in diverse European universities between 1988 and 1992. The first British seminar on Forensic linguistics which took place at the University of Birmingham in 1992 assembled delegates from Australia, Brazil, Eire, Holland, Greece, Ukraine and Germany as well as the UK. Among them there was consensus that an international association was needed and thus it could be said that from that seminar the IAFL was born (Turell 2008).

In the United States forensic work began slightly differently, but also concerned the rights of individuals with regard to the interrogation process. In 1963 Ernesto Miranda was convicted of armed robbery, but appealed on the grounds that he did not understand his right to remain silent or to have an attorney present at the time of questioning. The Court of Appeal overturned his conviction in 1966. Another early application of Forensic Linguistics in the United States related to the status of trademarks as words or phrases in the language. An early case involved a dispute surrounding an aspect of the brand name 'McDonald's', owners of the multi-national fast food chain. In this case the linguists were Genine Lentine and Roger Shuy (as reported in Levi 1994:5). Quality Inns International announced their intention of opening a chain of economy hotels to be called 'McSleep'. 'McDonald's' claimed that the attachment of the 'Mc' prefix to many unprotected nouns, such as 'Fries' in 'McFries' 'Nuggets' in 'McNuggets', etc., barred Quality Inns from use of the 'Mc' prefix. In this case the plaintiff was not just claiming implicit ownership of a name, but over a morphological principle, namely the attachment of a particular prefix to any noun. It appears that the claim was inherently one of a "formula for combination" (Levi 1994: 5) and it was this formula for which protection was being invoked. 'McDonald's' also claimed that they had originated the process of attaching unprotected words to the 'Mc' prefix and had run advertising campaigns which illustrated this. In their evidence Lentine and Shuy showed that the 'Mc' prefix had had previous commercial applications, and that as 'McDonald's' had not objected to any of these they had no grounds for doing so in the present instance. Despite the overwhelming evidence presented by Lentine and Shuy, judgement was for the plaintiff's and Quality International Inns were unable to launch their chain of motels under the 'McSleep' banner.

In Germany, an early case involved an alleged slander by a tenant in an apartment complex of a fellow tenant (Kniffka, 1981). The issue at stake was whether the word 'concubine' was an insult. Linguists advised that for some speakers, the word might be amusing, for others a way of addressing each other as a joke, while yet others might find it insulting under some circumstances: it was not possible to say that a given word or phrase, on its own, was an insult, or constituted verbal injury. Rather, the relationship between speaker and hearer, the context of situation, the speaker's education level — all needed to be taken into account. A word does not have a single, universally-agreed, meaning within a speech community.

Forensic linguistics is somewhat still in its developing phase on the Asian and African continents compared to Europe. So far there have been no high profile cases where linguistic expertise has been tendered as evidence to support the course of justice. There have however been isolated practices by university scholars especially in the area of legal translation and courtroom interpreting. Notwithstanding, the discipline has truly come of age. It has its own professional association, The International Association of Forensic Linguists, its own journal, International Journal of Speech, Language and the Law, founded in 1994; and biennial international conference. Modules in forensic linguistics and/or language and the law are taught to undergraduate and Masters level students in a rapidly increasing number of universities worldwide.

Forensic Linguistics in Practice

Forensic linguists are involved in many areas that relate to crime, both solving crime and absolving people wrongly accused of committing crimes. Some of these areas of research and expertise include: authorship analysis, speech act and pragmatic analysis, forensic phonetics and legal language. These distinct domains of research have varying degrees of acceptability or reliability within the ambit of the law. For example, voice identification (a component of forensic phonetics) if done by a qualified phonetician, who understands the limitations of the methodology and findings, is generally accepted as being relatively reliable.

Authorship Analysis

This refers to a systematic linguistic analysis aimed at identifying whether the fabrication of parts or an entire text can be linked to an individual. It relies on the analysis of suspect's idiolect, or particular patterns of language use such as vocabulary, collocations, pronunciation, spelling and grammar. A distinction may be made on the kinds of cases that would require a linguist's expertise in authorship analysis. The first being, where considerable material is available against which anonymous or disputed texts can be compared and secondly, where comparison texts are unavailable or where an investigation is not yet narrowly focused on a small pool of suspects (Coulthard *et al.* 2010).

In the former, there may be a small pool of suspect authors from whom sample texts may have been collected. The task of the forensic linguist is to compare these texts for linguistic clues that narrow the list of suspects down to the most probable whose known samples share the most measurable similarity to the disputed text. Shuy (2002) posits that such stylistic analysis centres on a writer's habitual language features over which he/she has little or no conscious awareness, such as patterns of clause embedding, use of parallel structures, deletion of "that" incomplementizer constructions, mechanical errors, punctuation, discourse features and organization, and print features such as underlining, bolding, or italicizing.

In situations where comparison texts are unavailable, the linguist is essentially being asked whether they can determine anything about the writer from their writing style and sometimes to elaborate potential meanings from unclear or ambiguous communications. To do this, linguists call on their knowledge of language indicators of such things as regional and social dialect, age, gender, education, and occupation, linguists analyze documents for broad clues to the identity of the writer.

It is important to point out that the job of the linguist is not to label any suspect guilty or otherwise, rather it is to create a profile that effectively narrows down the list of likely authors of the text solely on the bases of their linguistic nuances and nothing else. This is not to say that such positive identification is impossible but, rather, that the potential for variability in language use is great and the texts offered for comparison are sometimes dissimilar in genre, register, and size.

Case Study

Leonard (2005) offers an example of such an authorship analysis case that came the way of linguist, Roger Shuy, who was presented with a "pencil-scrawled ransom note, left at the doorstep of the parents of an abducted juvenile" (Shuy 2001). Shuy, almost immediately was able to observe, and infer, crucial elements of the kidnapper's identity. He examined the ransom note and asked the authorities if they had on their suspect list a well educated man from Akron, Ohio, as the language data suggested it was such a person who wrote the ransom note. They did. Using the language clues Shuy gave them, the police questioned the man, who was arrested and confessed. The note read:

> Do you ever want to see your precious little girl again? Put $10,000 cash in a diaper bag. Put it in the green trash kan on the devil strip at corner 18th and Carlson.
> Don't bring anybody along.
> No kops!! Come alone! I'll be watching you all the time. Anyone with you, deal is off and dautter is dead!!!

What does the language in this "pencil-scrawled" letter say about the author? Quite a bit. As Dr. Shuy noticed first off, there are a number of misspellings—*kops*, *dautter*, and *kan*. Who can't spell *cops* and *can*? More to the point, who can't spell *cops* and *can* but is able to spell *precious*? If someone can spell *precious*, it's pretty likely he can spell *daughter* as well, to say nothing of *cops* or *can*. Further, when uneducated people do actually misspell these words, they don't normally come up with *dautter*, *kops* or *kan*. So why would someone pretend to misspell? Probably in an attempt to mask his or her identity and appear uneducated. But the evidence suggests the writer is fairly educated--aside from being able to spell *precious* and *diaper* and *watching* as well, we can note that the punctuation is fairly standard, and the sentence structure demonstrates fluency and practice in writing English. But the clincher in identifying the man, Shuy says, was the phrase *devil strip*. If the kidnapper hadn't written this, he might be a free man today. *Devil strip* means the grass strip between the sidewalk and the road--but only in Akron, Ohio. Even in nearby Cleveland the term is not used. Devil strip specifically situated the writer of the ransom note as coming from Akron. And there was only one man on the police's short list of suspects who was from Akron and well-educated. And he was the one who handwritten the note (Shuy, 2001; Leonard, 2005)

Speech Act and Pragmatic Analysis

Austin(1962) and Searle's (1969) discussion of "speech acts" has also drawn interest from forensic linguists. Especially in the area of how discourse is structured, by what speakers are trying to do with their words, and how their intentions are recognised by their interlocutors. Speech acts, such as promising, offering, denying, agreeing, threatening, warning, and apologizing, have been well documented as central to conversations used as evidence in criminal cases (Shuy 1993).

Case Study

One example of how speech act analysis was used in civil litigation took place in Fort Worth, Texas. In an effort to price a used car, a congenitally deaf man charged the dealership with the infliction of false imprisonment, fraud, emotional distress, and violating the state's deceptive trade practices act as well as the human resources code's protection of the handicapped. Handwritten exchanges between the customer and the salesperson constituted the evidence for the charges. During the four hours of this event, he made it clear that he would not buy that day, but his only promise was to think about it and come back when he was ready. Nevertheless, the salesperson took the keys to the customer's current car and refused to return them. The salesperson also solicited, and got, a returnable check from the customer which was allegedly to be used to convince the supervisor that the customer was interested, supposedly to produce a better deal in the long run. After less than an hour of this, the customer requested that his check and keys be returned. By the second hour, he was demanding. By the fourth hour, he took matters into his own hands, scooped up all the written exchanges, rifled the salesperson's desk until he found his check, and headed for the door, only to be blocked by the salesperson, who smiled and dangled the keys tauntingly. The customer snatched the keys out of the salesperson's hand and headed straight for an attorney.

Speech act analysis of all of the hundred or so written exchanges made it clear that the customer gave no indication that he would buy that day. He reported facts about his financial status seven times, requested information about the vehicle six times, promised to return at a later date three times, disagreed with the salesman's offers 14times, requested his check back 12 times, and clearly said "no" to the salesperson's offer 11 times. Despite this evidence, the dealership claimed that the customer was, indeed, interested in buying that day and, even worse, that he had agreed to purchase the vehicle, which is why they justified keeping him there so long. This rather simple use of speech act analysis complemented other linguistic analyses in this case & contributed to the ultimate jury finding for the customer (Shuy, 1994).

References

Ariania, M. G., Sajedi, F. and Sajedi, M. (2014) Forensic linguistics: A brief overview of the key elements Procedia - Social and Behavioral Sciences 158 pp. 222 – 225

Austin, J.L. (1962) *How to Do Things with Words*. Oxford and New York: Oxford University Press.

Coulthard, M. and Johnson, A. (2007) *An Introduction to Forensic Linguistics: Language in Evidence*. London: Routledge

Coulthard, M. and Johnson, A. (2010) *The Routledge Handbook of Forensic Linguistics*, London: Routledge

Coulthard, M., Grant, T. and Kredens, K. (2010) "Forensic Linguistics" in SAGE Handbook of Sociolinguistics, Wodak, Ruth; Johnstone, Barbara;Kerswill, Paul (eds) SAGE Publications Ltd. Retrieved 26 September 2015, from <http://www.myilibrary.com?ID=381254>

Gibbons, J. and Turell, M. T. (eds.) (2008) *Dimensions of Forensic Linguistics* Amsterdam: John Benjamins

Leonard, R. A. (2005) "Forensic Linguistics" The International Journal of the Humanities Melbourne, Australia by Common Ground Publishing Pty Ltd

McMenamin, G. R. (1993) *Forensic Stylistics*. Amsterdam: Elsevier
Mellinkoff, D. (1963) *The Language of the Law*. Boston: Little, Brown and Company.
Olsson, J. (2004) *Forensic linguistics: An introduction to language, crime and the law*, London: Continuum.
Philbrick, F. A. (1949) *Language and the Law: The Semantics of Forensic English*, New York: Macmillan.
Rock, F. (2011) "Forensic linguistics", *The Routledge Handbook of Applied Linguistics*, James Simpson (ed) Routledge New York
Searle, J. (1969) *Speech Acts: An Essay in the Philosophy of Language*, London: Cambridge University Press
Shuy, R. W. (2002) "Forensic Linguistics" *The Handbook of Linguistics*, Aronoff, Mark and Janie Rees-Miller (eds). Blackwell Publishing
Shuy, R. W. (2001)"Discourse Analysis in theLegal Context" in *The Handbook of Discourse Analysis*, Deborah Schiffrin, Deborah Tannen, and Heidi E. Hamilton (eds.) Oxford: Blackwell Publishers Ltd. Pp. 437-452
Svartvik, J. (1968) *The Evans Statements: A case for forensic linguistics, Gothenburg*: Gothenburg University Press.
Tiersma, P. (1999*) Legal Language*, Chicago: University of Chicago Press
Tosi, O. (1979) *Voice Identification*. Baltimore: University Park Press.
Turell, M. T. (2008) Review of Malcolm Coulthard and Alison Johnson 2007: An Introduction to Forensic Linguistics: Language in Evidence. *Journal of the Spanish Association of Anglo-American Studies*. 30.2 pp. 155-160
Wood, L. and Kroger, R. (2000) *Doing Discourse Analysis: Methods for Studying Action in Talk and Text*, Thousand Oaks, CA: Sage Publications, Inc.

Chapter 14

A Multimodal Discourse Analysis of Selected Campaign Posters in Abuja

- Joy Aworo-Okoroh

Introduction

Multimodal Discourse argues that semiotic tools such as photographs, colour, framing, focus, and font style are deliberately used by visual designers in advertisements to communicate with viewers. Political Campaign Posters are examples of such medium which rely on combination of visuals and grammar to create not just an effect but meaning. This chapter therefore critically analysed selected campaign posters used in the 2015 Nigerian General Elections. Using a descriptive research method, six political posters were randomly selected from different bill boards in the Federal Capital Territory, Abuja and its environs. The six selected posters were drawn from the two major political parties in Nigeria-All Progressives Congress and People's Democratic Party. Kress and Van Leeuwen theory of Visual and Grammar design was used to analyse the posters. Emphasis was on information value, colour, gaze, pose and social distance. It was discovered that just as Kress postulated visuals are selected for a particular purpose and intent, to understand its meaning all elements must be interpreted vis-à-vis the grammar. The analysis also revealed that the different design patterns used indicated different levels of supremacy and power between the contestants and the viewers. The study concludes that visual designs are not merely for creating effects they are embodiments of meaning and interpreting them would aid in understanding the communicative value of the text under consideration.

Politics is essentially concerned with power and authority: how to obtain and appropriate it; how to make decisions and control resources within a jurisdiction; how to control and manipulate the perceptions, behaviour and values of those who are governed, among other things. In order to do all these, politicians rely on one key resource: language. This means that politics is inherently dependent on language; hence the notion that "language is an instrument of power" (Michara, 1). It is pertinent to understand the nature and uses of language in political advertorials, and become aware of the ways in which this language can be used to influence viewer opinion:

> One ought to recognize that the present political chaos is connected with the decay of language, and that one can probably bring about some improvement by starting at the verbal end. – George Orwell, "Politics and the English Language." 1946

Communication as a versatile process of transmission of ideas, thought and feelings comprises verbal and non-verbal components. While the verbal form attracts both oral and written medium of expressions, the non-verbal aspect encompasses signs (iconic-diagrams, images/pictures); gestures (body languages/paralanguages) and other symbolic representations (coded languages). The most common one used for interaction in human societies is the non-verbal. The role that non-verbal cues plays in conveying a message should heighten our interest in posters, since it is one of the leading non-verbal means of communication in the society today. They are used by commercial and political advertisers to persuade targeted audience, familiarize a candidate with the electorate and lure them to vote for the candidate.

Political advertising as a communication process aims in attracting the attention of viewers towards what a candidate or a party has to say with the 'intention of influencing their political attitudes, beliefs and/or behaviours" (Kaid, 2004). In electoral photography, the candidate does not only attempt to establish a program with the voters but also a 'personal link' with them, articulated through 'a style of life of which he is at once the product, the example and the bait,' heroized through the iconography of his appearance in familiar social settings, gestures and other predetermined set ups' (Barthes, 1993).

Dumitrescu (2010) identified two communication roles that political posters play: the first is to provide "factual" information about the candidates whilst the second is to present "nonverbal" information through pictures of the candidate, signalling behavioural intent. Political posters can also significantly alter their motivational and persuasive power simply by using images that elicit emotions such as fear or enthusiasm (Brader, 2005). Different feelings and preferences can be elicited through the image of the candidate alone.

So, what do candidates know about posters that the electorates do not? In other words, what are posters intended to communicate? What visual and textual strategies do political parties/ candidates use to portray their ambitions and to increase the awareness of the electorates? While it is true that posters restrict verbal communication, there is significant evidence pointing to the importance of non-verbal (visual) communication in the evaluation of candidates by voters.

Posters are an important part of the visual battleground of election campaigns around the world. Political parties and candidates spend substantial proportions of their campaign finances on them. Accordingly, posters are a kind of discourse that in its centre, power and ideology interact; and they can be used to express, or impose on one's ideology. Examples have also shown that when displayed in the right location, the combination of word and image on a poster can make for a powerful message.

Nowadays political poster as a means of political communication has received great prominence due to its proximity and accessibility to the populace. Technically posters are important forms of multimodal communications which present pictures with underlying meaning. Voters cannot avoid taking note of them since they are given durable entrenchment in the well-defined space of a community to send information about parties/candidates involved in the election. The communicative power of this simple visual display should not be taken lightly. It is pertinent to note that underlying every campaign poster is language; and politicians combine images with words in order to persuade the electorate to accept their political ideologies, thereby winning their votes. Political campaign posters have long been used as a simple but effective way for politicians to communicate their intention and attempt to influence the election process. Due to their relatively low cost, ease of production, broad visibility and ability to quickly convey a message, posters are often the medium of choice for the typical politician in times of election. During political campaigns, political leaders speak in public places, television and the radio. However, even when they are not present, their political posters represent them from cities and towns all over the country.

This chapter therefore seeks to critically analyse election posters in Nigeria in order to ascertain the multimodal functions of images in political posters. How the visual images and patterns in these posters combine with the grammar to portray the aspirants purpose and intention. It also explains how these choices work together by entering into relationships to create meaning.

An Overview of Multimodal Discourse

Multimodality, according to Ideema (2003), does not give a priori privilege to language over images, but shows how the two are heavily dependent on each other in meaning making. Multimodality treats the meanings of text as potential rather than as fixed since meaning does not so much depend on language or visuals, but through their membership of a code which is 'visual grammar' which gives the poster the potential to convey meaning. When we are confronted with texts with visual images, meaning is conveyed not just in the way the text describes itself through words and grammar but also through the use of images, colour, photographic styles and borders. Multimodality argues that these visuals are necessary in making meaning out of the texts. David Machin (10) argues that multimodal discourse has to do with harnessing of visual resources to communicate coherent messages, moods, styles and value in visual communication. When we are confronted with visual advertisement we often talk about how good, lively ,romantic or appealing the text is ,these words merely describe the effect of the visuals on us the readers/viewers but does not account for how the visuals/images and design decisions contribute to the overall meaning of the text.

Multimodality deals with this by providing a method that aids in understanding the different roles the composite elements of a visual text perform towards the overall meaning of the text. Multimodality, therefore, describes the grammar of visual communication, analyzing the rules and principles that allows viewers to understand the meaning –meaning created by visuals and how these interrelate with those created by a text. Multimodal discourse though similar to semiotic study is different because according to Kress and Leeuvwen, it tries to explain how combinations realize the meaning potentials of their choices, visual elements to them do not connote particular meanings but have communicative uses.

Kress and Van Leeuwen's Multimodal Grammar of Visual Design Theory approach as propounded by Gunther Kress and Theo van Leeuwen (2006) is derived from Halliday's (1994) Systemic Functional Linguistics. Multimodality which is also referred to as 'multimodal analysis' or 'multimodal semiotics' (O'Halloran:2011) according to Kress and Van

Leeuwen, occurs when a text communicates through a number of modes by combination. Typically, election campaign posters are multimodal in that they communicate through graphic and textual elements.

The grammar of visual design, like that of linguistic structure, can be interpreted through analysis of cues and signs that have individual meaning and may string together to create a larger layered effect. The grammar is history and culture specific. By using different modes, meaning is conveyed through design, production and interpretation (Kress & van Leeuwen, 1996).

Kress and van Leeuwen (1996) define two components for visual discourse: represented participants and interactive participants. By represented participants they mean people or things that are mapped on an image, while by interactive participants they mean producers and viewers. Among all these participants exists relations. The relation between the represented participants can be considered as syntactic, between the represented and the interactive participants as semantic and between the interactive participants as pragmatic:

> Interactive participants are [...] real people who produce and make sense of images in the context of social institutions which, to different degrees and in different ways, regulate what may be 'said' with images, and how it should be said and how it should be interpreted (Kress & van Leeuwen, 1996:119).

Therefore, we can say that there are four main relations in the advertising discourse. These relations interfere with each other and are not completely separable. The first relation is related to the relations between the images (or between the represented participants). The next two are related to the position of the producer and then the position of the receiver towards the image, and the last part is related to these processes as a whole in social sphere.

The social sphere and environment are stimuli for the producer. As a result by the stimulation from environment, the producer intends to publish certain message, and by using her/his available codes and knowledge, s/he composes the message to formulate the intention. The receiver by using her/his codes and knowledge interprets the message. If her/his codes are shared with the producer, the communication has taken place. And the effect of the message will return to the social sphere as a reaction of the receiver which can be for example a change of behaviour.

The important note is that the communication or (better to say) the interaction between producer and receiver is (in mass media/print as production) indirect, because of separated production-/reception contexts. However, the social sphere can help to determine this interaction. To identify the producer in mass media production is very confusing, because many persons and organizations work together. The company itself, the advertising company, the designer of the ad, the photographer, the depicted places and objects and so on seem to be all involved in the production process.

Another form of positioning works through different horizontal or vertical angles, in which the represented participants occur. The horizontal angles decide to what extent the viewers are *involved* in (frontal angle) or rather *detached* from (oblique angle) the depicted scenario. These different degrees of involvement or detachment correspond, to some extent to possessive pronouns in language, with the differentiation, that in images these degrees are not fixed, while in language exist no different levels of 'ourness' or 'theirness'. The vertical angle represents a relation of power between represented participant and viewer (this is also adopted from film technology): a high angle depicts a higher power of the interactive participant towards the represented participants, i.e. images shown from below, or with a high angle, depict a sense of power or importance, as the subject is shown larger than life and looming over the viewers' eye line. While a lower angle shows a higher power of the receiver, i.e. images seen from above or produced by an angle pointing down usually depict a relationship of inferiority or distance. If they are in the same height, the power relation is balanced.

Describing the position of viewers versus images does not explain the whole of the receiving process. A receiver is not only positioned by the image but also by himself as an individual, which means that receivers always have their own complex framework of codes, knowledge about the world, attitudes, beliefs and expectations towards the received image, which additionally can differ in the contexts and situations, the receiving takes place. So, it can never be clearly defined, how the reader's reception and reaction will constitute, thus there does not exist anything like "the" reader.

In multimodal texts both textual and visual resources take part in coding a message, hence their interaction is very important for understanding the overall meaning. Van Leeuwen (2005) argues that when analyzing visual communication, it is essential to consider "two verbal and visual modes of communication in print advertising with complex interaction between them" (8).

Research Methodology

It is a descriptive research. The data primarily consists of six campaign posters for Nigeria 2015 Election. The six posters were purposively selected from campaign posters distributed in Abuja, the Federal Capital Territory and its environs. The purposive sampling is to ensure that the six posters are drawn from the two major political parties in Nigeria-All Progressives Congress (APC) and Peoples Democratic Party (PDP).The posters are analysed using Kress and Van Leewen's Grammar of Visual Design, the aspects analysed are information value, colours, gaze, pose as well as social distance of the photographic image.

Data Analysis

Analysis of Datum 1

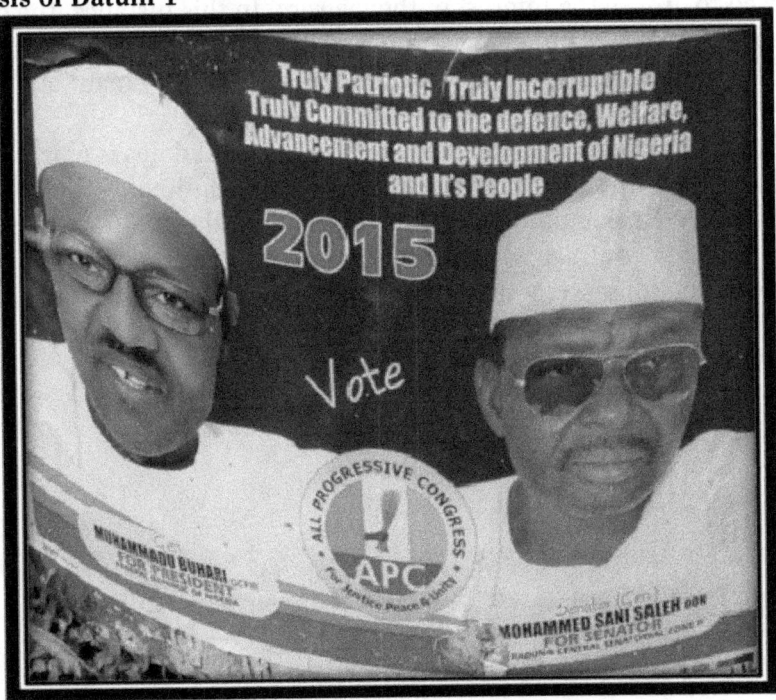

Multimodal Analysis

i.   **Information Value:** The information is from left to right. The left presents the given item which in this poster is Muhammad Buhari. This is the given information because it is familiar and known. So the reader reads from the left (Given) to the Right (i.e. the New). The new here is the contestant. He is new, someone not yet known by the viewers. This information value in this poster is placed as described above because the New needs the Given to gain acceptability.

ii. **Pose:** The photograph chosen for this poster is a smiling Buhari; this is an attempt to debunk the opinion that he is a harsh/stern fellow. The point of light on the poster is on the 'given' candidate.

iii. **Gaze:** The Given image "Buhari" gazes directly into the eyes of the viewer. This posture presents Buhari as a demand image. This is because his gaze faces directly the viewer thus enabling the viewer to have an imaginary relationship with the viewer. This demand image is different from that of the contestant, his image and pose is an offer image. We find that the eye contact is not direct. This offer image is used to arouse the interest of the viewers. In this instance, the object is not the viewers rather it is the image. Thus as the object the viewer finds him/herself scrutinizing the represented participant and what he represents.

iv. **Social Distance:** The individuality of the candidates is emphasized by using close up shots. They are presented at an intimate social distance.

v.   **Colour:** Background colour is black and the white attires of the candidates contrast with the background. The black colour probably gives an impression that the country is in darkness and needs the services of the candidates to improve the situation.

Analysis of Appendix II

Multimodal Analysis

i. **Information Value:** The information value of the composition shows that the poster is divided into two sections: the written text appears on the right and the photograph on the left. It is read from top to bottom because the candidate's head appears at the top of the composition. The candidate appears on the left, the place where the 'given' information is positioned.

ii. **Gaze:** He looks directly at the audience requesting an action, a vote. This is a demand visual in which the politician requests a direct answer from the viewer: his/her vote.

iii. **Colour:** The background of the upper part of the poster is teal blue and the bottom part is sky blue which is the party colour. The colours chosen for the written text are those of the party; blue, white, red and black. There is a cohesive use of colour.

iv. **Pose:** This political poster shows a candidate who appears alone. The candidate is a young man who is smartly dressed and his dress contrasts with the background. He is a man who appears without promises except for the party flag, and without references that can connect him with any prominent party personality.

v. **Social Distance:** The social distance is intimate because only the head and the shoulders are visible. This is a close shot.

Analysis of Appendix III

Multimodal Analysis

i. **Information Value**: The information value is divided into two sections: the written text on the left and the photographs on the right. It is read from top to bottom because the main candidate's head appears at the top of the composition. The social actors in the text appear on the right, the place where the 'new' and most important information is positioned.

ii. **Gaze:** They look directly at the audience interacting with them. It is a demand image, thereby creating a sort of relation between them and the viewers.

iii. **Colour:** The background of the poster is blue which contrasts with the attires of the candidates.

iv. **Pose:** Again, the smiling image of Muhammadu Buhari is used and he is dressed in native Kaftan which is to emphasize the fact that he is now a civilian. This picture contradicts with the stern military look people are used to. Prof Osinbajo is smartly dressed in suit. This is to give emphasis to the academic title of 'Prof'.

v. **Social Distance:** They are presented in an intimate social distance, at a close shot because only their heads and shoulders are visible.

Analysis of appendix IV

Multimodal Analysis
i. **Information Value:** As the viewers begin to interact with the poster; their attention is drawn to the image on the left hand side. The information value could be read from top to bottom and the composition structure of the poster presents it as an integrated text. The candidate is presented as 'given' while the party logo, candidate's passion/value is presented as 'New' on the right hand side. The candidate's image is clearly the most salient feature.
ii. **Social Distance:** The candidate is portrayed at a close personal distance creating an imaginary relationship between the viewer and the candidate.
iii. **Pose:** He is in a frontal shot, while the friendly smiling expression functions as a kind of visual invitation to interact with the candidate.
iv. **Gaze:** This a 'demand' image as the candidate confidently engages the viewer with full eye contact.
v. **Colour:** The colour background is sombre: green and black which contrast with the brightness (white) of the candidate's attire.

Analysis of Appendix V

Multimodal Analysis

i. **Information Value:** The information value of this poster is read from top to bottom. We have multiple images of the candidate in the poster. There are also some other images which are back grounded therefore foregrounding the candidate.

ii. **Pose:** The images are photographs of the main candidate in different cultural attires depicting some geo-political zones in the country. This gives the viewers the impression of a detribalized leader. Though he is not smiling broadly, he is relaxed and does not look stern. The background images play an important role as secondary participants. They depict projects that have been carried out by the Good luck administration.

iii. **Gaze:** The photograph of the candidate is a 'demand' image. He is in a frontal shot and the friendly smiling expression functions as a visual invitation.
iv. **Colour:** The colour combination brings about coherence in the sense that the party colours are used.
v. **Social Distance:** The candidate is portrayed at a close personal distance; creating an imaginary relationship between the viewer and the candidate, allowing the viewer to imaginarily come close to the public figure as if they were friends.

Analysis of Appendix VI

Multimodal Analysis
i. **Information Value:** The information value of this poster is read from left to right in the first instance and then from top to bottom. On the left is President Goodluck Jonathan as 'given' and on the right is Senator Solomon Ewuga as 'New'. Part of the head of Goodluck

Jonathan appears at the top of the poster which makes the reader want to read from the top after having looked at the content from 'Given' to 'New'. The photograph of Goodluck Jonathan is the most salient element due to its size. That of Solomon Ewuga is also salient but smaller in size.

ii. **Pose:** It is outstanding that they are smiling which contributes to giving a positive impression to the audience. The posture of the hand of Goodluck Jonathan (waving at the viewer) is significant, presenting him as a friendly and approachable politician. The positioning of the hand is important in the composition since it acts as connector between his name at the bottom and his head.

iii. **Social Distance:** The social distance suggests social familiarity because the shot is almost to the waist.

iv. **Colour:** The attire of Goodluck Jonathan contrasts with the background colour of the poster, whereas that of Ewuga blends in.

v. **Gaze:** Their pictures are 'demand' images.

Conclusion

As stipulated by Kress and Leeuwen images are carefully selected to conjoin with the grammar to communicate. In the posters we discovered that interpretation is incomplete if the grammar is described in isolation from the visuals. Thus there is need to understand that visual elements do not just connote particular meanings but have communicative uses. Political posters are not mere pictorial drawings. The research discovered that every choice made on a poster is a result of careful selection to reflect the person's ideology, intention and his persona. The pictures, positions, colours, gaze, postures and social distance of the posters are careful choices made in tandem with rules and patterns to create intended meaning.

Works cited

Barthes, R., *Mythologies*, London: Vintage, 1993. Print.

Brader, T. Striking a Responsive Chord: How Political Ads Motivate and Persuade Voters by Appealing to Emotions. *American Journal of Political Science*, 49(2), 2005. Print.

David Machin, *Introduction to Multimodal Analysis*, London: Hodder Education, 2007. Print

Dumitrescu, Delia. *Know Me, Love Me, Fear Me: The Anatomy of Candidate Poster Design in the 2007 French Legislative Elections*. Routledge, 2010. Print.

Halliday, M. A. K., *An Introduction to Functional Grammar*. London: Edward Arnold, 1994.

~ *Linguistic Studies of Text and Discourse*. London: Continuum, 2002. Print.

Kaid, Linda Lee, ed. *Handbook of Political Communication Research*, Lawrence Erlbaum Associates, 2004. Print.

Kress, Gunther and Theo van Leeuwen. *Reading Images: the Grammar of Visual Design*, Routledge, 1996. Print.

~ *Multimodal Discourse*. Bloomsbery Academy, 2001. Print.

Kress, Gunther. *Multimodality: A Social Semiotic Approach to Contemporary Communication*, Routledge, 2010. Print.

Michira, James Nyachae. "The Language of Politics: CDA of the 2013 Kenyan Presidential Campaign Discourse," *International Journal of Education and Research*. Vol. 2, No. 1: January 2014.

Index

Abubakar Shekau; 215-216
Adaptors; 72-73
Anthropology; 206
Authorship analysis; 234-235
Bach and Harnish; 26, 53, 71, 79, 87-89, 91, 92, 161
Boko Haram; 91
Chibok Schoolgirls; 216
Coherence; 4, 9, 12, 212,
Cohesion; 4, 9, 144
Common Ground; 118, 120, 121, 124, 156-192
Communicative competence; 22, 79
Context of culture; 2, 21-23
Context of situation; 2, 3, 17, 23, 54, 85, 233
Context; 9-13, 15-32, 37-39, 46-48, 55-58, 72-73-77, 79, 83-86, 90-96, 99-110, 117-118, 122, 124, 127, 134, 136-158, 160, 190, 219
Contextual Beliefs Model; 49
Conventional Implicature; 68-69
Conversation; 8, 11, 13, 18, 21, 23, 28, 29, 35-43, 49, 57, 61, 65-70, 87, 102-104, 118, 141, 156-179, 198,
Conversational analysis; 35-44
Conversational implicature; 22, 68, 69, 142-143,181
Critical Discourse Analysis; 201-214
Critical Discourse Studies; 206
Critical Language Studies; 296

Critical Linguistics; 201-202, 204-205
Critical Social Theory; 202-205
Cross reference; 5, 6, 8
Deixis; 99-116
Dialectologists; 231
Discourse context; 25-26,31
Discourse; 1-14,17,18,19, 24-32,37,57,62-67,74, 80-84,93, 96, 119, 122, 124, 134, 140, 141, 147, 160, 162, 183-193,201-212, 215, 216, 217-219, 229-230, 241-243
Discourse-Historical Approach; 210-211
Ethnography; 15
Ethnomethodology; 206
Face Management Act ; 61
Faucauldian Discourse Theory; 202
Ferdinand de Saussure; 9
Field; 2, 25, 31
Geoimplicature; 68, 84, 89
Grammar; 12, 46, 50, 57, 110, 135, 137, 138, 191-234, 239, 242, 243, 245, 252,
Hedging; 49, 72-73,169
Implicature; 22, 48, 68, 86, 89, 92-95,142-145,177
Institutional context; 24-25
Interactional discourse; 5
Interpersonal context; 23-24
Intertextuality; 5-9, 221, 223
J. R. Firth; 17
John Searle; 45, 52

Kidnap ; 216, 235-236
Linguistic competence; 79
Linguistic Context; 17, 18, 122
Malinowsky; 2, 3
Material process; 220-223
Metaphor; 22, 57, 64, 68, 136, 142, 145,146,147-148, 150
Metaphorical expression; 8,144, 148, 208
Mode; 2, 26, 31
Morris, Charles; 45
Multimodal Discourse Analysis; 239-252
Multimodal Semiotics; 242
Multimodality; 242
Neo-Gricean Pragmatics; 49
Noam Chomsky; 201
Norman Fairclough; 206
Odebunmi; 49, 69,
Pentecostal discourse; ix
Performance; 42
Politeness Principle; 22, 49, 57, 59
Pollyanna Principle; 57, 61
Practs; 55-56
Pragma-crafting Theory; 79, 81-97
Pragmadeviants; 82, 84
Pragmatic Act Theory; 49, 53-55, 57
Pragmatic Act Theory; 49, 53-57
Pragmeme; 54-57
Presupposition; 70,-71, 82, 84, 90-94, 117-132, 158, 177, 183, 191-192

Propaganda; 9, 185-189
Public relation; 183-200
Relevance Theory; 49
Rounders; 72-73
Ruth Wodak; 206
Semantics; 11, 12, 45, 46, 75-76, 117-118, 126-127,232
Semiotics; 59, 206, 215, 219, 242
Shields ; 72-73
Socio-cognitive model; 208-210
Socio-cultural context; 6, 19, 21, 23, 29
Speech Act; 79-98,139-142, 156-182, 191, 234, 236-237
Structural Linguistics; 9
Supra-segmental features; 85
Syntax; 1, 3, 45, 139, 144
Systemic Functional Linguistics; 47, 242
Tenor; 2, 25, 31
Terrorism; 215-227
Text Linguistics; 206, 208,
Text; 3-12, 26, 27-28, 55, 83, 177, 190, 206, 208, 217, 232-237, 242-248
Textual analysis; 217
Transactional discourse; 5
Transformational -Generative Grammar; 201
Truth value; 99-100,133-154
Van Dijk; 206-212
Visual Communication; 241,242
Visual Design Theory; 242,

www.ingramcontent.com/pod-product-compliance
Lightning Source LLC
Chambersburg PA
CBHW071405300426
44114CB00016B/2192